DAILY DEVOTIONAL FOR MEN 2025

365 Days Daily Inspirational Words Of Wisdom, Scripture Readings, Action Plans, Prayers, To Discover Purpose And Draw Strength From God.

Mount Hermon Publication

COPYRIGHT

PREFACE

Life can be complex, filled with joys and challenges, responsibilities and dreams. As you navigate this intricate tapestry, we invite you to take a moment each day to pause, to reflect, and to be inspired. Our hope is that these devotions will be a source of encouragement, wisdom, and inspiration as you strive to live a life aligned with your faith and values.

Whether you are seeking courage to face your fears, clarity to pursue your calling, strength to endure trials, joy in giving, wisdom in your thoughts, or purpose in your reflection, this book is designed to meet you where you are and walk with you in your journey.

Each day, you'll find a short exploration of a specific theme followed by actionable steps to apply these principles to your life. Our desire is for you to not only read but also practice, as faith without action is like a ship without a sail—beautiful but motionless.

We invite you to make this devotional a part of your daily routine—a moment to center yourself, to connect with your faith, and to draw inspiration for the day ahead. May it serve as a faithful companion, a steady guide, and a wellspring of hope throughout the year.

HOW TO USE THIS GUIDE

We've crafted this book with the aim of making it a valuable and practical resource for your spiritual growth and daily life. Here's a simple guide on how to make the most of this devotional:

1. Set a Daily Routine: Choose a specific time each day to engage with this devotional. It could be in the morning to start your day with inspiration or in the evening as a reflective way to end your day. Consistency is key in establishing a routine that works for you.

2. Find a Quiet Space: Select a quiet and comfortable space where you can focus without distractions. It could be your favorite chair, a peaceful corner of your home, or even a spot outdoors where you can connect with nature.

3. Read the Daily Entry: Start by reading the daily devotional entry. Each day presents a specific theme, a scripture reference, and a creative exploration of that theme. Take your time to absorb the message and reflect on its relevance to your life.

4. Meditate on Scripture: After reading the devotional, take a moment to meditate on the scripture reference provided. Consider how it aligns with the theme and how it can guide your thoughts and actions throughout the day.

5. Reflect and Apply: Following the devotional and scripture, spend a few moments reflecting on how the theme relates to your life. What insights or lessons can you draw from it? Then, consider the actionable steps provided and think about how you can apply them in your daily life.

6. Journal Your Thoughts: Consider keeping a journal or notebook alongside this devotional. Use it to jot down your reflections, insights, and personal experiences related to each day's theme. Journaling can be a powerful tool for self-discovery and growth.

7. *Take Action:* Faith without action is incomplete. The action steps provided in each devotional are designed to help you apply the principles discussed. Commit to taking action on at least one of the suggested steps each day, whether it's a practical act of kindness, a moment of prayer, or a change in your thought patterns.

8. *Share and Discuss:* Consider sharing your daily reflections and experiences with a friend, family member, or a small group of like-minded individuals. Engaging in discussions can deepen your understanding of the daily themes and provide additional insights.

9. *Make It Your Own:* Feel free to adapt this devotional to suit your needs. You can revisit previous entries, skip ahead, or use it as a springboard for deeper Bible study and prayer. Make it a personalized experience that aligns with your unique spiritual journey.

10. *Embrace Grace:* Remember that the journey of faith is not about perfection but progress. There may be days when you miss a reading or stumble in your actions. Embrace grace and keep moving forward, knowing that each day is an opportunity for growth and renewal.

As you embark on this daily journey of faith, may you find inspiration, wisdom, and transformation. May your heart be filled with courage, your mind with clarity, and your spirit with purpose. Above all, may you draw closer to the Creator and discover the fullness of your calling as a man of faith in 2025.

Heavenly Father,

As I embark on this journey of spiritual growth and reflection, I come before You with open hearts and humble spirits. Grant me the wisdom to seek Your guidance, the strength to face life's challenges, and the gratitude to appreciate Your countless blessings.

May this time of devotion be a source of inspiration, purpose, and connection with You. Bless my efforts as I meditate on Your word.

In Your holy name, I begin this journey. Amen.

DAY 01

The Power of Faith

"Now faith is the substance of things hoped for, the evidence of things not seen." — Hebrews 11:1 (KJV)

Faith is more than just a belief; it is a powerful force that propels us forward, even in the face of adversity. It is the confidence in things we hope for and the certainty in things we cannot see. For men, faith can be the cornerstone of strength and resilience, guiding us through life's challenges and uncertainties.

Imagine a ship navigating through a storm. The captain relies not on what he sees but on the compass that directs him towards safe harbor. Similarly, faith is our spiritual compass. When life's storms hit, faith keeps us anchored, providing assurance that God is in control and that His promises will come to pass. It is through faith that we gain the courage to take risks, pursue our dreams, and overcome obstacles.

Action Plan

Today, identify one area in your life where you feel uncertain or fearful. Write down a Bible verse that encourages faith and place it somewhere you'll see it daily, like your wallet or phone. Let it be a constant reminder to trust in God's plan.

Dear Heavenly Father, thank You for the gift of faith. Help me to trust in Your promises and rely on Your strength. When I face challenges and doubts, remind me of Your unfailing love and guidance. Strengthen my faith, Lord, and let it be a light in my life and an inspiration to others. In Jesus' name, I pray. Amen.

DAY 02

Trusting God in Uncertainty

"Trust in the LORD with all your heart and lean not on your own understanding." — Proverbs 3:5 (NIV)

Life is full of uncertainties. As men, we often feel the pressure to have all the answers and control every situation. However, true strength and wisdom come from trusting in God, especially when the path ahead is unclear.

Consider the story of Abraham, who was called to leave his home and go to an unknown land. He didn't have a roadmap or detailed instructions, but he trusted God's promise and followed His lead.

When we choose to trust God, we let go of the need to control and instead, find peace in His guidance. This trust transforms our worries into confidence, knowing that God is with us every step of the way.

Action Plan

Identify a current situation where you feel uncertain or anxious. Spend time in prayer, asking God to help you trust Him more. Write down Proverbs 3:5 and place it somewhere visible. Each time you feel doubt creeping in, read the verse and reaffirm your trust in God.

Heavenly Father, thank You for Your unfailing love and wisdom. Help me to trust You fully, especially in times of uncertainty. Teach me to lean on Your understanding rather than my own. Strengthen my faith, and guide my steps according to Your perfect plan. In Jesus' name, I pray. Amen.

DAY 03

Overcoming Fear with Courage

"Have I not commanded you? Be strong and courageous. Do not be afraid; do not be discouraged, for the Lord your God will be with you wherever you go." — Joshua 1:9 (NIV)

Fear is a powerful emotion that can paralyze and hinder us from achieving our true potential. However, as men of faith, we are called to rise above fear with courage. God's command to Joshua to be strong and courageous resonates with us today, reminding us that we are never alone in our battles.

Courage stems from our faith in God's presence and promises. When we trust that God is with us, fear loses its grip. Like a warrior going into battle, we can face our challenges head-on, knowing that God equips us with the strength we need. Whether it's a difficult decision at work, a personal struggle, or an uncertain future, courage allows us to take bold steps forward, confident in God's unwavering support.

<u>Action Plan</u>

Identify one fear that has been holding you back. Write it down and next to it, jot down Joshua 1:9. Take one small step today to confront this fear, whether it's having a difficult conversation, making a bold decision, or stepping out of your comfort zone.

Dear Heavenly Father, thank You for Your promise to be with me always. Help me to trust in Your presence and guidance, knowing that I am never alone. Fill my heart with boldness and peace, and let Your love cast out all fear. In Jesus' name, I pray. Amen.

DAY 04

The Importance of Prayer

"Pray without ceasing." — 1 Thessalonians 5:17 (KJV)

Prayer is our direct line of communication with God, a lifeline that keeps us connected to our Creator. It is through prayer that we express our gratitude, seek guidance, and find comfort in times of trouble. For men, prayer is an essential tool that equips us with the strength and wisdom needed to navigate the complexities of daily life.

Imagine facing a day without speaking to your closest friend or mentor. You would miss out on valuable advice, encouragement, and support. Similarly, when we neglect prayer, we miss out on the divine guidance and strength that God provides. Prayer is not just about asking for things; it is about building a relationship with God, aligning our will with His, and gaining the spiritual fortitude to face life's challenges.

Action Plan

Today, set aside a specific time for prayer, even if it's just five minutes. Share your worries, express your gratitude, and ask for His guidance. Make this a daily habit, and watch how your perspective and strength grow.

Dear Heavenly Father, thank You for the privilege of prayer. Help me to prioritize this time with You each day. Teach me to rely on Your wisdom and strength through prayer. May my relationship with You deepen and my faith grow stronger. In Jesus' name, I pray. Amen.

DAY 05

Living with Integrity

"The righteous man walks in his integrity; his children are blessed after him." — Proverbs 20:7 (NKJV)

Living with integrity is about consistently aligning our actions with our values, even when no one is watching. It's a commitment to truth, honor, and moral uprightness. For men, integrity is the bedrock of character and leadership, influencing how we interact with our families, colleagues, and communities.

Integrity isn't about perfection but about striving to do the right thing, even in small matters. It's being honest in our dealings, reliable in our commitments, and steadfast in our principles.

Consider integrity as a guiding light in a dark world. It may not always be easy to follow, but it leads to a life of fulfillment and honor. Integrity shapes not only our own lives but also the lives of those who look up to us.

Action Plan

Identify an area in your life where you may have compromised your integrity. Make a conscious decision today to correct it. Whether it's being more honest in your communication or fulfilling a commitment you've neglected, take one concrete step to align your actions with your values.

Dear Lord, thank You for being the perfect example of integrity. Help me to walk in Your ways, living a life that honors You. Let my integrity be a testimony of Your goodness and a blessing to those around me. In Jesus' name, I pray. Amen.

DAY 06

Strength in Weakness

"My grace is sufficient for you, for my power is made perfect in weakness." — 2 Corinthians 12:9 (NIV)

The Apostle Paul learned this profound truth when he was struggling with his "thorn in the flesh." Despite his pleas for relief, God responded with a powerful reminder: His grace is sufficient, and His power is perfected in our weakness.

Admitting our weaknesses is not a sign of defeat but a step towards true strength. When we acknowledge our limitations and turn to God, we open ourselves to His mighty power working within us. It is in our weakest moments that we experience His grace most profoundly, allowing us to accomplish what we could never achieve on our own.

Action Plan

Reflect on an area in your life where you feel inadequate or weak. Instead of hiding it, bring it before God in prayer. Ask for His strength to be made perfect in your weakness. Write down how God has helped you in past struggles, and let it encourage you to trust Him more deeply.

Dear Heavenly Father, thank You for Your promise that Your grace is sufficient for me. Help me to embrace my weaknesses and rely on Your strength. Strengthen my faith and courage, and let Your grace sustain me in all circumstances. In Jesus' name, I pray. Amen.

DAY 07

The Role of a Godly Man

"Be on your guard; stand firm in the faith; be courageous; be strong." — 1 Corinthians 16:13 (NIV)

A godly man is called to be a leader, protector, and provider, not just for his family but also within his community. Standing firm in faith and exhibiting strength and courage are essential qualities that reflect God's character through us.

A godly man is defined by his commitment to God's principles. He seeks to live out the teachings of Christ in every aspect of his life. This means showing love, patience, and humility in relationships, being honest and ethical in work, and maintaining integrity in all decisions.

Being a godly man doesn't mean being perfect; it means striving to grow in faith and character daily. It means being aware of one's weaknesses and seeking God's help to overcome them.

Action Plan

Reflect on an area in your life where you can better demonstrate godly character. Whether it's in your family, at work, or within your community, make a conscious effort to embody the qualities of a godly man.

Heavenly Father, thank You for the example of what it means to be a godly man. Help me to stand firm in my faith, be courageous, and lead with integrity. Empower me to be a positive influence and a source of light to those around me. In Jesus' name, I pray. Amen.

DAY 08

Embracing Forgiveness

"Bear with each other and forgive one another if any of you has a grievance against someone. Forgive as the Lord forgave you." - Colossians 3:13 (NIV)

To embrace forgiveness is to liberate oneself from the chains of bitterness and resentment, allowing the light of healing and renewal to flood our souls.

Forgiveness is not easy; it demands courage and humility. It's a choice to let go of the hurts and pains inflicted upon us, recognizing that harboring grudges only poisons our own hearts. When we forgive, we emulate the boundless compassion of our Creator, who forgives us unconditionally.

Action Plan:

Today, commit to forgiving someone who has wronged you. It may be a small offense or a deep wound, but choose to release the burden of unforgiveness. Write a letter to that person (even if you don't send it), expressing your forgiveness and prayers for their well-being. As you extend forgiveness, experience the freedom it brings to your spirit.

Heavenly Father, grant me the strength to embrace forgiveness as You have forgiven me. Help me to release the weight of bitterness and extend grace to those who have wronged me. May Your love fill my heart and guide my actions. In Jesus' name, Amen.

DAY 09

Embracing Forgiveness

"Be kind to one another, tenderhearted, forgiving one another, as God in Christ forgave you." - Ephesians 4:32 (ESV)

Forgiveness is not a weakness but a strength, a choice that reflects the depth of our character and the extent of our faith. When we choose to embrace forgiveness, we step into the realm of divine grace, mirroring the mercy bestowed upon us by our Creator.

To forgive is to unshackle ourselves from the burden of resentment and bitterness, to free our hearts from the chains of anger and hurt. It's a declaration of our willingness to let go of past wounds and embrace the possibility of reconciliation and healing.

Action Plan:

Today, take a moment to reflect on someone you need to forgive. It might be a friend, a family member, or even yourself. Write down their name and the offense they committed against you. Then, consciously choose to release the hurt and extend forgiveness. Pray for them, asking for God's blessings upon their lives.

Heavenly Father, grant me the courage to forgive as You have forgiven me. Help me to let go of bitterness and embrace the freedom found in forgiveness. Fill my heart with Your love and grace, that I may extend the same to others. In Jesus' name, Amen.

DAY 10

Serving Others Selflessly

"For even the Son of Man did not come to be served, but to serve, and to give his life as a ransom for many." - Mark 10:45 (NIV)

Serving others selflessly is a calling that echoes the very essence of Christ's ministry on Earth. It's an act of love that transcends personal gain, a humble offering of ourselves to uplift and bless those around us.

When we serve selflessly, we emulate the example set by Jesus Himself. He didn't seek recognition or status; instead, He humbly washed the feet of His disciples, demonstrating the heart of a servant leader. True greatness, as Jesus taught, lies in serving others with sincerity and compassion.

Action Plan:

Today, seek out an opportunity to serve someone in need without expecting anything in return. It could be a simple act of kindness like helping a neighbor with their groceries or volunteering at a local charity. Whatever it may be, do it wholeheartedly and with genuine love.

Lord, instill in me a servant's heart, motivated by love and compassion. Show me opportunities to serve others selflessly, just as You served during Your time on Earth. May my actions bring glory to Your name and reflect Your unconditional love. In Jesus' name, Amen.

DAY 11

The Fruit of the Spirit

"But the fruit of the Spirit is love, joy, peace, forbearance, kindness, goodness, faithfulness, gentleness and self-control. Against such things there is no law." - Galatians 5:22-23 (NIV)

The Fruit of the Spirit is not merely a checklist of virtues; it's the vibrant evidence of a life surrendered to God's transformative power. These fruits—love, joy, peace, patience, kindness, goodness, faithfulness, gentleness, and self-control—are not produced by our own efforts but by the Spirit working within us.

Joy fuels our spirits even in the midst of trials. Peace anchors us in the stormy seas of life. Patience teaches us to endure with grace. Kindness softens the hardest hearts. Goodness compels us to do what is right. Faithfulness keeps us steady on the path of righteousness. Gentleness tempers our strength with humility. Self-control empowers us to master our desires.

Action Plan:

Today, choose one fruit of the Spirit to focus on nurturing in your life. Whether it's practicing patience with your family, showing kindness to a stranger, or exercising self-control in your habits, intentionally cultivate that fruit throughout your day.

Heavenly Father, empower me by Your Spirit to bear the fruit of love, joy, peace, patience, kindness, goodness, faithfulness, gentleness, and self-control in my life. Help me to reflect Your character in all I do. In Jesus' name, Amen.

DAY 12

Walking in Humility

"He has shown you, O mortal, what is good. And what does the Lord require of you? To act justly and to love mercy and to walk humbly with your God." - Micah 6:8 (NIV)

Humility is not a sign of weakness but of strength. It's the recognition of our limitations and the acknowledgment of God's sovereignty in our lives. To walk in humility is to journey with grace, embracing a posture of openness and teachability.

In a world that often celebrates self-promotion and pride, humility shines as a beacon of authenticity and genuine connection. It's about putting others before ourselves, seeking to understand rather than to be understood. When we walk in humility, we reflect the character of Christ, who humbled Himself even unto death.

Action Plan:

Today, practice humility by intentionally listening more than speaking. Whether in conversations with loved ones or colleagues, prioritize understanding their perspectives without the need to assert your own. Seek opportunities to serve others without seeking recognition or praise. Let humility guide your actions and interactions throughout the day.

Gracious God, teach me to walk humbly in Your ways. Help me to set aside my pride and ego, and to embrace humility as a virtue worth pursuing. May Your Spirit empower me to serve others with grace and compassion, following the example of Jesus Christ.
Amen.

DAY 13

God's Guidance in Decisions

"Trust in the Lord with all your heart and lean not on your own understanding; in all your ways submit to him, and he will make your paths straight." - Proverbs 3:5-6 (NIV)

Life often presents us with crossroads, where decisions loom large and uncertainty abounds. Yet, in the midst of our confusion, we find solace in knowing that God offers guidance to those who seek Him earnestly. His wisdom illuminates our path, leading us towards the fulfillment of His purpose for our lives.

Trusting in God's guidance requires surrendering our limited understanding and placing our faith in His infinite wisdom. It's a journey of humility, acknowledging that we cannot navigate life's complexities alone. As we submit our plans and desires to Him, He orchestrates our steps, aligning them with His perfect will.

Action Plan:

Today, take time to seek God's guidance in a specific decision you're facing. Set aside moments of quiet reflection and prayer, asking Him to reveal His direction clearly. Listen attentively to His voice through scripture, wise counsel, and the gentle nudges of the Holy Spirit. Trust that He will lead you in the way you should go.

Heavenly Father, I surrender my decisions into Your capable hands. Grant me clarity and wisdom as I seek Your guidance. Help me to trust in Your leading, knowing that Your plans for me are good. May Your will be done in every aspect of my life. In Jesus' name, Amen.

DAY 14

The Beauty of Creation

"The heavens declare the glory of God; the skies proclaim the work of his hands." - Psalm 19:1 (NIV)

In the symphony of existence, nature sings a melody of divine craftsmanship. The beauty of creation surrounds us, from the majestic mountains to the delicate petals of a flower. Each element whispers of the Creator's love and artistry, inviting us to marvel at His handiwork.

Amidst the hustle and bustle of life, it's easy to overlook the wonders of creation. Yet, when we pause and behold the splendor around us, our hearts are stirred with awe and gratitude. In the beauty of a sunrise or the tranquility of a forest, we glimpse the infinite wisdom and creativity of God.

Action Plan:

Today, take a moment to immerse yourself in nature. Whether it's a stroll in the park or a gaze at the stars, intentionally seek out moments of connection with the natural world. As you do, reflect on the beauty and complexity of creation, and offer a prayer of thanksgiving to the Creator for His marvelous works.

Gracious God, thank You for the breathtaking beauty of creation that surrounds us. Open my eyes to see Your handiwork in every sunrise, every mountain peak, and every living creature. May I never cease to marvel at Your greatness and express my gratitude for the wonders You have made. Amen.

DAY 15

Patience in Trials

"Be joyful in hope, patient in affliction, faithful in prayer." -
Romans 12:12 (NIV)

Life's trials often test our patience, stretching us beyond our limits. Yet, in the midst of adversity, we're called to embrace patience as a virtue that strengthens our character and deepens our faith.

Patience in trials doesn't mean passive acceptance of suffering; rather, it's an active endurance fueled by hope and trust in God's promises. It's a resilient spirit that perseveres through hardships, knowing that every trial has the potential to refine us and draw us closer to Him.

When faced with challenges, we have a choice: to succumb to frustration and despair or to cultivate patience and resilience. Choosing the latter empowers us to navigate life's storms with grace and courage.

Action Plan:

Today, when confronted with a trial or difficulty, practice patience by pausing before reacting. Take a moment to breathe deeply and pray for strength. Remind yourself of God's faithfulness and the assurance that He is working all things together for your good.

Heavenly Father, in the midst of trials, grant me the gift of patience. Help me to trust in Your timing and to remain steadfast in hope. May Your peace guard my heart and Your presence sustain me through every challenge. In Jesus' name, Amen.

DAY 16

The Armor of God

"Put on the full armor of God, so that you can take your stand against the devil's schemes." - Ephesians 6:11 (NIV)

As men of faith, we are called to equip ourselves with the armor of God, a spiritual defense against the adversities and temptations of this world. Just as a soldier prepares for battle, we must arm ourselves with truth, righteousness, peace, faith, salvation, and the Word of God.

The armor of God is not merely symbolic; it is our safeguard in the spiritual realm. Truth exposes the lies of the enemy, righteousness protects our integrity, peace guards our hearts, faith shields us from doubt, salvation secures our eternal hope, and the Word of God guides our steps.

Action Plan:

Today, take a moment to intentionally put on the armor of God. Reflect on each piece and its significance in your life. Pray for God's strength and guidance to walk confidently in His armor throughout the day, facing challenges with courage and resilience.

Heavenly Father, I thank You for the armor You provide to protect and empower me in my spiritual journey. Help me to daily put on each piece, standing firm in Your truth and righteousness. Strengthen me to resist the schemes of the enemy and to walk in victory. In Jesus' name, Amen.

DAY 17

Daily Gratitude

"Give thanks in all circumstances; for this is God's will for you in Christ Jesus." - 1 Thessalonians 5:18 (NIV)

Gratitude is a powerful force that can transform our perspective and enrich our lives. It's easy to get caught up in the hustle and bustle of daily life, but amidst the chaos, cultivating a spirit of gratitude opens our eyes to the countless blessings surrounding us.

When we practice daily gratitude, we shift our focus from what we lack to what we have been given. It's a mindset that breeds contentment and joy, even in the midst of challenges. Gratitude reminds us of the goodness of God and His faithfulness in every season of our lives.

Action Plan:

Today, start a gratitude journal. Set aside a few minutes each day to reflect on the things you're thankful for. Write down three things you're grateful for, big or small. It could be a supportive friend, a warm cup of coffee, or the beauty of nature. As you make gratitude a habit, watch how it transforms your outlook on life.

Heavenly Father, thank You for the countless blessings You have bestowed upon me. Help me to cultivate a heart of gratitude, even in the midst of difficulties. Open my eyes to Your goodness and faithfulness each day. In Jesus' name, Amen.

DAY 18

The Value of Scripture

"Your word is a lamp for my feet, a light on my path." - Psalm 119:105 (NIV)

The value of scripture is immeasurable, for within its pages lies wisdom, guidance, and the very essence of God's voice speaking to our hearts.

Through scripture, we discover the promises of God, the stories of faith-filled individuals, and the timeless truths that transcend generations. It is not merely a collection of words on paper but a living, breathing testament to God's love and faithfulness.

As men seeking to live lives of integrity and purpose, we must cherish the value of scripture. Regularly immersing ourselves in God's Word empowers us to navigate life's challenges with clarity and confidence. It shapes our thoughts, molds our character, and strengthens our faith.

Action Plan:

Commit to spending time daily in scripture. Whether it's reading a chapter before bed or reflecting on a verse during your lunch break, prioritize engaging with God's Word. Consider starting a scripture journal to record insights, prayers, and reflections as you journey through the pages of the Bible.

Heavenly Father, thank you for the gift of your Word. May it be a lamp unto my feet and a light unto my path, guiding me each step of the way. Help me to treasure scripture and to apply its truths in my daily life. In Jesus' name, Amen.

DAY 19

Confession and Repentance

"If we confess our sins, he is faithful and just and will forgive us our sins and purify us from all unrighteousness." - 1 John 1:9 (NIV)

When we confess our sins, we acknowledge our humanity and our need for divine grace. Repentance goes beyond remorse; it's a decisive turning away from wrongdoing and a commitment to walk in righteousness.

Through confession, we lay bare our hearts before God, knowing that His love and mercy await us. It's a courageous act that breaks the chains of guilt and shame, allowing us to experience the fullness of His forgiveness. Repentance, then, is the natural response to confession—a deliberate choice to align our lives with God's will, to pursue holiness and integrity.

Action Plan:

Today, take time for personal reflection and confession. Write down any sins or shortcomings weighing on your conscience. Then, in prayer, confess them to God, asking for His forgiveness and strength to walk in a new direction.

Gracious Father, I come before You with a contrite heart, acknowledging my faults and seeking Your forgiveness. Grant me the courage to confess my sins and the wisdom to turn away from them. Fill me with Your Spirit, that I may live a life pleasing to You. In Jesus' name, Amen.

DAY 20

Seeking God's Wisdom

"If any of you lacks wisdom, you should ask God, who gives generously to all without finding fault, and it will be given to you."
- James 1:5 (NIV)

In our quest for purpose and direction, seeking God's wisdom is paramount. His wisdom transcends human understanding, offering clarity amidst life's complexities. When we humbly seek His guidance, we tap into a wellspring of insight that illuminates our path.

God's wisdom surpasses mere knowledge; it encompasses discernment, understanding, and divine revelation. It enables us to navigate challenges with grace, make sound decisions, and live with purposeful intent.

Action Plan:

Today, set aside time for prayer and meditation. Quiet your heart and mind, and earnestly seek God's wisdom for a specific area of your life where you need clarity. Listen attentively for His gentle guidance, trusting that He will illuminate your path with His divine insight.

Gracious God, I come before You seeking Your wisdom and guidance. Open my heart and mind to receive Your divine insight as I navigate life's challenges. Grant me the discernment to make wise decisions that honor You and bless others. In Your wisdom, may I find strength, purpose, and peace. Amen.

DAY 21

Building Strong Relationships

"Two are better than one because they have a good return for their labor: If either of them falls down, one can help the other up. But pity anyone who falls and has no one to help them up." - Ecclesiastes 4:9-10 (NIV)

God designed us for community, for relationships that uplift and support us through life's journey. Strong relationships are foundational to our well-being, providing companionship, encouragement, and accountability.

Building strong relationships requires intentional effort. It involves investing time and energy into nurturing connections with others, prioritizing communication, empathy, and vulnerability. It's about being present for one another, offering a listening ear, and extending grace and forgiveness when needed.

Action Plan:

Today, reach out to someone you care about and express your appreciation for them. It could be a family member, friend, or colleague. Make plans to spend quality time together, whether it's through a conversation over coffee or engaging in a shared activity.

Gracious God, thank You for the gift of relationships. Help me to cultivate strong bonds with those around me, built on love, trust, and mutual support. Guide my words and actions to foster deeper connections and bring glory to Your name. In Jesus' name, Amen.

DAY 22

Faith in Action

"What good is it, my brothers and sisters, if someone claims to have faith but has no deeds? Can such faith save them?" - James 2:14 (NIV)

True faith is not merely a set of beliefs we hold in our hearts; it's a force that propels us into action. It's the courage to step out, trusting in God's promises and power to guide us. Faith in action is a dynamic force that transforms lives and impacts the world around us.

When we put our faith into action, we become vessels of God's love and agents of change in our communities. It's about embodying the principles of compassion, generosity, and service in our daily lives. Through acts of kindness, words of encouragement, and deeds of mercy, we demonstrate the reality of our faith.

Action Plan:

Today, choose one practical way to live out your faith. It could be volunteering at a local charity, reaching out to someone in need, or simply offering a listening ear to a friend. Whatever it may be, let your actions reflect the love and compassion of Christ.

Heavenly Father, empower me to put my faith into action each day. Give me eyes to see the needs around me and the courage to respond with love and compassion. May my life be a testimony to Your grace and goodness. In Jesus' name, Amen.

DAY 23

Understanding Grace

"For it is by grace you have been saved, through faith—and this is not from yourselves, it is the gift of God." - Ephesians 2:8 (NIV)

Grace, a concept so vast and profound, lies at the heart of our faith journey. It's the unmerited favor of God, freely given to us despite our shortcomings and failures. Understanding grace transforms our lives, reminding us that we are loved beyond measure, not because of anything we've done, but because of who God is.

Grace teaches us humility, for it humbles us to acknowledge that we cannot earn God's love or salvation through our own efforts. Instead, it invites us to receive with open hearts the gift that God offers, knowing that we are fully accepted and cherished.

Action Plan:

Today, meditate on the depth of God's grace in your life. Take a few moments to reflect on specific instances where you've experienced God's unmerited favor and love. Write them down, and thank God for each one. Then, extend grace to someone in your life who may not deserve it, just as God has done for you.

Gracious God, thank you for your boundless love and unmerited favor. Help me to grasp the depth of your grace in my life and to extend it to others. May your grace transform my heart and guide my actions today and always. In Jesus' name, Amen.

DAY 24

Being a Light in the World

"You are the light of the world. A town built on a hill cannot be hidden. Neither do people light a lamp and put it under a bowl. Instead, they put it on its stand, and it gives light to everyone in the house. In the same way, let your light shine before others, that they may see your good deeds and glorify your Father in heaven." - Matthew 5:14-16 (NIV)

As men of faith, we are called to be beacons of light in a world often overshadowed by darkness. Just as a lamp illuminates a room, our actions, words, and attitudes should radiate the love and truth of God. We are called to stand out, not blend in—to be a guiding force, leading others towards goodness and righteousness.

Being a light in the world means living with integrity, compassion, and kindness. It means being a source of encouragement and hope to those around us, even in the face of adversity. Our light shines brightest when we reflect the character of Christ in our daily lives, inspiring others to seek Him.

Action Plan:

Today, purposefully seek out opportunities to be a light in someone's life. Whether it's through a kind gesture, a word of encouragement, or a helping hand, let your actions reflect the love of God.

Heavenly Father, thank you for calling me to be a light in the world. Give me the strength and courage to shine brightly for you, even in the midst of darkness. Help me to embody your love and grace in all that I do. In Jesus' name, Amen.

DAY 25

The Importance of Community

"Two are better than one because they have a good return for their labor: If either of them falls down, one can help the other up. But pity anyone who falls and has no one to help them up." -
Ecclesiastes 4:9-10 (NIV)

God designed us for community, weaving the fabric of our lives with threads of connection and support. In a world that often fosters individualism, the importance of community cannot be overstated. It is within the embrace of community that we find strength, encouragement, and purpose.

True community offers companionship in times of joy and solace in times of sorrow. It provides a safe space for vulnerability and authenticity, where we can share our burdens and celebrate our victories together. Through community, we discover that we are not alone in our struggles and triumphs, but rather part of a larger tapestry of humanity.

Action Plan:

Today, reach out to someone in your community who may be feeling isolated or in need of support. Offer a listening ear, a helping hand, or a word of encouragement. Take intentional steps to deepen your connections within your community, whether through joining a small group, volunteering, or simply spending quality time with others.

Gracious God, thank You for the gift of community, where we find strength, belonging, and love. Help us to nurture and cherish the relationships You have blessed us with, and may we always seek to support and uplift one another. In Jesus' name, Amen.

DAY 26

God's Promises

"For no matter how many promises God has made, they are 'Yes' in Christ." - 2 Corinthians 1:20a (NIV)

God's promises are the anchor in the stormy seas of life, a beacon of hope that never dims. In a world often fraught with uncertainty, His promises stand firm, unchanging and unwavering. They serve as reminders of His faithfulness, His unending love, and His unfailing presence.

Despite the challenges we face, we can cling to the promises of God with unwavering faith. From His promise to never leave nor forsake us (Hebrews 13:5) to His assurance of peace that surpasses all understanding (Philippians 4:7), His word is a source of strength and encouragement.

Action Plan:

Today, choose to meditate on one specific promise of God. Write it down and carry it with you throughout the day. Whenever doubt or fear creeps in, remind yourself of that promise and speak it aloud. Allow it to permeate your heart and mind, filling you with renewed confidence and trust in God's faithfulness.

Heavenly Father, thank You for Your promises that sustain us in every season of life. Help us to hold fast to Your word and to trust in Your unfailing goodness. May Your promises be our guiding light, leading us closer to You each day. In Jesus' name, Amen.

DAY 27

Overcoming Temptation

"No temptation has overtaken you except what is common to mankind. And God is faithful; he will not let you be tempted beyond what you can bear. But when you are tempted, he will also provide a way out so that you can endure it." - 1 Corinthians 10:13 (NIV)

In a world filled with distractions and allurements, the battle against temptation is a daily struggle. Yet, as men of faith, we are not alone in this fight. God's promise is clear: He will never allow us to face temptation beyond what we can handle, and He always provides a way out.

Temptation often disguises itself as pleasure or instant gratification, but its consequences can be detrimental to our spiritual well-being. However, by staying rooted in our faith and seeking God's strength, we can overcome even the most persistent temptations.

Action Plan:

Today, identify one specific temptation that frequently challenges you. Pray for strength and discernment to recognize the way out that God provides. Surround yourself with supportive friends or mentors who can encourage you in your journey.

Heavenly Father, in the midst of temptation, I turn to You for strength and guidance. Help me to recognize the way out that You provide and grant me the courage to resist temptation. Surround me with Your love and support. In Jesus' name, Amen.

DAY 28

The Gift of Salvation

"For God so loved the world that he gave his one and only Son, that whoever believes in him shall not perish but have eternal life."
- John 3:16 (NIV)

In a world filled with turmoil and uncertainty, the gift of salvation stands as a beacon of hope and redemption. It's a reminder of God's unfathomable love for us, demonstrated through the sacrifice of Jesus Christ. Salvation offers us the opportunity to be reconciled with our Creator, to experience true peace and purpose amidst life's chaos.

The gift of salvation is freely available to all who believe. It's not earned through our own efforts or merits but received through faith in Christ. Through salvation, we are forgiven, renewed, and empowered to live a life of meaning and significance.

Action Plan:

Today, take a moment to reflect on the gift of salvation and its impact on your life. Consider how you can share this gift with others, whether through acts of kindness, sharing your faith story, or inviting someone to church.

Heavenly Father, thank you for the gift of salvation that you have freely given us through your Son, Jesus Christ. Help us to fully grasp the magnitude of this gift and to live in gratitude and obedience. May we boldly share the message of salvation with those around us, that they too may experience the joy of knowing you. In Jesus' name, Amen.

DAY 29

Stewardship and Generosity

"Each of you should give what you have decided in your heart to give, not reluctantly or under compulsion, for God loves a cheerful giver." - 2 Corinthians 9:7 (NIV)

Stewardship and generosity are not just acts of charity but reflections of our gratitude for the abundant blessings bestowed upon us. As men of faith, we are called to be faithful stewards of the resources entrusted to us by our Creator. Our possessions, talents, and time are gifts meant to be shared for the betterment of the world around us.

Generosity flows from a heart that acknowledges the providence of God and seeks to mirror His generosity in our interactions with others. When we embrace stewardship, we recognize that our resources are not solely for our own benefit but are instruments for advancing God's kingdom on earth.

Action Plan:

Today, identify one area where you can practice stewardship and generosity. It could be volunteering your time at a local charity, donating to a cause you're passionate about, or simply offering a listening ear to someone in need. Whatever it may be, do it wholeheartedly and with joy, knowing that you are participating in God's work of love and compassion.

Gracious God, thank You for the abundance of blessings You have bestowed upon me. Guide me in using my resources to bless others and glorify Your name. In Jesus' name, Amen.

DAY 30

Pursuing Holiness

"But just as he who called you is holy, so be holy in all you do; for it is written: 'Be holy, because I am holy.'" - 1 Peter 1:15-16 (NIV)

As men of faith navigating the complexities of the world, the pursuit of holiness stands as our noble quest. Holiness is not about isolation or withdrawal but about being set apart for God's purposes in the midst of our daily lives. It's about reflecting the character of our holy God in every thought, word, and action.

In a world that often glorifies self-interest and compromise, pursuing holiness requires intentional effort and unwavering commitment. It means aligning our lives with God's standards of righteousness, seeking purity of heart, integrity in relationships, and righteousness in all endeavors.

Action Plan:

Today, commit to one specific area of your life where you can pursue holiness more intentionally. It could be in your speech, your relationships, your work ethic, or your leisure activities. Set aside time for prayer and reflection, asking God to reveal any areas where you need to realign your priorities and values to reflect His holiness.

Gracious Father, empower me to pursue holiness wholeheartedly in the midst of the world's distractions and temptations. Give me the strength to live with integrity and righteousness, honoring You in all I do. May Your holy presence guide and sustain me each day. In Jesus' name, Amen.

DAY 31

The Power of Words

"The tongue has the power of life and death, and those who love it will eat its fruit." - Proverbs 18:21 (NIV)

Words hold immense power. They have the ability to build up or tear down, to inspire or discourage. As men of faith, we must recognize the weight of our words and wield them with wisdom and kindness.

Our words shape our reality and the reality of those around us. With a word of encouragement, we can ignite hope in someone's heart. Conversely, with a word of criticism or negativity, we can inflict wounds that may linger for a lifetime.

Let us choose our words carefully, speaking life and love into every situation. Let our speech be seasoned with grace, lifting others up and pointing them towards the source of all goodness and truth.

Action Plan:

Today, make a conscious effort to speak words of encouragement and affirmation to those around you. Whether it's a compliment to a coworker, a word of appreciation to a family member, or an affirmation of faith to a friend, let your words be a source of light and joy.

Heavenly Father, thank You for the gift of speech. Help me to use my words to build up rather than tear down, to encourage rather than discourage. May Your love flow through my words, bringing hope and healing to all who hear them. In Jesus' name, Amen.

DAY 32

Facing Challenges with Faith

"I can do all this through him who gives me strength." -
Philippians 4:13 (NIV)

Life is a journey filled with peaks and valleys, triumphs and trials. Yet, in the face of every challenge, our faith becomes our anchor, our source of unwavering strength and resilience.

When we face challenges with faith, we recognize that we are not alone. God walks alongside us, empowering us to overcome obstacles that seem insurmountable.

In the midst of adversity, it's easy to feel overwhelmed and discouraged. But as men of faith, we are called to rise above our circumstances, trusting in God's plan for our lives. With faith as our guide, we can navigate through the darkest of times with courage and hope.

Action Plan:

Today, when faced with a challenge, choose to lean on your faith. Take a moment to pray and surrender your worries to God. Then, boldly step forward, knowing that He is with you every step of the way. Allow your faith to fuel your actions, and watch as God works wonders in your life.

Heavenly Father, in times of difficulty, help me to hold fast to my faith. Strengthen me with Your power and grant me the courage to face every challenge with confidence. Thank you for being my constant source of hope and strength. In Jesus' name, Amen.

DAY 33

God's Faithfulness

"Know therefore that the Lord your God is God, the faithful God who keeps covenant and steadfast love with those who love him and keep his commandments, to a thousand generations." -
Deuteronomy 7:9 (ESV)

God's faithfulness is an unshakable pillar in our lives, a rock on which we can confidently stand amidst life's storms. It's a testament to His unwavering commitment to His promises, never faltering, never failing.

In every season, God's faithfulness endures. In times of joy, He celebrates with us. In times of sorrow, He comforts us with His presence. Even when we falter, His faithfulness remains steadfast, guiding us back to His loving embrace.

Action Plan:

Today, reflect on moments in your life where you've seen God's faithfulness at work. Take time to journal or meditate on these experiences, acknowledging His presence and provision. Then, choose one area of your life where you're struggling to trust in God's faithfulness, and surrender it to Him in prayer.

Gracious God, thank You for Your unwavering faithfulness in my life. Help me to trust in Your promises and rely on Your strength, especially in times of uncertainty. I surrender my fears and doubts to You, knowing that You are always faithful. In Jesus' name, Amen.

DAY 34

The Blessing of Obedience

"If you fully obey the Lord your God and carefully follow all his commands I give you today, the Lord your God will set you high above all the nations on earth." - Deuteronomy 28:1 (NIV)

Obedience to God's commands is not merely an obligation; it is the pathway to blessings beyond measure. When we align our lives with His will, we position ourselves to receive His favor and experience His abundant provision.

The blessing of obedience flows from a heart surrendered to God's authority. It's a conscious decision to trust His wisdom and follow His guidance, even when it seems counterintuitive or challenging. Through obedience, we demonstrate our love for God and acknowledge His sovereignty over every aspect of our lives.

Action Plan:

Today, choose one area of your life where you've been hesitant to obey God's command. It could be in your relationships, finances, career, or personal growth. Commit to obeying His instruction in that area, trusting that His way is best. Take practical steps to align your actions with His will, seeking His guidance through prayer and Scripture.

Heavenly Father, give me the strength and wisdom to obey Your commands wholeheartedly. Help me to trust in Your goodness and surrender my will to Yours. May my obedience bring glory to Your name and lead to abundant blessings in my life. In Jesus' name, Amen.

DAY 35

Living with Purpose

"For we are God's handiwork, created in Christ Jesus to do good works, which God prepared in advance for us to do." - Ephesians 2:10 (NIV)

Living with purpose is a journey of discovery and fulfillment. It's about understanding that each of us is uniquely crafted by the hands of God, endowed with talents and passions to make a difference in the world around us.

To live with purpose means to live intentionally, with clarity of vision and direction. It's about seeking God's guidance in every decision and allowing His purpose to shape our ambitions, careers, relationships, and daily actions. When we live with purpose, even the simplest tasks become infused with meaning, and every challenge becomes an opportunity for growth.

Action Plan:

Take time today to reflect on your life's purpose. Consider your passions, talents, and the needs of the world around you. Whether it's serving others, pursuing a new opportunity, or deepening your relationship with God, take a deliberate step forward with faith and conviction.

Heavenly Father, thank You for creating me with a purpose. Help me to discern Your will for my life and to live each day with intentionality and passion. Guide me as I seek to fulfill the good works You have prepared for me. In Jesus' name, Amen.

DAY 36

The Power of Worship

"God is spirit, and his worshipers must worship in the Spirit and in truth." - John 4:24 (NIV)

Worship is not merely a ritual; it's a gateway to experiencing the presence and power of God in our lives. When we lift our hearts in adoration and praise, we align ourselves with the divine purpose, tapping into a source of strength and inspiration beyond ourselves.

In worship, we surrender our worries, fears, and burdens at the feet of the Almighty, exchanging them for peace and joy that surpasses understanding. It's a transformative encounter that reshapes our perspective, reminding us of God's sovereignty and goodness even in the midst of life's challenges.

Action Plan:

Today, set aside time for intentional worship. Create a playlist of worship songs that resonate with your soul or simply offer up your own heartfelt prayers and praises. Focus on God's attributes and the blessings He has bestowed upon you. Allow the atmosphere of worship to permeate your surroundings and your spirit, inviting God to move in your life in new and profound ways.

Heavenly Father, I thank You for the gift of worship, through which we draw near to You. Help me to cultivate a heart of worship, one that honors You in spirit and truth. May my life be a continual offering of praise unto Your holy name. In Jesus' name, Amen.

DAY 37

Understanding God's Love

"See what great love the Father has lavished on us, that we should be called children of God! And that is what we are!" - 1 John 3:1a (NIV)

Understanding God's love is akin to discovering a boundless ocean whose depths we can never fully fathom. It's a love so profound, so relentless, that it defies human comprehension. Yet, in its simplicity lies its beauty – a love that calls us His children, heirs to His kingdom.

God's love is not contingent on our achievements or merits; it's freely given, unconditionally. It's a love that pursues us in our brokenness, gently drawing us close to Him. When we grasp the depth of His love, we find our true identity and purpose.

Action Plan:

Today, take a moment to meditate on God's love for you. Reflect on the ways He has shown His love in your life, whether through blessings, moments of peace, or acts of grace. Then, choose to share that love with others. Reach out to someone in need, offer a kind word or gesture, and let God's love flow through you.

Heavenly Father, thank You for the incomprehensible love You have lavished upon me. Help me to grasp the depth of Your love and live in the reality of being Your beloved child. Empower me to extend Your love to those around me, that they too may experience Your grace. In Jesus' name, Amen.

DAY 38

The Importance of Honesty

"The Lord detests lying lips, but he delights in people who are trustworthy." - Proverbs 12:22 (NIV)

Honesty is the foundation upon which integrity stands tall. In a world clouded by deceit and half-truths, the importance of honesty cannot be overstated. When we commit to truthfulness, we align ourselves with God's will, for He is the ultimate source of all truth.

Being honest requires courage. It means choosing transparency even when it's easier to conceal. Honesty builds trust, fostering deeper, more meaningful relationships with others and with God. It's a reflection of our character and a testament to our commitment to righteousness.

Action Plan:

Today, commit to being completely honest in all your interactions. Whether in your words or actions, let truth be your guiding principle. Practice self-reflection, acknowledging areas where dishonesty may have crept in, and strive to rectify them. Remember, honesty is not just about speaking truth; it's also about living it.

Heavenly Father, help me to walk in honesty and integrity each day. Give me the strength to speak truth and the wisdom to discern right from wrong. May my words and actions reflect Your truth, bringing glory to Your name. In Jesus' name, Amen.

DAY 39

The Role of a Father

*"Fathers, do not exasperate your children; instead, bring them up
in the training and instruction of the Lord." - Ephesians 6:4 (NIV)*

The role of a father is one of profound significance. Just as God is
our Heavenly Father, earthly fathers are called to mirror His love,
guidance, and provision in the lives of their children. A father's
influence extends far beyond mere provision; it shapes the
character, values, and destinies of the next generation.

Fathers have the unique privilege and responsibility of nurturing,
teaching, and guiding their children. Their presence is a source of
strength and stability, offering both protection and encouragement.
Through their words and actions, fathers impart invaluable lessons
of faith, resilience, and love.

Action Plan:

Today, commit to being a present and engaged father. Spend
quality time with your children, listening to their joys, fears, and
dreams. Take an active role in their upbringing, modeling integrity,
kindness, and perseverance. Prioritize their spiritual growth,
leading by example and sharing the timeless truths of God's Word.

*Heavenly Father, thank You for the gift of fatherhood. Grant me
the wisdom and grace to fulfill this sacred role with love and
diligence. Help me to be a beacon of Your light, guiding my
children in Your ways. May my life reflect Your love and
compassion, shaping the hearts of my children for Your glory. In
Jesus' name, Amen.*

DAY 40

Embracing God's Plan

"For I know the plans I have for you," declares the Lord, "plans to prosper you and not to harm you, plans to give you hope and a future." - Jeremiah 29:11 (NIV)

Embracing God's plan is an act of surrender, a declaration of trust in His wisdom and goodness. Though our own plans may seem clear and enticing, it's in relinquishing control that we find true fulfillment and purpose. God's plan surpasses our understanding, crafted with a love that knows no bounds.

When we embrace God's plan, we step into a journey marked by divine guidance and providence. It's a path paved with grace, leading us towards our ultimate destiny. Though the road may be winding and challenging, every twist and turn serves a greater purpose in shaping us into who God intends us to be.

Action Plan:

Today, surrender your plans to God. Take time to pray and seek His guidance for your life. Reflect on areas where you may have been resisting His plan and ask for the strength to let go. Trust that His plan for you is far greater than anything you could imagine, and commit to following where He leads.

Heavenly Father, I surrender my plans to You today. Help me to trust in Your perfect timing and wisdom. Guide me along the path You have set before me, and grant me the courage to embrace Your plan wholeheartedly. In Jesus' name, Amen.

DAY 41

Contentment in Christ

"I have learned to be content whatever the circumstances." - Philippians 4:11b (NIV)

Contentment in Christ is not about complacency but about finding peace and fulfillment in His presence regardless of our circumstances. It's a state of heart and mind anchored in the unchanging love of God. In a world that constantly whispers discontentment, we are called to fix our eyes on Jesus, the source of true satisfaction.

Contentment doesn't mean we stop striving or pursuing our goals. Instead, it empowers us to pursue them with a sense of peace, knowing that our worth and identity are found in Christ alone. When we find contentment in Him, we release the grip of comparison, envy, and greed that often entangle us.

Action Plan:

Today, practice gratitude for the blessings in your life, both big and small. Take time to reflect on God's faithfulness and provision, thanking Him for His goodness. Cultivate contentment by focusing on what you have rather than what you lack. Whenever feelings of discontentment arise, intentionally shift your perspective back to the abundance found in Christ.

Gracious Father, teach me to find contentment in You alone. Help me to trust Your plan for my life and to rest in Your unfailing love. May I be filled with gratitude and joy, knowing that You are more than enough for me. In Jesus' name, Amen.

DAY 42

Enduring Hardships

"Consider it pure joy, my brothers and sisters, whenever you face trials of many kinds, because you know that the testing of your faith produces perseverance." - James 1:2-3 (NIV)

Enduring hardships is a journey marked by faith and resilience. In life, we inevitably encounter challenges that test our strength and character. Yet, it is through these trials that our faith is refined like gold in fire.

Hardships are not meant to break us but to build us. They cultivate perseverance, teaching us to endure with unwavering resolve. When we face adversity with courage and faith, we grow stronger, drawing closer to God in the process.

Action Plan:

Today, when faced with a hardship, choose to embrace it as an opportunity for growth. Instead of being discouraged, view it as a chance to strengthen your faith and character. Lean on God for guidance and strength, trusting that He will carry you through every trial.

Heavenly Father, in the midst of hardships, I turn to You for strength and courage. Help me to see beyond the challenges and to trust in Your plan for my life. Grant me perseverance to endure, knowing that through every trial, You are refining me into the person You created me to be. Amen.

DAY 43

Living by the Spirit

"So I say, walk by the Spirit, and you will not gratify the desires of the flesh." - Galatians 5:16 (NIV)

Living by the Spirit is about surrendering to the divine guidance that leads us towards righteousness and away from the temptations of the flesh. It's a conscious choice to align our thoughts, words, and actions with the will of God, allowing His Spirit to dwell within us and transform our lives.

When we live by the Spirit, we experience true freedom. No longer slaves to our own selfish desires, we find liberation in serving others and glorifying God. The Spirit empowers us to love unconditionally, to show kindness and compassion even in the face of adversity.

Action Plan:

Today, commit to walking by the Spirit in all aspects of your life. Begin each day with prayer and meditation, inviting the Holy Spirit to guide your thoughts and actions. Throughout the day, consciously seek opportunities to demonstrate love, joy, peace, patience, kindness, goodness, faithfulness, gentleness, and self-control—the fruits of the Spirit.

Heavenly Father, fill me with Your Spirit and lead me on the path of righteousness. Help me to surrender my will to Yours and to walk in obedience to Your Word. May Your Spirit empower me to live a life that honors and glorifies You. In Jesus' name, Amen.

DAY 44

The Value of Work

"Whatever you do, work at it with all your heart, as working for the Lord, not for human masters." - Colossians 3:23 (NIV)

Work is not merely a means to an end; it's a calling, a way to honor God through our diligence and dedication. When we approach our tasks with wholehearted commitment, we reflect the image of our Creator, who Himself is a God of purposeful action.

Every job, no matter how mundane or grand, carries inherent value. Through our work, we contribute to the betterment of society and fulfill our role in God's divine plan. Whether we're tilling fields, leading teams, or caring for families, our labor is an offering to Him.

Action Plan:

Today, strive to excel in your work, whatever it may be. Commit to giving your best effort, not for the praise of men, but as an expression of gratitude to God. Seek opportunities to serve others through your work, recognizing that every task, no matter how small, has the potential to glorify Him.

Heavenly Father, thank You for the privilege of work. Help me to approach each task with diligence and dedication, knowing that I work ultimately for You. Grant me the wisdom to recognize the significance of my labor and the strength to carry it out joyfully. In Jesus' name, Amen.

DAY 45

The Importance of Rest

"Come to me, all you who are weary and burdened, and I will give you rest." - Matthew 11:28 (NIV)

Rest is not just a physical necessity; it's a spiritual discipline. In a world that glorifies busyness and productivity, the importance of rest often gets overlooked. Yet, God Himself set the example of rest when He rested on the seventh day after creating the heavens and the earth.

Rest rejuvenates our bodies, refreshes our minds, and renews our spirits. It's a time to recharge, to realign our priorities, and to draw closer to God. When we neglect rest, we risk burnout and spiritual stagnation. Rest is not a sign of weakness but of wisdom, acknowledging our limitations and our need for God's sustenance.

Action Plan:

Today, prioritize rest in your life. Set aside time each day for quiet reflection, prayer, and meditation. Disconnect from the noise of the world and find solace in God's presence. Additionally, make space in your schedule for adequate sleep and relaxation. Trust that in surrendering to rest, you are entrusting your cares to a faithful God who sustains you.

Gracious Father, thank You for the gift of rest. Teach me to embrace rest as a holy practice, recognizing its importance in my physical, mental, and spiritual well-being. Help me to find peace in Your presence and strength in Your promises. In Jesus' name, Amen.

DAY 46

God's Provision

"And my God will meet all your needs according to the riches of his glory in Christ Jesus." - Philippians 4:19 (NIV)

God's provision is abundant and unwavering. He is the ultimate provider, meeting our needs in ways beyond our comprehension. In times of scarcity or abundance, His provision remains constant, a testament to His faithfulness and love for us.

Understanding God's provision goes beyond material blessings. It encompasses every aspect of our lives – physical, emotional, and spiritual. He provides comfort in times of distress, strength in moments of weakness, and guidance in the midst of uncertainty. Our role is to trust in His timing and His ways, knowing that He always has our best interests at heart.

Action Plan:

Today, practice gratitude for God's provision in your life. Take a moment to reflect on the ways He has provided for you – whether through tangible blessings or spiritual guidance. Write down three things you are grateful for and spend time in prayer, thanking God for His faithfulness and provision.

Heavenly Father, thank you for your abundant provision in my life. Help me to trust in your timing and to remain grateful for your blessings, both big and small. Guide me to rely on your provision with unwavering faith, knowing that you always provide for your children. In Jesus' name, Amen.

DAY 47

Joy in the Lord

"Rejoice always, pray continually, give thanks in all circumstances; for this is God's will for you in Christ Jesus." - 1 Thessalonians 5:16-18 (NIV)

Joy in the Lord is not just an emotion; it's a state of being rooted in our relationship with Him. It transcends circumstances, flowing from the deep wellspring of God's presence within us. When we find our joy in the Lord, we discover a source of strength and resilience that sustains us through life's trials.

Choosing joy in the Lord is a deliberate act of faith. It's a decision to focus on God's goodness and faithfulness, even in the midst of adversity. This joy empowers us to rise above our circumstances, knowing that God is with us every step of the way.

Action Plan:

Today, make a conscious effort to cultivate joy in the Lord. Start by spending time in prayer and meditation, reflecting on His promises and faithfulness. Throughout the day, practice gratitude, intentionally thanking God for the blessings in your life, both big and small. As you do, allow His joy to fill your heart and overflow into every aspect of your day.

Gracious God, thank You for the gift of joy that comes from knowing You. Help me to rejoice always, even when faced with challenges. May Your presence fill me with a joy that surpasses all understanding, guiding my steps and shining brightly for others to see. In Jesus' name, Amen.

DAY 48

Practicing Self-Control

"Like a city whose walls are broken through is a person who lacks self-control." - Proverbs 25:28 (NIV)

Self-control is a hallmark of strength and wisdom. It's the ability to govern our desires, impulses, and emotions, even in the face of temptation. When we exercise self-control, we demonstrate mastery over ourselves, allowing us to pursue our goals and live in alignment with God's will.

Practicing self-control is not always easy. It requires discipline and commitment. Yet, the rewards are immeasurable. Through self-control, we cultivate resilience and perseverance, essential qualities for navigating life's challenges. We become stewards of our actions, making choices that honor God and uplift others.

Action Plan:

Today, choose one area of your life where you struggle with self-control. It could be your temper, your eating habits, or your use of time. Identify triggers that lead to indulgence or excess, and commit to exercising restraint. Lean on God's strength and seek accountability from a trusted friend or mentor. With each victory, celebrate the growth and progress you've made.

Heavenly Father, grant me the strength to practice self-control in all aspects of my life. Help me to resist temptation and align my desires with Your perfect will. May my actions bring glory to Your name and inspire others to walk in discipline and obedience. In Jesus' name, Amen.

DAY 49

The Power of Community

"Two are better than one, because they have a good return for their labor: If either of them falls down, one can help the other up. But pity anyone who falls and has no one to help them up." - Ecclesiastes 4:9-10 (NIV)

The power of community is a gift from God, a source of strength, support, and encouragement. In the company of fellow believers, we find solace in shared experiences, strength in unity, and inspiration to press on in our faith journey.

Community reminds us that we are not meant to walk alone. It provides a safe space to be vulnerable, to share our joys and struggles, knowing that we are surrounded by brothers who will lift us up when we stumble and celebrate with us in our victories.

Action Plan:

Today, reach out to a fellow brother in faith. Whether through a phone call, a text, or a face-to-face meeting, extend a hand of friendship and support. Take the initiative to strengthen your bonds within your community by actively engaging in conversations, offering help where needed, and being present in both times of joy and times of trial.

Gracious God, thank You for the gift of community. Help me to cherish and nurture the relationships I have with my fellow brothers in faith. May our community be a beacon of Your love and grace. In Jesus' name, Amen.

DAY 50

The Impact of Kindness

"Be kind and compassionate to one another, forgiving each other, just as in Christ God forgave you." - Ephesians 4:32 (NIV)

Kindness is a language that transcends barriers and touches hearts. It has the power to heal wounds, mend broken spirits, and bring light into the darkest of days. When we choose kindness, we reflect the love of Christ, who showed us the ultimate act of kindness by sacrificing Himself for our redemption.

The impact of kindness is profound. A simple act of kindness can ripple outwards, spreading joy and hope to those around us. It has the power to transform lives, inspiring others to pay it forward and create a chain reaction of positivity.

Action Plan:

Today, purposefully seek out opportunities to show kindness to others. It could be as simple as offering a listening ear to a friend in need, giving a compliment to a stranger, or performing a random act of kindness for someone in your community. Let your actions be guided by love and compassion, knowing that even the smallest gesture can make a difference.

Heavenly Father, thank You for the gift of kindness. Help me to be a vessel of Your love, spreading kindness wherever I go. Give me eyes to see the needs of others and a heart willing to respond with compassion. May my life be a reflection of Your kindness and grace. In Jesus' name, Amen.

DAY 51

Guarding Your Heart

"Above all else, guard your heart, for everything you do flows from it." - Proverbs 4:23 (NIV)

Guarding your heart is not just a suggestion; it's a commandment rooted in wisdom. Your heart is the wellspring of your life, the source from which your thoughts, words, and actions flow. Protecting it is crucial to maintaining spiritual health and vitality.

In a world filled with distractions and temptations, guarding your heart means being vigilant about what you allow to influence you. It involves filtering out negativity, guarding against harmful influences, and cultivating a mindset focused on truth and righteousness.

Action Plan:

Today, take inventory of what you allow into your heart and mind. Identify any sources of negativity, whether it be certain media, toxic relationships, or destructive thought patterns. Then, intentionally replace those with positive influences—scripture, uplifting music, supportive friendships—anything that nurtures your spiritual growth and strengthens your connection with God.

Heavenly Father, help me to guard my heart diligently, for it is the wellspring of my life. Grant me discernment to recognize harmful influences and the strength to resist them. Fill my heart with Your love and truth, guiding me in all that I do. In Jesus' name, Amen.

DAY 52

The Call to Evangelize

"And he said to them, 'Go into all the world and proclaim the gospel to the whole creation.'" - Mark 16:15 (ESV)

The call to evangelize is not just a suggestion; it's a commandment from our Lord Jesus Christ Himself. As men of faith, we are entrusted with the invaluable task of sharing the Good News with others. This mission is not reserved for a select few but is a responsibility placed upon every believer.

Evangelism is about spreading the message of salvation, extending the invitation to experience the transformative power of God's love. It's about shining the light of Christ in a world that is often shrouded in darkness. Through evangelism, we participate in God's redemptive work, inviting others into a relationship with Him.

Action Plan:

Today, commit to sharing your faith with at least one person. It could be a friend, family member, colleague, or even a stranger. Be intentional about opportunities to speak about Jesus, whether through conversation, acts of kindness, or sharing your own testimony. Trust in the Holy Spirit to guide your words and actions.

Heavenly Father, empower me to be a bold and faithful witness for You. Open doors for me to share the gospel and grant me the words to speak with clarity and conviction. Use me as Your instrument to bring others into Your kingdom. In Jesus' name, Amen.

DAY 53

Developing Spiritual Disciplines

"But seek first his kingdom and his righteousness, and all these things will be given to you as well." - Matthew 6:33 (NIV)

Spiritual disciplines are the training ground for the soul, the means by which we draw closer to God and grow in our faith. They encompass practices such as prayer, meditation, fasting, study of scripture, and worship. Just as athletes train rigorously to excel in their sport, so too must we discipline ourselves spiritually to thrive in our walk with God.

Developing spiritual disciplines is essential for cultivating a deeper intimacy with God. They help us align our priorities with His kingdom purposes and empower us to live lives of greater purpose and impact. Through these practices, we open our hearts to receive the abundant blessings and guidance that God promises to those who seek Him first.

Action Plan:

Start by committing to a daily quiet time with God. Set aside a specific time each day for prayer, meditation, and reading scripture. Begin with just a few minutes and gradually increase the duration as you build consistency. Keep a journal to track your progress and insights gained during your quiet time.

Heavenly Father, guide me as I embark on this journey of developing spiritual disciplines. Grant me the discipline and dedication to seek You first in all things. May my heart be open to receive Your wisdom and grace each day. In Jesus' name, Amen.

DAY 54

Trusting God's Timing

"For I know the plans I have for you," declares the Lord, "plans to prosper you and not to harm you, plans to give you hope and a future." - Jeremiah 29:11 (NIV)

Trusting God's timing is an act of faith that requires patience and surrender. In a world of instant gratification, we often find ourselves struggling with impatience, wanting things to happen according to our own timetable. Yet, God's timing is perfect, guided by His infinite wisdom and love for us.

When we trust God's timing, we acknowledge His sovereignty over our lives. We release our desires and plans into His hands, confident that He knows what is best for us. Even in moments of waiting and uncertainty, we can find peace knowing that God is working all things together for our good.

Action Plan:

Today, surrender your timeline to God. Reflect on areas of your life where you've been impatient or anxious about the future. Surrender those desires to God's care, trusting that He has a perfect plan in store for you. Practice patience and faith as you wait for His timing to unfold.

Heavenly Father, teach me to trust Your timing in all things. Help me to surrender my desires and plans to Your will, knowing that Your timing is perfect. Give me patience and faith as I wait for Your promises to be fulfilled. In Jesus' name, Amen.

DAY 55

Embracing Change

"See, I am doing a new thing! Now it springs up; do you not perceive it? I am making a way in the wilderness and streams in the wasteland." - Isaiah 43:19 (NIV)

Change is inevitable in life, for it is the catalyst of growth and transformation. Yet, many fear change, clinging to the familiar even when it hinders progress. Embracing change requires faith and courage, trusting that God is orchestrating a beautiful new beginning.

Change challenges us to step out of our comfort zones, to relinquish control and surrender to the divine plan unfolding before us. It invites us to adapt, to learn, and to evolve into the person God intended us to be.

Action Plan:

Today, embrace change with an open heart and a willing spirit. Identify an area in your life where change is needed—a habit to break, a mindset to shift, or a new opportunity to pursue. Take a small, intentional step toward embracing this change, trusting that God will guide you through the process.

Heavenly Father, thank You for the promise of new beginnings and the opportunity for growth through change. Grant me the courage to embrace the changes You bring into my life, trusting in Your perfect plan. May Your presence be my constant comfort and strength. In Jesus' name, Amen.

DAY 56

God's Unfailing Love

"But God demonstrates his own love for us in this: While we were still sinners, Christ died for us." - Romans 5:8 (NIV)

God's love is boundless, reaching far beyond our understanding. It's a love that knows no bounds, a love that pursues us relentlessly, even in our darkest moments. Despite our flaws and shortcomings, God's love remains constant and unwavering.

Understanding God's unfailing love brings us immense comfort and strength. It reminds us that we are never alone, that we are deeply cherished by the Creator of the universe. This love empowers us to face life's challenges with courage and confidence, knowing that we are held securely in God's embrace.

Action Plan:

Today, meditate on God's unfailing love for you. Take a few moments to reflect on the ways in which God has shown His love in your life. Write down your thoughts or share them with a friend. Allow yourself to bask in the warmth of God's love, letting it renew your spirit and inspire you to love others in return.

Gracious God, thank you for your unfailing love that surrounds me each day. Help me to grasp the depth of your love and to live in its truth. May I be a beacon of your love to others, sharing your grace and compassion with everyone I encounter. In Jesus' name, Amen.

DAY 57

The Importance of Reflection

"Let us examine our ways and test them, and let us return to the Lord." - Lamentations 3:40 (NIV)

Reflection is a vital practice on our spiritual journey. It's the pause button in the hustle of life, allowing us to evaluate our actions, attitudes, and beliefs in the light of God's truth. Through reflection, we gain insight into our strengths and weaknesses, drawing closer to God's intended path for us.

In the midst of our busy lives, it's easy to lose sight of our purpose and drift away from God's will. But through intentional reflection, we realign our hearts with His, seeking His guidance and correction. It's a humbling yet empowering process, as we surrender our pride and open ourselves to transformation.

Action Plan:

Set aside time each day for quiet reflection. Find a peaceful space where you can be alone with your thoughts and with God. Reflect on your day, examining your thoughts, words, and actions in light of God's Word. Ask Him to reveal areas where you need to grow and seek His guidance in making necessary changes.

Heavenly Father, thank You for the gift of reflection. Help me to be diligent in examining my ways and aligning them with Your will. Grant me the wisdom to discern Your voice amidst the noise of the world. May my reflections draw me closer to You and strengthen my faith. In Jesus' name, Amen.

DAY 58

Walking in the Light

"But if we walk in the light, as he is in the light, we have fellowship with one another, and the blood of Jesus, his Son, purifies us from all sin." - 1 John 1:7 (NIV)

Walking in the light signifies living a life of truth, righteousness, and purity. It's about embracing God's guidance and allowing His truth to illuminate our path. When we walk in the light, we align ourselves with the divine purpose and experience the fullness of fellowship with God and others.

Choosing to walk in the light requires a conscious decision to live according to God's Word. It means casting aside the darkness of sin and embracing the brilliance of His love and grace. As we walk in the light, we become beacons of hope and inspiration to those around us, drawing others closer to God's presence.

Action Plan:

Today, commit to walking in the light by actively seeking God's presence in your life. Spend time in prayer and meditation, allowing His Word to penetrate your heart. Reflect on areas where you may be walking in darkness and seek His forgiveness and guidance to lead you back into the light.

Heavenly Father, thank You for the light of Your presence that guides me each day. Help me to walk in Your truth and righteousness, that I may experience the fullness of fellowship with You and others. Shine Your light upon my path and lead me in Your ways. In Jesus' name, Amen.

DAY 59

The Role of a Husband

"Husbands, love your wives, just as Christ loved the church and gave himself up for her." - Ephesians 5:25 (NIV)

As husbands, we are called to emulate the sacrificial love of Christ in our marriages. Our role is not merely to lead or provide, but to love our wives selflessly, just as Christ loved the church. This love is characterized by empathy, understanding, and a willingness to lay down our lives for the well-being of our spouse.

Being a husband means being a partner in every sense of the word. It means cherishing our wives, honoring their needs and aspirations, and walking alongside them through life's joys and challenges. Our love should be a beacon of strength and support, a reflection of the divine love that binds us to one another.

Action Plan:

Today, make a deliberate effort to show love and appreciation to your wife. Take time to listen to her thoughts and feelings, validate her experiences, and affirm her worth. Whether it's through a kind word, a thoughtful gesture, or simply being present, let your love shine brightly.

Heavenly Father, thank You for the gift of marriage. Help me to be a husband who loves my wife selflessly, just as Christ loved the church. Give me the grace to honor and cherish her each day, and to continually grow in love and unity. In Jesus' name, Amen.

DAY 60

Overcoming Doubt

"Jesus said to him, 'If you can believe, all things are possible to him who believes.'" - Mark 9:23 (NKJV)

Doubt can be a formidable adversary on our journey of faith, casting shadows of uncertainty over our hearts and minds. Yet, in the face of doubt, we are called to stand firm in the promises of God, trusting in His unfailing love and boundless power.

Overcoming doubt requires a steadfast belief in God's faithfulness. It means choosing to anchor our souls in His Word, even when circumstances seem bleak. For it is in our moments of doubt that our faith is tested and strengthened, forging within us a resilience that can withstand any storm.

Action Plan:

Today, confront your doubts head-on by immersing yourself in Scripture and prayer. Identify areas of uncertainty or fear in your life and surrender them to God, asking Him to replace doubt with unwavering faith. Surround yourself with fellow believers who can offer support and encouragement as you navigate through doubt.

Heavenly Father, grant me the courage to overcome doubt and trust in Your promises. Help me to cling to Your Word as a beacon of hope in times of uncertainty. Strengthen my faith, Lord, and guide me along the path of righteousness. In Jesus' name, Amen.

DAY 61

The Power of Praise

"I will extol the Lord at all times; his praise will always be on my lips." - Psalm 34:1 (NIV)

Praise has the power to transform our hearts and circumstances. When we lift our voices in praise, we invite the presence of God into our lives, ushering in peace, joy, and strength. It's a declaration of faith, acknowledging God's sovereignty and goodness, even in the midst of trials.

Praise is not contingent on our circumstances; it flows from a heart overflowing with gratitude. In times of joy, it magnifies our blessings, and in times of sorrow, it brings comfort and hope. Through praise, we shift our focus from our problems to the greatness of our God, who is worthy of all honor and glory.

Action Plan:

Today, make a conscious effort to incorporate praise into your daily routine. Start by setting aside a few moments each morning to praise God for His faithfulness and goodness. Throughout the day, cultivate a habit of praise by acknowledging God's presence in every situation, whether big or small.

Heavenly Father, I thank You for the gift of praise. Help me to cultivate a heart of worship, recognizing Your greatness in all things. May my lips always be quick to praise Your name, for You alone are worthy of all honor and glory. In Jesus' name, Amen.

DAY 62

Living Out Your Faith

"In the same way, let your light shine before others, that they may see your good deeds and glorify your Father in heaven." - Matthew 5:16 (NIV)

Living out your faith is more than mere words; it's a vibrant expression of your relationship with God. It's about allowing His love to permeate every aspect of your life, transforming your thoughts, words, and actions.

When you live out your faith, you become a beacon of hope and inspiration to those around you. Your life becomes a living testimony to God's grace and power, drawing others closer to Him. Through acts of kindness, compassion, and service, you reflect the character of Christ and shine His light into the world.

Action Plan:

Today, purposefully seek opportunities to live out your faith in practical ways. Whether it's lending a helping hand to someone in need, offering words of encouragement to a friend, or simply being a listening ear, let your actions speak volumes about your faith. Ask God to guide you and empower you to live boldly for Him each day.

Heavenly Father, thank You for the gift of faith. Help me to live out that faith in ways that honor and glorify You. Give me the courage to step out in obedience, trusting You to work through me to touch the lives of others. May my life be a reflection of Your love and grace. In Jesus' name, Amen.

DAY 63

The Call to Righteousness

"But as for you, O man of God, flee these things. Pursue righteousness, godliness, faith, love, steadfastness, gentleness." - 1 Timothy 6:11 (ESV)

The call to righteousness is a beckoning to embody God's character in every aspect of our lives. It's not merely about following a set of rules, but rather about cultivating a heart that seeks after God's own heart. Righteousness is the cornerstone of a life lived in alignment with God's will.

To pursue righteousness is to choose the path of moral excellence and uprightness, even when it's unpopular or difficult. It's about standing firm in our convictions, resisting the temptations that seek to lead us astray. Righteousness is a commitment to honor God in all that we do, knowing that He delights in those who walk blamelessly before Him.

Action Plan:

Today, commit to living out righteousness in one specific area of your life. Whether it's in your relationships, your work, or your personal habits, identify an area where you can align your actions more closely with God's standards.

Heavenly Father, help me to pursue righteousness with all my heart, soul, and strength. Give me the courage to stand firm in my convictions and the wisdom to discern Your will in every situation. May my life be a testimony to Your righteousness, bringing glory to Your name. In Jesus' name, Amen.

DAY 64

God's Sovereignty

"I am the Alpha and the Omega," says the Lord God, "who is, and who was, and who is to come, the Almighty." - Revelation 1:8 (NIV)

God's sovereignty reigns supreme over all creation. He is the Alpha and the Omega, the beginning and the end, the One who holds the universe in His hands. Understanding God's sovereignty brings peace and assurance, knowing that He is in control of every situation, even when it seems chaotic or uncertain.

In acknowledging God's sovereignty, we surrender our own desires and plans, trusting in His perfect wisdom and timing. It's a humbling recognition that we are not the masters of our fate, but rather servants of the Almighty God who orchestrates all things according to His divine will.

Action Plan:

Today, surrender any areas of your life where you've been striving for control. Release your worries and fears into God's hands, trusting that His sovereignty will guide you through every circumstance. Practice letting go and allowing God to work His perfect plan in your life.

Heavenly Father, I acknowledge Your sovereignty over all things. Help me to trust in Your wisdom and surrender my will to Yours. May Your perfect plan be accomplished in my life, bringing glory to Your name. In Jesus' name, Amen.

DAY 65

The Value of Perseverance

"Let us not become weary in doing good, for at the proper time we will reap a harvest if we do not give up." - Galatians 6:9 (NIV)

Perseverance is the relentless pursuit of our goals despite challenges and setbacks. It's the unwavering determination to press on, even when the journey seems long and arduous. In our walk of faith, perseverance is not merely a virtue; it's a necessity.

Life is filled with obstacles and trials that threaten to derail us from our path. But it's through perseverance that we find strength to overcome. It's the resilience to stand firm in the face of adversity, trusting in God's faithfulness to see us through.

Action Plan:

Today, choose one area in your life where you've been tempted to give up. Whether it's a personal goal, a relationship, or a spiritual pursuit, commit to persevering despite the challenges. Take small, consistent steps towards your objective, trusting that each effort brings you closer to your desired outcome.

Heavenly Father, grant me the endurance to persevere in the face of trials. Help me to trust in Your unfailing love and to keep my eyes fixed on You, knowing that You are my strength and my refuge. Give me the courage to press on, even when the road ahead seems daunting. In Jesus' name, Amen.

DAY 66

Building a Strong Faith

"For we live by faith, not by sight." - 2 Corinthians 5:7 (NIV)

Building a strong faith is like constructing a sturdy fortress in the midst of life's storms. It requires a firm foundation rooted in God's promises and a steadfast commitment to trust Him, even when circumstances seem bleak.

Faith is not merely a passive belief; it's an active, unwavering confidence in the unseen. It's choosing to anchor our souls in the unchanging truth of God's Word, regardless of what our senses perceive. As we nurture our faith through prayer, study, and fellowship, we fortify ourselves against doubt and fear.

Action Plan:

Today, take a step of faith by entrusting a specific concern or dream to God. Write it down and commit it to prayer, surrendering your anxieties and uncertainties to Him. Then, actively seek opportunities to strengthen your faith, whether through reading Scripture, attending worship services, or engaging in conversations with fellow believers.

Heavenly Father, I surrender my doubts and fears to You, trusting in Your faithfulness and goodness. Help me to cultivate a strong and unwavering faith that surpasses my circumstances. May my life be a testimony to Your power and grace. In Jesus' name, Amen.

DAY 67

Loving Your Enemies

"But I say to you who hear, love your enemies, do good to those who hate you." - Luke 6:27 (ESV)

Loving your enemies challenges the very core of human nature. It's easy to love those who love us, but to extend love to those who oppose or mistreat us requires divine strength. Yet, this is precisely what Jesus calls us to do.

Loving our enemies doesn't mean condoning their actions or agreeing with their beliefs. Instead, it's a radical act of compassion that transcends boundaries and transforms hearts. When we love our enemies, we break the cycle of hatred and resentment, paving the way for reconciliation and healing.

Action Plan:

Today, choose one person whom you consider an enemy or someone who has wronged you. Purposefully extend an act of kindness or forgiveness towards them. It could be a simple gesture, a word of encouragement, or even a prayer for their well-being. Let love be your response, knowing that it has the power to overcome even the deepest animosity.

Heavenly Father, grant me the grace to love my enemies as You have loved me. Help me to extend compassion and forgiveness, even to those who may oppose me. May Your love shine through me, breaking down barriers and bringing reconciliation. In Jesus' name, Amen.

DAY 68

The Blessing of Giving

"Remember this: Whoever sows sparingly will also reap sparingly, and whoever sows generously will also reap generously." - 2 Corinthians 9:6 (NIV)

The act of giving is not merely a duty; it's a privilege and a blessing. When we give, whether it be our time, resources, or love, we participate in God's work of generosity and abundance. Giving is an expression of gratitude for all that we have received and a demonstration of our faith in God's provision.

Giving opens our hearts to the needs of others, fostering compassion and empathy within us. It reminds us of our interconnectedness and the importance of community. As we give freely and generously, we experience the joy and fulfillment that comes from making a positive impact in someone else's life.

Action Plan:

Today, find a way to give to someone in need. It could be a financial donation to a charity, volunteering your time at a local shelter, or simply offering a listening ear to a friend going through a difficult time. Whatever you choose, do it with a cheerful heart and a spirit of generosity.

Heavenly Father, thank You for the countless blessings You have bestowed upon me. Help me to be a cheerful giver, freely sharing the abundance You have provided. May my acts of generosity bring hope and joy to those in need, reflecting Your love to the world. In Jesus' name, Amen.

DAY 69

The Power of Testimony

"They triumphed over him by the blood of the Lamb and by the word of their testimony." - Revelation 12:11a (NIV)

Our testimonies hold immeasurable power. They are the stories of God's faithfulness, His grace, and His transformative work in our lives. When we share our testimonies, we not only testify to the goodness of God but also inspire and encourage others in their faith journey.

Testimonies serve as reminders of God's presence in our lives, even in the darkest of times. They reveal His faithfulness in the midst of adversity and His ability to turn our trials into triumphs. Our testimonies become powerful weapons against the enemy, for they declare the victory we have in Christ.

Action Plan:

Today, take some time to reflect on your own testimony. Write it down, detailing the ways God has worked in your life and the miracles He has performed. Then, share your testimony with someone—a friend, family member, or even a stranger. Your story has the potential to touch hearts and transform lives.

Heavenly Father, thank You for the incredible work You have done in my life. Give me the boldness to share my testimony with others, that Your name may be glorified and hearts may be encouraged. May my story be a testament to Your power and faithfulness. In Jesus' name, Amen.

DAY 70

Finding Peace in God

"Peace I leave with you; my peace I give you. I do not give to you as the world gives. Do not let your hearts be troubled and do not be afraid." - John 14:27 (NIV)

In the midst of life's storms and chaos, finding peace can seem elusive. Yet, true peace is not found in external circumstances but in the steadfast presence of God. It's a peace that surpasses understanding, a tranquil assurance that God is in control and that His love surrounds us.

To find peace in God is to surrender our worries and fears at His feet, trusting in His faithfulness and goodness. It's a conscious choice to dwell in His presence, seeking solace in prayer and meditation on His Word. In God's embrace, we find rest for our weary souls and strength to face each day with courage and hope.

Action Plan:

Today, take a moment to quiet your heart and mind in God's presence. Spend time in prayer, pouring out your concerns and burdens before Him. Meditate on Scripture passages that speak of His peace and promises. As you commune with God, allow His peace to fill you, knowing that He is with you in every circumstance.

Heavenly Father, thank You for the gift of Your peace, which transcends all understanding. In the midst of life's challenges, help me to find refuge in Your presence. Grant me the strength to trust in Your unfailing love and the courage to walk in Your peace each day. In Jesus' name, Amen.

DAY 71

Developing a Servant's Heart

"For even the Son of Man did not come to be served, but to serve, and to give his life as a ransom for many." - Mark 10:45 (NIV)

A servant's heart is a reflection of Christ's own heart. It's a humble posture of selflessness and compassion, motivated by love for others. As men of faith, cultivating a servant's heart is essential to following in the footsteps of Jesus and fulfilling our purpose in God's kingdom.

Developing a servant's heart requires a shift in perspective. Instead of seeking recognition or accolades, we strive to meet the needs of those around us with genuine humility and grace.

When we embrace a servant's heart, we embody the essence of Christ's teachings. We become vessels of His love and instruments of His peace, making a tangible difference in the lives of those we encounter. Through acts of service, we demonstrate the transformative power of God's love to a world in need.

Action Plan:

Today, seek out opportunities to serve others in your community. It could be as simple as lending a helping hand to a neighbor or volunteering at a local charity. Look for ways to meet the needs of those around you with humility and compassion.

Gracious God, thank You for the example of Jesus, who came not to be served but to serve. Show me how to serve others with humility and grace, bringing glory to Your name. In Jesus' name, Amen.

DAY 72

The Joy of the Lord

"You make known to me the path of life; you will fill me with joy in your presence, with eternal pleasures at your right hand." - Psalm 16:11 (NIV)

The joy of the Lord is not just a fleeting emotion; it's a deep, abiding sense of contentment and fulfillment that comes from being in His presence. It's a joy that transcends circumstances, rooted in the unshakeable truth of God's love and faithfulness.

When we abide in God's presence, our hearts are filled with a joy that surpasses understanding. It's a joy that sustains us through the trials and challenges of life, reminding us that we are never alone. Even in the midst of sorrow or pain, the joy of the Lord remains our strength and our refuge.

<u>Action Plan:</u>

Today, take a moment to meditate on God's goodness and faithfulness. Spend time in prayer and worship, opening your heart to His presence. As you draw near to Him, allow His joy to fill you to overflowing. Choose to embrace His joy as your strength, regardless of what circumstances may come your way.

Heavenly Father, thank You for the gift of Your joy that fills my heart and sustains me each day. Help me to abide in Your presence, finding true joy and contentment in You alone. May Your joy overflow in my life, shining brightly for all to see and drawing others closer to You. In Jesus' name, Amen.

DAY 73

The Importance of Fellowship

"And let us consider how we may spur one another on toward love and good deeds, not giving up meeting together, as some are in the habit of doing, but encouraging one another—and all the more as you see the Day approaching." - Hebrews 10:24-25 (NIV)

Fellowship is more than just gathering together; it's a sacred bond that strengthens our faith and lifts our spirits. In fellowship, we find encouragement, support, and accountability. It's a reminder that we are not alone in our journey of faith but are part of a community united by love for God and one another.

When we engage in fellowship, we create opportunities for growth and transformation. Through meaningful conversations, shared experiences, and mutual prayer, we inspire and uplift each other, spurring one another on toward love and good deeds.

Action Plan:

Today, reach out to a fellow brother in Christ and arrange a time to meet for coffee or a walk. Use this time to share your joys, struggles, and prayers with one another. Be intentional about listening and offering support, and allow God's presence to permeate your conversation.

Heavenly Father, thank You for the gift of fellowship and the community of believers You have placed in my life. Help me to cherish and nurture these relationships, seeking to encourage and uplift others as we journey together in faith. May our fellowship be a reflection of Your love and grace. In Jesus' name, Amen.

DAY 74

Renewing Your Mind

"Do not conform to the pattern of this world, but be transformed by the renewing of your mind. Then you will be able to test and approve what God's will is—his good, pleasing and perfect will." -
Romans 12:2 (NIV)

Renewing your mind is the process of aligning your thoughts with God's truth. In a world inundated with distractions and negativity, this renewal is essential for spiritual growth and discernment. It involves letting go of harmful thought patterns and embracing the wisdom found in God's Word.

When we renew our minds, we break free from the limitations imposed by the world and open ourselves to the limitless possibilities of God's kingdom. Our perspectives shift, allowing us to see ourselves, others, and the world through the lens of grace and love.

Action Plan:

Today, commit to renewing your mind through daily meditation on Scripture. Set aside time each day to reflect on God's Word, allowing it to penetrate your heart and mind. As you immerse yourself in Scripture, ask God to reveal His truth to you and empower you to live it out in your daily life.

Heavenly Father, thank You for the gift of Your Word, which has the power to renew our minds and transform our lives. Help me to prioritize time spent in Your presence, meditating on Your truth and seeking Your wisdom. In Jesus' name, Amen.

DAY 75

The Strength of Gentleness

"But the fruit of the Spirit is love, joy, peace, forbearance, kindness, goodness, faithfulness, gentleness and self-control. Against such things there is no law." - Galatians 5:22-23 (NIV)

In a world often marked by toughness and aggression, the strength of gentleness shines brightly. Gentleness is not weakness; rather, it is a demonstration of inner strength under control. It is the ability to respond with kindness and compassion even in the face of adversity.

Choosing gentleness requires humility and patience. It means setting aside our pride and ego to show empathy and understanding towards others. Gentleness allows us to build bridges instead of walls, fostering harmony and reconciliation in our relationships.

Action Plan:

Today, practice gentleness in your interactions with others. Before reacting in anger or frustration, pause and choose to respond with gentleness and grace. Seek opportunities to show kindness and compassion, especially towards those who may not deserve it. Let your words and actions be guided by love and understanding.

Heavenly Father, teach me the ways of gentleness and humility. Help me to respond to others with kindness and compassion, reflecting Your love in all that I do. May my life be a testimony to the strength that comes from gentleness. In Jesus' name, Amen.

DAY 76

God's Presence in Your Life

"The Lord himself goes before you and will be with you; he will never leave you nor forsake you. Do not be afraid; do not be discouraged." - Deuteronomy 31:8 (NIV)

God's presence in our lives is an ever-present reality, a constant source of strength, comfort, and guidance. His promise to never leave us nor forsake us is a reassurance that we are never alone, no matter the circumstances we face.

When we acknowledge God's presence in our lives, we invite His peace to dwell within us. His presence brings clarity amidst confusion, hope amidst despair, and courage amidst fear. In every moment, He is there, walking alongside us, ready to carry us through life's challenges.

Action Plan:

Today, take a moment to cultivate awareness of God's presence in your life. Pause and reflect on His faithfulness and goodness. Practice gratitude for His continuous presence, acknowledging His hand at work in your life. Throughout the day, intentionally seek His guidance and lean on His strength.

Heavenly Father, thank You for Your constant presence in my life. Help me to always be aware of Your nearness and to trust in Your unfailing love. Guide me in every step I take, and may Your presence fill me with peace and joy. In Jesus' name, Amen.

DAY 77

Walking in Forgiveness

"Be kind and compassionate to one another, forgiving each other, just as in Christ God forgave you." - Ephesians 4:32 (NIV)

Forgiveness is not just a one-time act; it's a daily practice, a conscious decision to release the grip of bitterness and resentment from our hearts. When we walk in forgiveness, we mirror the unconditional love and grace that God has extended to us through Christ.

Choosing forgiveness frees us from the bondage of past hurts, allowing healing to take place in our lives. It's a powerful act of self-love, as it releases the weight of anger and pain, paving the way for peace and reconciliation. Walking in forgiveness doesn't mean forgetting the offense but rather choosing to let go of its power over us.

Action Plan:

Today, make a commitment to forgive someone who has wronged you. It may not be easy, but choose to let go of any grudges or resentments you've been holding onto. Write down the name of the person you need to forgive and pray for them, asking God to help you release any negative feelings.

Heavenly Father, grant me the strength and grace to walk in forgiveness each day. Help me to let go of bitterness and extend love and grace to those who have hurt me. May Your mercy flow through me, bringing healing and reconciliation to broken relationships. In Jesus' name, Amen.

DAY 78

The Call to Holiness

"But just as he who called you is holy, so be holy in all you do; for it is written: 'Be holy, because I am holy.'" - 1 Peter 1:15-16 (NIV)

The call to holiness is a divine invitation to live a life set apart for God's purposes. It's not about perfection, but rather about a continual striving towards righteousness and purity of heart. As men of faith, we are called to reflect the character of our holy Creator in every aspect of our lives.

Holiness begins with a heart surrendered to God, willing to be transformed by His grace and guided by His Spirit. It's a journey of obedience and self-discipline, choosing to align our thoughts, words, and actions with God's will. In a world that often promotes self-indulgence and moral compromise, embracing holiness sets us apart as beacons of light and truth.

Action Plan:

Today, commit to living a life of holiness in one specific area. It could be guarding your speech, practicing purity in your relationships, or seeking reconciliation where there is conflict. Choose one aspect of your life where you can grow in holiness, and ask God for the strength and wisdom to walk in His ways.

Heavenly Father, thank You for calling me to a life of holiness. Give me the grace to surrender myself fully to Your will, and the courage to live in obedience to Your commands. May my life be a reflection of Your holiness, drawing others closer to You. In Jesus' name, Amen.

DAY 79

The Blessing of Family

"Behold, children are a heritage from the Lord, the fruit of the womb a reward." - Psalm 127:3 (ESV)

Family is a precious gift from God, a source of love, support, and strength. In a world that often feels chaotic and uncertain, our families provide a sanctuary of stability and belonging. They are the cornerstone of our lives, shaping us into the men we are meant to be.

Our families teach us invaluable lessons about love, sacrifice, and forgiveness. They celebrate our victories and stand by us in our trials. Through the laughter and the tears, they remind us of the power of unconditional love and the importance of standing together through life's challenges.

Action Plan:

Today, take a moment to express gratitude to your family members. Write a note, make a phone call, or spend quality time together. Let them know how much they mean to you and how grateful you are for their presence in your life.

Heavenly Father, thank You for the gift of family. Bless each member with Your love and protection. Help us to cherish and nurture our relationships, growing closer together in faith and love. Guide us as we support and encourage one another on this journey of life. In Jesus' name, Amen.

DAY 80

Embracing God's Mercy

"But God, being rich in mercy, because of the great love with which he loved us, even when we were dead in our trespasses, made us alive together with Christ—by grace you have been saved." - Ephesians 2:4-5 (ESV)

God's mercy is a beacon of hope in our lives, a divine gift that knows no bounds. It is through His mercy that we find forgiveness and redemption, despite our shortcomings and failures. Embracing God's mercy requires humility, acknowledging our need for His grace and surrendering ourselves to His loving embrace.

God's mercy is not earned; it is freely given out of His boundless love for us. It's a reminder that no matter how far we may have strayed, His arms are always open wide, ready to welcome us back into His embrace. When we accept God's mercy, we experience the transformative power of His love, healing our wounds and restoring our souls.

Action Plan:

Today, take a moment to reflect on the mercy that God has shown you in your life. Consider the ways He has forgiven you and lifted you up in times of need. Then, extend that same mercy to others.

Heavenly Father, thank You for Your endless mercy and grace. Help me to embrace Your mercy fully, trusting in Your unfailing love. May Your mercy overflow in my life, guiding my actions and shaping my character. In Jesus' name, Amen.

DAY 81

The Importance of Wisdom

"The fear of the Lord is the beginning of wisdom, and knowledge of the Holy One is understanding." - Proverbs 9:10 (NIV)

Wisdom is a precious gift, born from reverence for God and a deep understanding of His ways. It surpasses mere knowledge, encompassing discernment, prudence, and insight. In a world filled with complexities and uncertainties, the importance of wisdom cannot be overstated.

Seeking wisdom requires humility and a willingness to learn. It involves listening to the counsel of others, studying God's Word, and allowing His Spirit to illuminate our minds and hearts. Through wisdom, we navigate life's challenges with grace and confidence, making choices that honor God and bless those around us.

Action Plan:

Today, commit to pursuing wisdom in all areas of your life. Take time to pray for wisdom, asking God to grant you understanding and insight. Seek out mentors or wise counsel to guide you in important decisions. Be intentional about learning from both successes and failures, allowing each experience to shape you into a wiser individual.

Heavenly Father, grant me wisdom as I navigate life's journey. Open my eyes to see things from Your perspective and guide my steps in paths of righteousness. May Your wisdom dwell richly within me, empowering me to live a life that brings glory to Your name. In Jesus' name, Amen.

DAY 82

Trusting God's Provision

"And my God will meet all your needs according to the riches of his glory in Christ Jesus." - Philippians 4:19 (NIV)

Trusting in God's provision is an act of faith that acknowledges His sovereignty over our lives. It's understanding that He is our ultimate provider, caring for us with a love that surpasses all understanding. When we place our trust in Him, we release the burden of worry and anxiety, knowing that He will never fail us.

God's provision extends far beyond our material needs; it encompasses every aspect of our lives. He provides strength in our weakness, comfort in our sorrow, and guidance in our uncertainty. As we lean on Him in faith, He sustains us with His unfailing love and grace.

Action Plan:

Today, surrender your worries and anxieties to God. Take time to reflect on His faithfulness in the past and meditate on His promises for the future. Choose to trust in His provision, even when circumstances seem bleak. Practice gratitude for the blessings He has already bestowed upon you, knowing that He will continue to provide for all your needs.

Heavenly Father, thank You for Your faithfulness and provision in my life. Help me to trust in Your perfect timing and to surrender my worries to You. Strengthen my faith as I rely on Your unfailing love and grace. In Jesus' name, Amen.

DAY 83

The Power of Hope

"May the God of hope fill you with all joy and peace as you trust in him, so that you may overflow with hope by the power of the Holy Spirit." - Romans 15:13 (NIV)

Hope is not just a fleeting wish; it is an anchor for the soul, a source of strength in times of adversity. When we place our trust in God, we tap into the limitless reservoir of hope that He offers. This hope is not dependent on our circumstances but on the unchanging nature of God's love and faithfulness.

Hope sustains us through the darkest of nights, guiding us toward the promise of a brighter tomorrow. It fuels our perseverance, reminding us that no challenge is insurmountable with God by our side. In the face of uncertainty, hope whispers, "Keep going," urging us to press on with courage and determination.

Action Plan:

Today, choose to cultivate hope in your life. Spend time in prayer and meditation, seeking God's presence and the reassurance of His promises. Surround yourself with positive influences and uplifting messages that inspire hope. Reach out to someone who may be struggling and offer them words of encouragement and support.

Heavenly Father, thank You for being the God of hope who fills us with joy and peace. Strengthen my faith, Lord, and help me to anchor my hope in You alone. May Your presence be my constant source of assurance, guiding me through every trial and triumph. In Jesus' name, Amen.

DAY 84

Living with Integrity

"The integrity of the upright guides them, but the unfaithful are destroyed by their duplicity." - Proverbs 11:3 (NIV)

Living with integrity means aligning our actions with our values, even when no one is watching. It's about being true to ourselves and to God, striving to do what is right in every circumstance. Integrity is not just a moral standard; it's a way of life that reflects the character of Christ within us.

When we live with integrity, we build trust and credibility with others. Our words carry weight, and our actions speak louder than any promises we make. Integrity sets us apart in a world plagued by dishonesty and deceit, serving as a beacon of light and hope to those around us.

Action Plan:

Today, commit to living with unwavering integrity in every area of your life. Reflect on your values and beliefs, and consider how they influence your decisions and behaviors. Choose honesty, transparency, and accountability in all your interactions, both big and small.

Heavenly Father, thank You for the gift of integrity. Help me to walk in honesty and righteousness, honoring You in all that I do. Give me the strength to resist the temptations of deceit and the courage to stand firm in my convictions. May my life be a testimony to Your grace and truth. In Jesus' name, Amen

DAY 85

Embracing God's Peace

"Peace I leave with you; my peace I give you. I do not give to you as the world gives. Do not let your hearts be troubled and do not be afraid." - John 14:27 (NIV)

God's peace is a profound gift, unlike any the world can offer. It's a peace that surpasses understanding, a calm that prevails even in the midst of life's storms. Embracing God's peace means surrendering our anxieties and fears, trusting in His sovereignty and goodness.

In a world filled with chaos and uncertainty, God's peace serves as an anchor for our souls. It sustains us through trials and tribulations, reminding us that we are never alone. When we embrace God's peace, we experience a sense of wholeness and tranquility that can only come from Him.

Action Plan:

Today, take a moment to be still in God's presence. Set aside distractions and worries, and simply rest in His peace. Practice deep breathing and prayer, allowing God's peace to wash over you. As you cultivate a habit of seeking God's peace daily, you'll find yourself better equipped to face life's challenges with confidence and serenity.

Heavenly Father, thank You for the gift of Your peace. Help me to embrace it fully, trusting in Your love and faithfulness. May Your peace guard my heart and mind, guiding me through every season of life. In Jesus' name, Amen.

DAY 86

God's Grace in Your Life

"But he said to me, 'My grace is sufficient for you, for my power is made perfect in weakness.' Therefore I will boast all the more gladly about my weaknesses, so that Christ's power may rest on me." - 2 Corinthians 12:9 (NIV)

God's grace is a profound gift that sustains us through life's trials and triumphs. It's the unmerited favor and unconditional love that He showers upon us, regardless of our shortcomings. In our moments of weakness, His grace becomes our strength, lifting us up and carrying us through.

Understanding and acknowledging God's grace in our lives cultivates humility and gratitude. It reminds us that we are not deserving of His love, yet He chooses to bless us abundantly. God's grace empowers us to overcome obstacles, to forgive others, and to live with purpose and meaning.

Action Plan:

Reflect on the ways God's grace has manifested in your life. Take time to journal or meditate on moments where His grace has been evident, whether through answered prayers, unexpected blessings, or moments of divine intervention. Allow these reflections to deepen your appreciation for God's unending grace.

Heavenly Father, thank You for Your abundant grace that sustains me each day. May Your grace empower me to walk in faith and obedience, trusting in Your perfect plan for my life. In Jesus' name, Amen.

DAY 87

The Importance of Courage

"Be strong and courageous. Do not be afraid or terrified because of them, for the Lord your God goes with you; he will never leave you nor forsake you." - Deuteronomy 31:6 (NIV)

Courage is not the absence of fear, but the strength to overcome it. It's the willingness to step into the unknown, to face challenges head-on, trusting in God's presence and guidance. In a world filled with uncertainties and obstacles, courage is the fuel that propels us forward on our journey of faith.

Courage enables us to pursue our dreams and passions, even in the face of opposition or doubt. It empowers us to stand up for what is right, to speak out against injustice, and to be a beacon of hope in a darkened world. Courage is a virtue that distinguishes the ordinary from the extraordinary, the timid from the bold.

Action Plan:

Today, identify one area in your life where you need to exercise courage. It could be confronting a difficult situation, taking a leap of faith in your career or relationships, or stepping out of your comfort zone to pursue a new opportunity. Whatever it may be, trust in God's strength and take that courageous step forward.

Heavenly Father, thank You for Your promise to never leave nor forsake us. Grant me the courage to face whatever challenges come my way, knowing that You are always by my side. Help me to be bold and fearless in living out Your will for my life. In Jesus' name, Amen.

DAY 88

Seeking God's Kingdom

"But seek first his kingdom and his righteousness, and all these things will be given to you as well." - Matthew 6:33 (NIV)

Seeking God's kingdom is not merely a passive endeavor; it's an active pursuit of His will and His ways in our lives. When we prioritize God's kingdom above all else, we align ourselves with His divine purpose and experience the abundant life He promises.

Seeking God's kingdom means placing Him at the center of our thoughts, actions, and desires. It's a conscious decision to surrender our own ambitions and seek His guidance in every aspect of our lives. As we seek God's kingdom first, we find fulfillment, peace, and true joy that transcends earthly treasures.

Action Plan:

Today, take time to reflect on your priorities. Are you seeking God's kingdom above all else, or are you allowing worldly distractions to take precedence? Commit to making God the focal point of your life. Set aside dedicated time for prayer, study, and worship, seeking His guidance in all that you do.

Heavenly Father, I desire to seek Your kingdom above all else. Give me the wisdom and strength to align my life with Your will and Your ways. Help me to prioritize Your kingdom in my thoughts, actions, and desires, trusting that You will provide all that I need. In Jesus' name, Amen.

DAY 89

The Blessing of Humility

"Humble yourselves before the Lord, and he will lift you up." -
James 4:10 (NIV)

Humility is not weakness; it's strength under control. It's the recognition of our limitations and imperfections, coupled with a deep trust in God's wisdom and guidance. When we humble ourselves before the Lord, we open our hearts to His transformative power and invite His blessings into our lives.

Humility fosters unity and harmony in our relationships. It enables us to empathize with others, to listen with an open heart, and to extend grace and forgiveness. Through humility, we reflect the character of Christ, who humbled Himself to serve others and ultimately to sacrifice Himself for our redemption.

Action Plan:

Today, practice humility in your interactions with others. Instead of seeking recognition or praise, choose to serve with a humble heart. Look for opportunities to uplift those around you, putting their needs above your own. Allow humility to be your guiding light, leading you closer to God and to a deeper understanding of His will for your life.

Heavenly Father, teach me the way of humility, that I may walk in Your truth and grace. Help me to set aside my pride and ego, and to serve others with a humble heart. May Your presence fill me with strength and compassion, as I strive to follow the example of Your Son, Jesus Christ. Amen.

DAY 90

Developing a Thankful Heart

"Give thanks in all circumstances; for this is God's will for you in Christ Jesus." - 1 Thessalonians 5:18 (NIV)

A thankful heart is a magnet for blessings. It transforms our perspective, turning challenges into opportunities and ordinary moments into extraordinary blessings. Gratitude is not dependent on our circumstances; it's a choice we make to recognize the goodness of God in every aspect of our lives.

When we cultivate a thankful heart, we unlock the power of positivity and resilience. Instead of focusing on what we lack, we shift our attention to the abundance that surrounds us. Gratitude breeds contentment and joy, allowing us to live each day with a sense of purpose and fulfillment.

Action Plan:

Start a gratitude journal. Each day, write down three things you're thankful for, no matter how big or small. Take time to reflect on the blessings in your life and express gratitude to God for His goodness. Cultivate a habit of gratitude, and watch how it transforms your perspective and outlook on life.

Heavenly Father, thank You for the countless blessings You shower upon me each day. Teach me to have a heart overflowing with gratitude, even in the midst of trials. Help me to recognize Your hand at work in every area of my life and to give thanks in all circumstances. In Jesus' name, Amen.

DAY 91

The Role of Encouragement

"Therefore encourage one another and build each other up, just as in fact you are doing." - 1 Thessalonians 5:11 (NIV)

Encouragement is a powerful force that can uplift, inspire, and ignite hope within the hearts of others. It's about speaking life-giving words, offering support, and affirming the worth and potential of those around us. In a world filled with challenges and uncertainties, the role of encouragement becomes even more crucial.

When we encourage others, we become instruments of God's grace, spreading His love and light wherever we go. Encouragement has the power to transform lives, to instill confidence in the discouraged, and to reignite the fire within the weary soul. It's a reminder that we are not alone, that there are people cheering us on and believing in our ability to overcome obstacles.

Action Plan:

Today, make a conscious effort to encourage someone in your life. It could be a family member, a friend, a colleague, or even a stranger. Offer words of affirmation, a listening ear, or a helping hand. Let your encouragement be genuine and heartfelt, uplifting the spirits of those around you.

Heavenly Father, thank You for the gift of encouragement. Help me to be a beacon of hope and strength to those in need. Fill my words with kindness and my actions with compassion, that I may uplift and inspire others as You have done for me. In Jesus' name, Amen.

DAY 92

Living with Compassion

"Be kind and compassionate to one another, forgiving each other, just as in Christ God forgave you." - Ephesians 4:32 (NIV)

Living with compassion is a reflection of God's heart for humanity. It's about seeing others through the lens of empathy and kindness, just as Christ has shown us. When we embrace compassion, we become vessels of love in a world that often feels cold and indifferent.

Compassion compels us to reach out to those who are hurting, to offer a listening ear to the brokenhearted, and to extend a helping hand to the downtrodden. It's not merely a feeling but a call to action, urging us to be agents of healing and reconciliation in our communities.

Action Plan:

Today, make a deliberate effort to show compassion to someone in need. It could be a simple act of kindness, like offering words of encouragement to a struggling friend or lending a helping hand to a neighbor in need. Look for opportunities to demonstrate compassion in both big and small ways, and let your actions reflect the love of Christ.

Gracious God, thank You for Your boundless compassion towards us. Teach me to live with a heart full of compassion, ready to love and serve others as You have loved and served me. May Your compassion flow through me, bringing light and hope to those around me. In Jesus' name, Amen.

DAY 93

God's Plan for You

"For I know the plans I have for you," declares the Lord, "plans to prosper you and not to harm you, plans to give you hope and a future." - Jeremiah 29:11 (NIV)

God's plan for each of us is woven into the very fabric of our existence. It is a plan crafted with infinite wisdom and boundless love, designed to lead us toward a future filled with hope and purpose. Though we may not always understand His ways, we can trust that His plan for us is perfect and will ultimately bring about our good.

God's plan encompasses every aspect of our lives – our dreams, our relationships, our struggles, and our triumphs. He orchestrates every detail with precision and care, guiding us along the path He has laid out for us.

Action Plan:

Today, surrender your plans to God and seek His guidance for your life. Spend time in prayer, asking Him to reveal His will to you and give you the strength to follow where He leads. Trust that His plan is far greater than anything you could imagine, and commit to walking in faith and obedience.

Heavenly Father, thank You for the assurance that Your plans for me are good. Help me to trust in Your wisdom and surrender my will to Yours. Guide me along the path You have set before me, and grant me the courage to follow wherever You lead. In Jesus' name, Amen.

DAY 94

The Importance of Faithfulness

"His master replied, 'Well done, good and faithful servant! You have been faithful with a few things; I will put you in charge of many things. Come and share your master's happiness!'" - Matthew 25:23 (NIV)

Faithfulness is the steadfast commitment to our promises, responsibilities, and relationships. It is the quality that strengthens marriages, deepens friendships, and builds trust in all aspects of life. When we are faithful, we reflect the character of our unchanging God, who remains steadfast in His love and promises.

Being faithful requires discipline and perseverance. It means staying true to our convictions even in the face of challenges and temptations. In a world where instant gratification is often prioritized, faithfulness stands as a beacon of reliability and consistency.

Action Plan:

Today, commit to being faithful in one area of your life where you've been struggling. It could be in honoring your commitments at work, being present and attentive in your relationships, or staying true to your values and beliefs. Take small, intentional steps to cultivate faithfulness, and trust God to strengthen you in the process.

Heavenly Father, help me to be faithful in all areas of my life, just as You are faithful to Your promises. May my faithfulness bring glory to Your name and reflect Your unchanging love to those around me. In Jesus' name, Amen.

DAY 95

The Power of God's Word

"For the word of God is alive and active. Sharper than any double-edged sword, it penetrates even to dividing soul and spirit, joints and marrow; it judges the thoughts and attitudes of the heart." - Hebrews 4:12 (NIV)

The Word of God is not merely ink on paper; it is living and powerful. It has the ability to transform lives, renew minds, and restore souls. When we immerse ourselves in God's Word, we encounter His truth and experience His presence in a profound way.

God's Word serves as a guidebook for life, offering wisdom and direction for every situation we face. It brings clarity to confusion, strength to weakness, and hope to despair. Through Scripture, we discover the depth of God's love for us and His promises that never fail.

Action Plan:

Today, make a commitment to prioritize time spent in God's Word. Set aside a specific time each day for reading and meditating on Scripture. Allow God to speak to you through His Word, and be open to the transformation He wants to bring about in your heart.

Heavenly Father, thank You for the gift of Your Word. Help me to cherish it and to meditate on it day and night. May Your Word be a lamp to my feet and a light to my path, guiding me closer to You each day. In Jesus' name, Amen.

DAY 96

Trusting in God's Strength

"Trust in the Lord with all your heart and lean not on your own understanding; in all your ways submit to him, and he will make your paths straight." - Proverbs 3:5-6 (NIV)

Trusting in God's strength means surrendering our own weaknesses and limitations to His infinite power. It's acknowledging that we cannot navigate life's challenges alone and placing our faith in the One who holds all things together. When we trust in God's strength, we find courage to face adversity, resilience to overcome obstacles, and peace amidst turmoil.

God's strength is not merely a concept; it's a tangible reality that sustains us in our times of need. It's the assurance that we are never alone, for He walks beside us every step of the way. When we lean on His strength, we tap into an unshakeable source of hope and renewal.

Action Plan:

Today, take a moment to surrender your worries and fears to God. Trust in His strength to carry you through whatever challenges you may be facing. Then, step out in faith, knowing that His strength is more than sufficient for whatever lies ahead.

Heavenly Father, I thank You for Your unwavering strength that sustains me each day. Help me to trust in You wholeheartedly, knowing that Your power is made perfect in my weakness. Give me the courage to rely on Your strength, confident that You will guide me through every trial. In Jesus' name, Amen.

DAY 97

The Joy of Salvation

"Restore to me the joy of your salvation and grant me a willing spirit, to sustain me." - Psalm 51:12 (NIV)

The joy of salvation is a profound gift bestowed upon us by God's grace. It's not merely the relief from sin's burden but the exhilarating realization of being reconciled with our Creator. In our salvation, we find redemption, restoration, and a renewed purpose for our lives.

This joy is not fleeting or dependent on circumstances; it's rooted in the unchanging love of God. It's a joy that surpasses all understanding, filling our hearts with hope and peace even in the midst of trials. As men of faith, embracing the joy of salvation empowers us to live boldly, knowing that we are beloved children of God.

Action Plan:

Today, take a moment to reflect on the magnitude of your salvation. Consider the depths from which you've been rescued and the boundless love that made it possible. Then, share this joy with others. Whether through sharing your testimony, extending acts of kindness, or inviting someone to experience God's love, let the joy of your salvation shine brightly for all to see.

Heavenly Father, thank You for the indescribable gift of salvation. Restore unto me the joy of Your salvation, and fill me with Your Spirit so that I may overflow with gratitude and share this joy with others. May Your love and grace be evident in every aspect of my life. In Jesus' name, Amen.

DAY 98

Embracing God's Truth

"Jesus answered, 'I am the way and the truth and the life. No one comes to the Father except through me.'" - John 14:6 (NIV)

In a world filled with noise and confusion, embracing God's truth is our anchor. His truth is unwavering and timeless, providing us with guidance, wisdom, and purpose. When we align our lives with His truth, we find true freedom and fulfillment.

God's truth is not just a set of principles to follow; it's a person—Jesus Christ. He is the embodiment of truth, and in Him, we find the path to salvation and abundant life. Embracing God's truth means surrendering our own understanding and trusting in His perfect plan for us.

Action Plan:

Today, commit to spending time in God's Word, seeking His truth and wisdom. Set aside a few minutes to read a passage from the Bible and meditate on its meaning for your life. As you reflect on God's truth, ask Him to reveal any areas where you may be living contrary to His will, and commit to aligning your life with His truth.

Heavenly Father, thank You for Your Word, which is a lamp unto my feet and a light unto my path. Help me to embrace Your truth wholeheartedly and to live according to Your will. May Your truth guide my thoughts, words, and actions each day. In Jesus' name, Amen.

DAY 99

The Value of Patience

"But if we hope for what we do not yet have, we wait for it patiently." - Romans 8:25 (NIV)

Patience is a virtue often overlooked in today's fast-paced world. Yet, it is a quality that brings about profound transformation in our lives. Patience teaches us to trust in God's timing and to remain steadfast in the face of adversity.

In our journey of faith, patience is essential. It allows us to endure trials and tribulations with grace, knowing that God is working all things together for our good. Patience cultivates perseverance, enabling us to press on toward the goals God has set before us.

Action Plan:

Today, practice patience in one area of your life where you've been feeling rushed or anxious. Instead of giving in to impatience, choose to trust in God's timing. Take a moment to breathe deeply and remind yourself that God is in control. Use this opportunity to cultivate patience and resilience in your heart.

Heavenly Father, thank You for Your perfect timing and Your faithfulness to fulfill Your promises. Help me to cultivate patience in my life, especially in times of waiting and uncertainty. Grant me the strength to trust in Your plan and to wait upon You with hope and confidence. In Jesus' name, Amen.

DAY 100

Living a Christ-Centered Life

"I have been crucified with Christ and I no longer live, but Christ lives in me. The life I now live in the body, I live by faith in the Son of God, who loved me and gave himself for me." - Galatians 2:20 (NIV)

Living a Christ-centered life is a call to surrender our own desires and ambitions, and to allow Christ to reign supreme in every aspect of our being. It means making Jesus the focal point of our thoughts, actions, and decisions, and seeking to honor Him in all that we do.

When we live a Christ-centered life, we experience true freedom and fulfillment. Our lives are no longer driven by selfish pursuits, but by a desire to glorify God and serve others. We find purpose and meaning in following Christ's example of love, compassion, and sacrifice.

Action Plan:

Today, commit to making Jesus the center of your life. Take time to reflect on His teachings and example, and ask yourself how you can live more like Him. Choose to prioritize prayer, Bible study, and fellowship with other believers, allowing Christ to shape and transform you from the inside out.

Heavenly Father, thank You for the gift of Your Son, Jesus Christ, who is the center of our faith and our lives. Help me to surrender myself completely to Him, and to live each day with a heart devoted to following His example. May my life bring glory and honor to Your name. In Jesus' name, Amen.

DAY 101

The Importance of Repentance

"Repent, then, and turn to God, so that your sins may be wiped out, that times of refreshing may come from the Lord." - Acts 3:19 (NIV)

Repentance is the gateway to transformation and renewal. It's a humbling acknowledgment of our shortcomings and a turning away from sin toward God. Through repentance, we open ourselves to the boundless mercy and grace of our Heavenly Father.

Repentance is not merely about feeling sorry for our sins; it's about taking decisive action to change our ways. It requires sincerity and contrition, a genuine desire to be restored to right relationship with God. In repentance, we find forgiveness and the opportunity for a fresh start.

Action Plan:

Today, take time to reflect on areas of your life where you may have strayed from God's path. Confess any sins or wrongdoing to God, asking for His forgiveness and guidance. Then, commit to making amends and turning away from sinful behaviors. Seek accountability and support from a trusted friend or mentor as you strive to live a life pleasing to God.

Gracious God, forgive me for the times I have fallen short of Your glory. Give me the strength to repent wholeheartedly and turn to You with sincerity and humility. Help me to walk in Your ways and experience the fullness of Your grace and mercy. In Jesus' name, Amen.

DAY 102

God's Faithfulness in Trials

"The LORD himself goes before you and will be with you; he will never leave you nor forsake you. Do not be afraid; do not be discouraged." - Deuteronomy 31:8 (NIV)

In the midst of trials and tribulations, God's faithfulness shines brightest. He is a steadfast anchor in the storm, a constant presence in our darkest hours. Even when we feel overwhelmed by life's challenges, we can trust in God's unwavering love and faithfulness.

God's faithfulness in trials is a testament to His promise to never abandon us. He walks alongside us, providing strength, comfort, and guidance through every trial we face. Though the road may be difficult, we can take heart knowing that God is with us, working all things together for our good.

Action Plan:

Today, when faced with a trial or difficulty, choose to lean on God's faithfulness. Instead of relying on your own strength, surrender your burdens to Him and trust in His provision. Spend time in prayer, seeking His guidance and wisdom, and allow His peace to fill your heart.

Heavenly Father, thank You for Your faithfulness that sustains me through every trial and hardship. Help me to trust in Your promises and lean on Your strength when I am weak. May Your presence be my comfort and Your guidance be my light. In Jesus' name, Amen.

DAY 103

The Power of the Holy Spirit

"But you will receive power when the Holy Spirit comes on you; and you will be my witnesses in Jerusalem, and in all Judea and Samaria, and to the ends of the earth." - Acts 1:8 (NIV)

The Holy Spirit is not merely a concept or an idea; He is the dynamic, life-giving presence of God within us. When we open our hearts to Him, we tap into a power that transcends our human limitations. The Holy Spirit empowers us to live boldly for Christ, equipping us with wisdom, courage, and supernatural abilities to fulfill His purposes.

With the Holy Spirit dwelling within us, we are transformed from the inside out. He convicts us of sin, guides us into truth, and enables us to live holy and righteous lives. The same Spirit that raised Jesus from the dead resides in us, empowering us to overcome every obstacle and fulfill our God-given destiny.

Action Plan:

Today, invite the Holy Spirit to take control of every area of your life. Spend time in prayer, asking Him to fill you afresh and empower you for the tasks ahead. Listen attentively to His promptings and obey His leading, trusting that He will guide you every step of the way.

Heavenly Father, thank You for the gift of Your Holy Spirit. Fill me anew with Your presence and power today. May Your Holy Spirit guide, strengthen, and empower me to live a life that brings glory

DAY 104

Embracing God's Forgiveness

"If we confess our sins, he is faithful and just and will forgive us our sins and purify us from all unrighteousness." - 1 John 1:9 (NIV)

God's forgiveness is a gift beyond measure, a beacon of hope that illuminates even the darkest corners of our souls. It is a promise of redemption, a pathway to renewal, and a testament to His boundless love for us. Embracing God's forgiveness means letting go of the weight of guilt and shame, and accepting the freedom and grace that He offers.

No sin is too great for God's forgiveness. His mercy knows no bounds, and His love is unconditional. When we humbly come before Him, acknowledging our faults and shortcomings, He extends His hand of forgiveness, washing away our sins and restoring us to wholeness.

Action Plan:

Today, take a moment to reflect on areas in your life where you need God's forgiveness. As you receive His forgiveness, extend that same grace to others who may have wronged you, releasing any bitterness or resentment from your heart.

Heavenly Father, thank You for Your unfailing love and boundless mercy. Wash me clean, O Lord, and renew a right spirit within me. Help me to extend the same forgiveness to others as You have shown to me. In Jesus' name, Amen.

DAY 105

The Role of Discipline

"For the moment all discipline seems painful rather than pleasant, but later it yields the peaceful fruit of righteousness to those who have been trained by it." - Hebrews 12:11 (ESV)

Discipline is the cornerstone of success and spiritual growth. It requires a steadfast commitment to self-control and obedience to God's will. While discipline may seem difficult in the moment, its fruits are sweet and long-lasting.

In our journey of faith, discipline molds us into the men God intends us to be. It strengthens our character, fortifies our resolve, and empowers us to overcome life's challenges. Through discipline, we develop habits that honor God and lead to a life of righteousness.

Action Plan:

Today, choose one area of your life where you need more discipline. Whether it's in your prayer life, relationships, work, or personal habits, identify specific steps you can take to cultivate discipline in that area. Set realistic goals and hold yourself accountable, seeking God's strength to help you stay focused and committed.

Heavenly Father, grant me the strength and perseverance to embrace discipline in my life. Help me to surrender my will to Yours and to walk in obedience to Your commands. May Your Spirit empower me to cultivate habits that honor You and bring glory to Your name. In Jesus' name, Amen.

DAY 106

Living with Boldness

"For God has not given us a spirit of fear, but of power and of love and of a sound mind." - 2 Timothy 1:7 (NKJV)

Living with boldness is not about recklessness or arrogance; it's about courageously stepping into the plans and purposes that God has for us. It's about embracing our identity as children of the Most High and walking confidently in His strength.

Boldness is rooted in faith. It's the audacity to believe that God is who He says He is and that He will do what He has promised. When we live with boldness, we defy the limitations imposed by fear and doubt, trusting in God's ability to lead us triumphantly through any circumstance.

Action Plan:

Today, identify one area of your life where fear has been holding you back. It could be a dream you've been hesitant to pursue or a conversation you've been avoiding. Take a bold step forward in faith, trusting that God will equip you with everything you need to succeed. Step out of your comfort zone and into the boundless possibilities that await you.

Heavenly Father, thank You for the spirit of power, love, and sound mind that You have given me. Help me to live with boldness, trusting in Your strength and guidance in every aspect of my life. Give me the courage to step out in faith, knowing that You are with me always. In Jesus' name, Amen.

DAY 107

The Blessing of Service

"For even the Son of Man did not come to be served, but to serve, and to give his life as a ransom for many." - Mark 10:45 (NIV)

Service is not merely an obligation but a profound blessing bestowed upon us by God. Just as Jesus came not to be served but to serve, we are called to follow His example and serve others with humility and love.

When we engage in acts of service, we reflect the selfless love of Christ to the world. Service breaks down barriers, builds bridges, and fosters unity among God's people. It is through serving others that we experience true fulfillment and purpose in our lives.

Action Plan:

Today, seek out opportunities to serve others in your community. It could be volunteering at a local soup kitchen, helping a neighbor with yard work, or simply offering a kind word to someone in need. Look for ways to meet the needs of those around you with a heart of compassion and generosity.

Heavenly Father, thank You for the privilege of serving others in Your name. Help me to cultivate a servant's heart, always seeking to bless others and glorify You through my actions. May Your love shine brightly through me as I serve those in need. In Jesus' name, Amen.

DAY 108

The Importance of Listening

"My dear brothers and sisters, take note of this: Everyone should be quick to listen, slow to speak and slow to become angry." - James 1:19 (NIV)

Listening is a gift we can offer to others, a gesture of love and respect. In our fast-paced world, it's easy to rush through conversations, eager to share our own thoughts and opinions. Yet, true connection and understanding are born when we take the time to truly listen.

Listening goes beyond hearing words; it involves empathy and understanding. When we listen attentively, we honor the speaker and validate their experiences. It fosters deeper relationships and opens doors to growth and learning.

Action Plan:

Today, make a conscious effort to listen more attentively to those around you. Whether it's a friend sharing their joys and struggles or a colleague expressing their ideas, give them your full attention. Practice active listening by maintaining eye contact, nodding in understanding, and refraining from interrupting. Truly seek to understand before responding.

Gracious God, teach me the value of listening with an open heart and mind. Help me to set aside my own agenda and ego, and to truly hear the voices of those around me. May my listening be a reflection of Your love and compassion in this world. In Jesus' name, Amen.

DAY 109

Trusting God's Promises

"For no matter how many promises God has made, they are 'Yes' in Christ. And so through him the 'Amen' is spoken by us to the glory of God." - 2 Corinthians 1:20 (NIV)

God's promises are the bedrock of our faith, firm and unshakeable. In a world filled with uncertainty, we find solace in the promises of our Heavenly Father, knowing that He is faithful to fulfill every word He has spoken. When we trust in God's promises, we anchor our souls in His unfailing love and provision.

God's promises are not mere words; they are guarantees sealed by the blood of Jesus Christ. Through His death and resurrection, Christ has secured for us the inheritance of eternal life and abundant blessings. As we place our trust in Him, we can rest assured that every promise He has made will come to pass in His perfect timing.

Action Plan:

Today, choose to meditate on one of God's promises found in Scripture. Reflect on its significance for your life and personal circumstances. Whenever doubt or fear creeps in, hold fast to the promise and declare it aloud in faith.

Heavenly Father, thank You for Your unending faithfulness and the promises You have made to Your children. Help me to trust in Your word wholeheartedly, knowing that You are always true to Your promises. Strengthen my faith and fill me with hope as I cling to Your unfailing love. In Jesus' name, Amen.

DAY 110

The Power of God's Love

"For I am convinced that neither death nor life, neither angels nor demons, neither the present nor the future, nor any powers, neither height nor depth, nor anything else in all creation, will be able to separate us from the love of God that is in Christ Jesus our Lord."
- Romans 8:38-39 (NIV)

The power of God's love is boundless and unshakeable. It transcends all barriers and conquers all fears. It is the foundation of our faith, the source of our strength, and the essence of our existence. In a world filled with turmoil and uncertainty, God's love remains constant, unwavering, and eternal.

God's love is not just a feeling; it's an action—a relentless pursuit of our hearts, even in our darkest moments. It is a love that knows no bounds, reaching out to us with grace and mercy, drawing us into His embrace.

Action Plan:

Today, meditate on the vastness of God's love for you. Reflect on the ways He has shown His love in your life, both big and small. Then, choose to share His love with others. Whether through a kind word, a helping hand, or a simple act of kindness, let your actions be a reflection of God's love shining through you.

Heavenly Father, thank You for the incredible gift of Your love. Help me to fully grasp the depth and magnitude of Your love for me. Fill me with Your love so that I may overflow with compassion and kindness toward others. In Jesus' name, Amen.

DAY 111

The Role of the Church

"And let us consider how we may spur one another on toward love and good deeds, not giving up meeting together, as some are in the habit of doing, but encouraging one another—and all the more as you see the Day approaching." - Hebrews 10:24-25 (NIV)

The church plays a vital role in the life of every believer. It serves as a community of faith where individuals come together to worship God, grow in their relationship with Him, and support one another in their spiritual journey.

Being part of a church provides accountability and encouragement. It's a place where we can share our joys and struggles, knowing that we are surrounded by brothers and sisters who will uplift and pray for us. Through fellowship and worship, we are strengthened and equipped to live out our faith in the world.

Action Plan:

Today, make a commitment to actively participate in your church community. Attend worship services regularly, join a small group or Bible study, and look for opportunities to serve others within the church. By investing in your church family, you'll experience the blessings of unity and spiritual growth.

Heavenly Father, thank You for the gift of the church, where we can come together to worship You and support one another. Help me to be an active and engaged member of my church community, using my gifts to build up the body of Christ. May our fellowship be a reflection of Your love and grace. In Jesus' name, Amen.

DAY 112

Embracing God's Call

"For we are God's handiwork, created in Christ Jesus to do good works, which God prepared in advance for us to do." - Ephesians 2:10 (NIV)

God's call is not just a random summons; it's a divine invitation to fulfill our purpose and destiny. Each of us is uniquely crafted by God for a specific mission, designed to bring glory to His name and bless the world around us. Embracing God's call means recognizing and accepting our role in His grand design.

When we heed God's call, we step into the fullness of who He created us to be. We tap into our potential and unleash the gifts and talents He has bestowed upon us. It's a journey of faith and obedience, trusting that God's plans for us are good and that He will equip us for every task He sets before us.

Action Plan:

Today, take time to discern God's call on your life. Reflect on your passions, strengths, and the desires of your heart, seeking God's guidance through prayer and meditation. Ask Him to reveal His purpose for you and to give you the courage and wisdom to pursue it wholeheartedly.

Heavenly Father, thank You for calling me according to Your purpose. Give me ears to hear Your voice and a heart that is willing to obey. Help me to embrace Your call with faith and courage, knowing that You are with me every step of the way. In Jesus' name, Amen.

DAY 113

The Value of Simplicity

"But seek first his kingdom and his righteousness, and all these things will be given to you as well." - Matthew 6:33 (NIV)

In a world that often glorifies complexity and excess, the value of simplicity shines brightly as a guiding principle for a fulfilling life. Simplicity invites us to prioritize what truly matters, to strip away the distractions that cloud our vision and clutter our hearts.

Living simply doesn't mean living without; rather, it means living with intentionality and mindfulness. It's about focusing on the essentials, letting go of the unnecessary burdens that weigh us down. When we embrace simplicity, we find freedom from the relentless pursuit of material possessions and societal expectations.

Simplicity fosters gratitude and contentment, teaching us to find joy in the simple pleasures of life. It opens our eyes to the beauty of God's creation and the richness of relationships.

Action Plan:

Today, declutter one area of your life—whether it's your physical space, your schedule, or your digital devices. Take time to remove unnecessary items or commitments that no longer serve you.

Gracious God, teach me the value of simplicity in a world filled with distractions and noise. Help me to prioritize what truly matters and to find contentment in the abundance of Your blessings. Guide me in simplifying my life so that I may better serve You and others. In Jesus' name, Amen.

DAY 114

The Importance of Witnessing

"But you will receive power when the Holy Spirit comes on you; and you will be my witnesses in Jerusalem, and in all Judea and Samaria, and to the ends of the earth." - Acts 1:8 (NIV)

Witnessing is not just a call; it's a commandment given to us by our Lord Jesus Christ. As His disciples, we are tasked with sharing the good news of salvation with others, spreading the light of His love to the darkest corners of the world. Witnessing is an essential part of our faith journey, for it not only strengthens our own relationship with God but also brings others into His fold.

When we witness to others, we become vessels of God's grace, sharing the transformative power of His love and forgiveness. Through our words and actions, we have the opportunity to lead others to Christ, offering them hope and eternal life.

Action Plan:

Today, commit to sharing your faith with at least one person. It could be a friend, family member, or even a stranger. Look for opportunities to testify to God's goodness and share how He has worked in your life.

Heavenly Father, thank You for entrusting us with the privilege of witnessing for Your kingdom. Fill us with Your Holy Spirit, empowering us to boldly proclaim the good news of salvation to those around us. Open doors for fruitful conversations and opportunities to share Your love. In Jesus' name, Amen.

DAY 115

The Power of a Quiet Spirit

"But let your adorning be the hidden person of the heart with the imperishable beauty of a gentle and quiet spirit, which in God's sight is very precious." - 1 Peter 3:4 (ESV)

In a world that clamors for attention and noise, there is power in cultivating a quiet spirit. A quiet spirit is not one devoid of passion or strength; rather, it is a spirit anchored in peace and trust in God. It is an inner calmness that transcends external circumstances, allowing us to navigate life's challenges with grace and wisdom.

A quiet spirit speaks volumes without uttering a word. It reflects a deep confidence in God's sovereignty and a reliance on His strength. In the midst of chaos and turmoil, a quiet spirit stands as a beacon of hope and stability, drawing others closer to the peace that surpasses all understanding.

Action Plan:

Today, practice cultivating a quiet spirit in the midst of busyness and noise. Take moments throughout your day to pause, breathe, and center yourself in God's presence. Practice listening more than speaking, allowing space for God to speak to your heart. Let your actions be guided by a spirit of peace and gentleness, trusting in God's provision and guidance.

Heavenly Father, help me to cultivate a quiet spirit that reflects Your peace and presence. Teach me to trust in Your sovereignty and to find strength in Your presence. May my life be a testament to Your grace and goodness. In Jesus' name, Amen.

DAY 116

Living with Integrity

"The integrity of the upright guides them, but the unfaithful are destroyed by their duplicity." - Proverbs 11:3 (NIV)

Living with integrity means aligning our actions with our beliefs, even when no one is watching. It's about being honest, trustworthy, and morally upright in all aspects of our lives. When we live with integrity, we honor God and earn the respect of those around us.

Integrity is a rare and precious quality in today's world, but its importance cannot be overstated. It forms the foundation of strong relationships, both with God and with others. When we uphold our integrity, we build a reputation of reliability and authenticity that speaks volumes about our character.

Action Plan:

Today, commit to practicing integrity in all your dealings. Whether it's in your work, relationships, or personal life, strive to always do what is right, even when it's difficult. Hold yourself to the highest standards of honesty and integrity, knowing that your actions reflect your commitment to God.

Heavenly Father, I thank You for the gift of integrity. Help me to live with honesty and integrity in all that I do, honoring You with my words and actions. Give me the strength to resist temptation and the wisdom to always choose what is right. In Jesus' name, Amen.

DAY 117

Embracing God's Plan for Your Life

"For I know the plans I have for you," declares the Lord, "plans to prosper you and not to harm you, plans to give you hope and a future." - Jeremiah 29:11 (NIV)

God's plan for your life is a masterpiece crafted with love and purpose. It's a journey filled with divine guidance and fulfillment beyond measure. When you embrace God's plan, you step into the fullness of His blessings and experience the abundance of His grace.

God's plan may not always align with our own desires or expectations, but His ways are higher and His thoughts are greater. Trusting in His plan requires faith and surrender, knowing that He works all things together for the good of those who love Him.

Action Plan:

Today, surrender your plans and ambitions to God. Spend time in prayer, seeking His will for your life. Listen attentively to His voice and be open to His leading. As you discern His plan, take intentional steps to align your actions with His purposes, trusting that His ways are perfect.

Heavenly Father, thank You for the perfect plan You have for my life. Give me the faith and courage to trust in Your guidance, even when I cannot see the full picture. Help me to surrender my will to Yours and to walk in obedience to Your leading. In Jesus' name, Amen.

DAY 118

The Importance of Spiritual Growth

"But grow in the grace and knowledge of our Lord and Savior Jesus Christ. To him be glory both now and forever! Amen." - 2 Peter 3:18 (NIV)

Spiritual growth is the essence of our journey with God. It's the process of becoming more like Christ, deepening our relationship with Him, and maturing in our faith. Just as physical exercise strengthens our bodies, spiritual growth strengthens our souls, equipping us to face life's challenges with courage and resilience.

When we prioritize spiritual growth, we open ourselves to the transformative power of God's Word and His Spirit. We become more attuned to His voice, more sensitive to His leading, and more aligned with His purposes. Spiritual growth isn't just about acquiring knowledge; it's about experiencing a profound, life-changing encounter with the living God.

Action Plan:

Today, commit to cultivating spiritual growth in your life by establishing a regular time for prayer and Bible study. Set aside a few minutes each day to commune with God, seeking His presence and guidance.

Heavenly Father, thank You for the gift of spiritual growth. Help me to be intentional in my pursuit of You, seeking to know You more deeply and to become more like You each day. Guide me by Your Spirit and strengthen me for the journey ahead. In Jesus' name, Amen.

DAY 119

The Role of Accountability

"Therefore confess your sins to each other and pray for each other so that you may be healed. The prayer of a righteous person is powerful and effective." - James 5:16 (NIV)

Accountability is the cornerstone of growth and transformation in our spiritual journey. It's the recognition that we are not meant to walk alone but to journey together, supporting and encouraging one another along the way. When we embrace accountability, we invite others into our lives to hold us to a higher standard, to challenge us, and to help us become the men God has called us to be.

Being accountable means being vulnerable, allowing others to see our weaknesses and struggles. Through accountability, we experience the power of community, finding strength in numbers and comfort in knowing that we are not alone in our battles.

Action Plan:

Today, seek out an accountability partner or join a small group where you can share your joys, struggles, and victories in your faith journey. Commit to being transparent and honest with your accountability partner, and encourage them to do the same.

Heavenly Father, thank You for the gift of accountability and the community of believers You have placed in my life. May our relationships be strengthened through accountability, and may Your name be glorified in all that we do. In Jesus' name, Amen.

DAY 120

Trusting God in Difficult Times

"Trust in the Lord with all your heart and lean not on your own understanding; in all your ways submit to him, and he will make your paths straight." - Proverbs 3:5-6 (NIV)

In the midst of life's storms and trials, trusting God can be a challenge. Yet, it is in these difficult times that our faith is truly tested and strengthened. When we choose to trust God, we relinquish control and place our confidence in His unwavering love and sovereignty.

Trusting God in difficult times doesn't mean ignoring our struggles or pretending everything is fine. Instead, it means acknowledging our limitations and surrendering our fears and anxieties to Him.

Action Plan:

Today, when faced with a difficult situation, choose to trust God's plan. Take a moment to pray and surrender your worries to Him. Then, make a list of His promises from Scripture that speak to your current circumstances. Keep this list close by as a reminder of God's faithfulness, and whenever doubt creeps in, meditate on His promises and trust in His unfailing love.

Heavenly Father, in times of uncertainty and difficulty, help me to trust in Your goodness and faithfulness. Strengthen my faith and fill me with Your peace that surpasses all understanding. May I rest in the assurance of Your love and provision, knowing that You are always with me. In Jesus' name, Amen.

DAY 121

The Power of Confession

"Therefore, confess your sins to each other and pray for each other so that you may be healed. The prayer of a righteous person is powerful and effective." - James 5:16 (NIV)

Confession holds transformative power. It's not just admitting our wrongdoings but humbly laying them bare before God and others. Confession breaks down the walls of pride and self-righteousness, paving the way for healing and reconciliation.

When we confess our sins, we acknowledge our need for God's grace and mercy. It's a courageous act of vulnerability that opens the door to forgiveness and restoration. Confession frees us from the burden of guilt and shame, allowing us to experience the fullness of God's love and acceptance.

Action Plan:

Today, take time to confess your sins to God in prayer. Be honest and transparent, laying your heart bare before Him. Additionally, consider confiding in a trusted friend or mentor and asking for their support and accountability. By sharing your struggles with others, you invite God's healing into your life and strengthen your bonds of community.

Heavenly Father, I come before You with a humble and contrite heart, acknowledging my need for Your forgiveness. Grant me the courage to confess my sins and the strength to walk in Your ways. May Your mercy wash over me, bringing healing and restoration to my soul. In Jesus' name, Amen.

DAY 122

Living with Joy

"You make known to me the path of life; you will fill me with joy in your presence, with eternal pleasures at your right hand." - Psalm 16:11 (NIV)

Living with joy is not merely about experiencing fleeting happiness based on circumstances, but rather, it's about finding a deep and abiding sense of joy that comes from knowing and walking with God. True joy transcends external circumstances and is rooted in our relationship with Him.

Joy is a fruit of the Spirit, a gift freely given to those who abide in Christ. It is a source of strength and resilience, enabling us to face life's challenges with unwavering hope and positivity. When we live with joy, we reflect the light of Christ to the world around us, drawing others closer to Him.

Action Plan:

Today, choose joy in every situation. Practice gratitude by intentionally focusing on the blessings in your life, no matter how small they may seem. Take time to worship and praise God, allowing His presence to fill you with overflowing joy. Look for opportunities to spread joy to others through acts of kindness and encouragement.

Heavenly Father, thank You for the gift of joy that comes from knowing You. Help me to live each day with a joyful heart, regardless of my circumstances. Fill me with Your presence and guide me to spread joy to those around me. In Jesus' name, Amen.

DAY 123

Embracing God's Grace

"For it is by grace you have been saved, through faith—and this is not from yourselves, it is the gift of God." - Ephesians 2:8 (NIV)

God's grace is the cornerstone of our faith, the undeserved gift that transforms lives. It is the unmerited favor and love of God extended to us, despite our flaws and shortcomings. Embracing God's grace means acknowledging our need for His mercy and receiving the gift of salvation with humility and gratitude.

In a world that often demands perfection and self-sufficiency, God's grace offers us freedom from the burden of trying to earn our way into His love. It is a reminder that we are loved unconditionally, just as we are, and that nothing we can do will ever separate us from His love.

Action Plan:

Today, take a moment to reflect on the depth of God's grace in your life. Consider the ways in which He has shown you mercy and forgiveness, and give thanks for His unending love. Then, extend that same grace to others, forgiving those who have wronged you and showing kindness to those in need.

Heavenly Father, thank You for Your boundless grace and mercy. Help me to fully embrace Your love and to live in the freedom that comes from knowing I am saved by Your grace. Give me the strength to extend grace to others, just as You have graciously extended it to me. In Jesus' name, Amen.

DAY 124

The Importance of Self-Examination

"Search me, God, and know my heart; test me and know my anxious thoughts. See if there is any offensive way in me, and lead me in the way everlasting." - Psalm 139:23-24 (NIV)

Self-examination is a vital aspect of spiritual growth and maturity. It involves taking an honest look at our thoughts, attitudes, and actions in the light of God's truth. Through self-examination, we invite God to reveal areas in our lives that need refinement and transformation.

We acknowledge our weaknesses and vulnerabilities, allowing God's grace to work in and through us. Self-examination enables us to identify patterns of sin or harmful behaviors, leading to repentance and a deeper commitment to living in alignment with God's will.

Action Plan:

Today, set aside time for quiet reflection and self-examination. Take a journal or notebook and prayerfully ask God to reveal any areas in your life that need His healing touch. Be open and honest with yourself, and allow the Holy Spirit to guide you in identifying areas for growth and transformation.

Heavenly Father, thank You for Your grace and mercy that allows us to come before You with open hearts. Help me to engage in regular self-examination, that I may grow in spiritual maturity and become more like Your Son, Jesus Christ. Lead me in the path of righteousness and transformation. In His name, I pray. Amen.

DAY 125

Trusting God's Leadership

"Trust in the Lord with all your heart and lean not on your own understanding; in all your ways submit to him, and he will make your paths straight." - Proverbs 3:5-6 (NIV)

Trusting God's leadership is an act of surrendering our will to His divine wisdom and guidance. It requires us to let go of our desire for control and instead place our faith in His perfect plan for our lives. When we trust in God's leadership, we acknowledge His sovereignty and believe that He is working all things together for our good.

God's leadership is unlike any other; it is rooted in love, grace, and mercy. He leads us with compassion and understanding, always guiding us toward His best for us. Even in the midst of uncertainty and trials, we can trust that God is in control and that He will never leave us nor forsake us.

Action Plan:

Today, surrender your plans and desires to God's leadership. Take time to pray and seek His will for your life, trusting that He knows what is best for you. As you go about your day, listen for His voice and follow His prompting, knowing that He is leading you every step of the way.

Heavenly Father, thank You for Your perfect leadership in my life. Help me to trust in Your wisdom and guidance, knowing that You have my best interests at heart. Give me the strength to surrender my will to Yours and to follow wherever You lead. In Jesus' name, Amen.

DAY 126

The Role of Faith in Everyday Life

"Now faith is confidence in what we hope for and assurance about what we do not see." - Hebrews 11:1 (NIV)

Faith is not just a belief system; it's a way of life. It's the unwavering confidence in God's promises, even when circumstances seem bleak. In our everyday lives, faith serves as our compass, guiding us through the uncertainties and challenges we encounter.

When we live by faith, we acknowledge that we are not in control, but we trust in a higher power who is. Faith empowers us to step out of our comfort zones, knowing that God is with us every step of the way. It gives us the strength to persevere in the face of adversity and the courage to pursue our dreams with boldness.

Action Plan:

Today, choose to live out your faith in practical ways. Start by taking a moment to pray and surrender your worries and fears to God. Then, step out in faith by committing to one act of kindness or generosity towards someone in need. Whether it's offering a listening ear, lending a helping hand, or simply sharing a word of encouragement, let your actions reflect the love and compassion of Christ.

Heavenly Father, thank You for the gift of faith that sustains me each day. Help me to trust in Your unfailing love and to walk by faith, not by sight. Give me the courage to live boldly for You and the compassion to extend Your love to those around me. In Jesus' name, Amen.

DAY 127

The Power of Consistency

"Let us not become weary in doing good, for at the proper time we will reap a harvest if we do not give up." - Galatians 6:9 (NIV)

Consistency is the key that unlocks the door to success in every aspect of life. It's the steady, persistent effort we put forth day after day, even when we don't see immediate results. Just as a river carves its path through rock over time, consistency shapes our character and accomplishments.

In our spiritual journey, consistency is vital. It's the daily commitment to prayer, to studying God's Word, and to living out our faith in practical ways. Consistency deepens our relationship with God, strengthens our spiritual muscles, and equips us to face life's challenges with unwavering faith.

Action Plan:

Today, choose one area of your life where you desire to be more consistent. It could be in your prayer life, in serving others, or in pursuing a specific goal. Set realistic, achievable targets, and commit to taking small steps each day toward that goal. Remember, it's the cumulative effect of consistent effort that brings about lasting change.

Heavenly Father, thank You for Your faithfulness to us. Help us to mirror that faithfulness in our own lives through consistency. Give us the strength and determination to persevere, even when the journey seems long and challenging. May our consistency bring glory to Your name. In Jesus' name, Amen.

DAY 128

Embracing God's Faithfulness

"Know therefore that the Lord your God is God; he is the faithful God, keeping his covenant of love to a thousand generations of those who love him and keep his commandments." - Deuteronomy 7:9 (NIV)

God's faithfulness is an unshakable foundation upon which we can build our lives. In a world of uncertainty and change, His faithfulness remains steadfast and unwavering. He is true to His promises, never failing to fulfill His word.

Embracing God's faithfulness means placing our trust completely in Him, knowing that He will never leave us nor forsake us. It means looking back on our lives and recognizing the countless times He has shown up, even in the midst of our doubts and fears.

Action Plan:

Today, take some time to reflect on God's faithfulness in your life. Write down specific instances where you have seen His hand at work, whether it be answered prayers, unexpected blessings, or moments of divine intervention. As you recall these memories, let them serve as reminders of God's unfailing love and faithfulness.

Heavenly Father, thank You for Your faithfulness that endures through all generations. Help me to trust in Your promises and rely on Your steadfast love. May Your faithfulness strengthen my faith and fill me with hope for the future. In Jesus' name, Amen.

DAY 129

The Blessing of Contentment

"But godliness with contentment is great gain." - 1 Timothy 6:6
(NIV)

Contentment is a rare jewel in a world that constantly whispers discontentment into our ears. Yet, in the stillness of our hearts, we find that true wealth lies not in the accumulation of possessions, but in the peace that comes with contentment.

Contentment is not complacency; it's a deep-rooted satisfaction that transcends circumstances. It's an attitude of gratitude, recognizing the blessings we already possess rather than longing for what we lack. When we embrace contentment, we find joy in the simple things and serenity in the midst of life's storms.

Action Plan:

Today, practice gratitude. Take a few moments to reflect on the blessings in your life, both big and small. Write down three things you're thankful for and meditate on them throughout the day. Let gratitude cultivate a spirit of contentment within you, transforming your outlook on life.

Gracious God, teach me the secret of contentment in every situation. Help me to find joy in Your provision and peace in Your presence. Open my eyes to the abundance of blessings surrounding me, that I may live with a heart overflowing with gratitude. In Jesus' name, Amen.

DAY 130

Living with Purpose

"Commit to the Lord whatever you do, and he will establish your plans." - Proverbs 16:3 (NIV)

Living with purpose means living with intentionality, understanding that every breath we take is an opportunity to fulfill the unique calling God has placed on our lives. It's about seeking His will in all that we do and allowing His guiding hand to direct our steps. When we live with purpose, we find meaning in our daily activities, and our lives become a testament to God's glory.

To live with purpose, we must first seek clarity in our hearts. Reflect on your passions, talents, and the desires that God has placed within you. Consider how you can use these gifts to serve others and make a positive impact on the world around you.

Action Plan:

Today, take a moment to write down your life's mission statement. What is the overarching purpose that drives you? Once you've identified it, choose one specific action you can take to align your daily activities with this purpose. Whether it's volunteering at a local charity, mentoring someone in need, or simply approaching your work with a renewed sense of dedication, commit to living each day with purpose.

Heavenly Father, thank You for the purpose You have given me. Help me to live each day with intentionality, seeking Your will in all that I do. Guide me as I strive to fulfill the plans You have for me. In Jesus' name, Amen.

DAY 131

Trusting in God's Power

"But those who hope in the Lord will renew their strength. They will soar on wings like eagles; they will run and not grow weary, they will walk and not be faint." - Isaiah 40:31 (NIV)

Trusting in God's power is a cornerstone of our faith journey. In a world filled with uncertainty and challenges, it's easy to feel overwhelmed by our own limitations. Yet, the Bible reminds us that our strength and hope are found not in our abilities but in the limitless power of God. When we place our trust in Him, we tap into a source of strength that renews and uplifts us beyond our understanding.

God's power is not just for grand miracles; it is present in the daily moments of our lives. Trusting in His power means surrendering our fears and doubts, acknowledging that He is in control and that His plans for us are good.

Action Plan:

Today, identify one area of your life where you feel particularly challenged or powerless. Take a moment to pray, consciously surrendering that situation to God's mighty power. Replace your anxiety with faith, and look for small ways to act in alignment with your trust in Him.

Almighty God, I acknowledge Your power and sovereignty over my life. Renew my strength and guide me through every trial with Your unwavering power. In Jesus' name, Amen.

DAY 132

The Importance of Encouragement

"Therefore encourage one another and build each other up, just as in fact you are doing." - 1 Thessalonians 5:11 (NIV)

Encouragement is a powerful tool that can transform lives, uplift spirits, and inspire greatness. In a world where challenges and discouragement are commonplace, the act of encouraging others becomes a beacon of hope and strength. It's about recognizing the potential and worth in those around us and speaking life into their situations.

Encouragement goes beyond mere words; it involves listening, empathizing, and offering support. When we encourage others, we become instruments of God's love and grace, helping to build their faith and resilience. By fostering a culture of encouragement, we create an environment where individuals can thrive, knowing they are valued and supported.

Action Plan:

Today, make it a point to encourage at least one person. It could be a colleague, a friend, or a family member. Offer a genuine compliment, share a word of appreciation, or provide support in a way that lifts their spirit. Notice how this simple act not only impacts their day but also brings joy and fulfillment to your own heart.

Dear Lord, help me to be a source of encouragement to those around me. Open my eyes to see the needs of others and give me the words to uplift and inspire them. Let my actions reflect Your love and build up those who are weary. In Jesus' name, Amen.

DAY 133

God's Sovereignty in Your Life

"The Lord has established his throne in heaven, and his kingdom rules over all." - Psalm 103:19 (NIV)

Understanding God's sovereignty is about recognizing His ultimate control and authority over all aspects of our lives. It means trusting that He is in charge, even when circumstances seem chaotic or uncertain. God's sovereignty assures us that nothing happens without His knowledge or permission, and everything ultimately serves His divine purpose.

It reminds us that we are not alone, and our lives are not subject to random fate. God is actively involved, weaving every thread of our experiences into a tapestry that reveals His glory and our good. Embracing His sovereignty allows us to surrender our anxieties and uncertainties, knowing that He holds the entire universe—and our lives—in His capable hands.

Action Plan:

Reflect on a current challenge or uncertainty you are facing. Consciously choose to trust God's sovereignty in this situation. Write down your worries and then, in prayer, hand them over to God. Ask for His guidance and trust that He is working everything out for your good, even if you cannot see it yet.

Sovereign Lord, thank You for Your control and authority over my life. Help me to trust in Your plan and to surrender my anxieties to You. Strengthen my faith as I navigate life's challenges, knowing You are always in control. In Jesus' name, Amen.

DAY 134

The Power of a Positive Attitude

"Finally, brothers and sisters, whatever is true, whatever is noble, whatever is right, whatever is pure, whatever is lovely, whatever is admirable—if anything is excellent or praiseworthy—think about such things." - Philippians 4:8 (NIV)

The power of a positive attitude cannot be overstated. It's the lens through which we view our circumstances, transforming challenges into opportunities and setbacks into stepping stones. A positive attitude is rooted in faith, trusting that God is working all things for our good and His glory, even when we can't see it.

Embracing a positive attitude means choosing to focus on the blessings in our lives rather than dwelling on the negatives. It's about cultivating gratitude, seeing the good in others, and approaching each day with hope and enthusiasm.

Action Plan:

Today, make a conscious effort to shift your mindset toward positivity. Start by identifying three things you are grateful for and write them down. Throughout the day, whenever negative thoughts arise, counter them with positive affirmations and reminders of God's promises. Watch how this simple practice can transform your perspective and bring joy to your day.

Heavenly Father, thank You for the gift of a new day. Help me to embrace a positive attitude, focusing on the good and trusting in Your plan. May my attitude reflect Your love and light to those around me. In Jesus' name, Amen.

DAY 135

Embracing God's Timing

"For everything there is a season, and a time for every matter under heaven." - Ecclesiastes 3:1 (ESV)

Embracing God's timing is an act of faith and patience. In our fast-paced world, it's easy to get caught up in the rush and desire for immediate results. Yet, the Bible teaches us that there is a perfect time for every aspect of our lives, orchestrated by God's divine wisdom.

Waiting on God's timing requires trust. It's about believing that His plans for us are better than anything we could devise on our own. While it can be challenging to wait, especially during tough times, this waiting period is often where growth happens. It's in these moments of patience that God prepares us for the blessings ahead.

Action Plan:

Today, identify an area in your life where you feel impatient. It could be related to your career, relationships, or personal goals. Take a moment to surrender this impatience to God. Write down a prayer or a reflection, acknowledging your trust in His perfect timing and committing to wait with faith and patience.

Heavenly Father, help me to trust in Your perfect timing. Teach me patience and give me the strength to wait for Your plans to unfold in my life. I surrender my impatience to You and ask for peace in my heart as I trust Your divine schedule. In Jesus' name, Amen.

DAY 136

The Importance of Commitment

"Commit your work to the Lord, and your plans will be established." - Proverbs 16:3 (ESV)

Commitment is a powerful force that shapes our character and directs our path. It is the resolve to stay dedicated to a cause, a purpose, or a relationship, even when challenges arise. In our walk with God, commitment means entrusting our efforts and ambitions to Him, trusting that He will guide and strengthen us.

Being committed requires discipline, perseverance, and faith. It's easy to be swayed by distractions or discouraged by setbacks, but true commitment calls us to remain steadfast. When we commit our work to the Lord, we align our will with His, finding purpose and direction..

Action Plan:

Today, reflect on an area where your commitment might be wavering. It could be in your spiritual practices, your job, or a relationship. Take a tangible step to renew your dedication. This might involve setting a specific goal, creating a routine, or simply spending extra time in prayer, asking God to strengthen your resolve.

Heavenly Father, help me to embrace the importance of commitment in all areas of my life. Strengthen my resolve and guide my efforts, so that I may honor You in everything I do. Teach me to stay faithful and steadfast, trusting in Your plans for me. In Jesus' name, Amen.

DAY 137

Trusting in God's Love

"And so we know and rely on the love God has for us. God is love. Whoever lives in love lives in God, and God in them." - 1 John 4:16 (NIV)

Trusting in God's love is foundational to our faith. It's a powerful truth that can transform our lives, bringing peace and assurance even in the most challenging times. God's love is unconditional, unwavering, and everlasting. It's not based on our performance or circumstances but on His very nature.

When we truly grasp the depth of God's love, it changes how we view ourselves and the world around us. We no longer need to strive for acceptance or fear rejection because we are already fully loved by the Creator of the universe. This divine love empowers us to love others, to forgive, and to live with a sense of purpose and security.

Action Plan:

Today, take a moment to meditate on God's love for you. Find a quiet place, read 1 John 4:16, and reflect on what it means to be loved unconditionally by God. Write down three ways you have experienced His love in your life. Let this reminder fill you with confidence and peace as you go through your day.

Heavenly Father, thank You for Your unfailing love. Help me to trust in Your love more deeply each day. Remind me of Your presence and guide me to live out of the overflow of Your love. Fill my heart with confidence and peace, knowing I am cherished by You. In Jesus' name, Amen.

DAY 138

The Role of Perseverance

"Blessed is the man who remains steadfast under trial, for when he has stood the test he will receive the crown of life, which God has promised to those who love him." - James 1:12 (ESV)

Perseverance is a defining quality of a strong, faithful man. Life presents us with numerous challenges and obstacles, and it is in these moments that our true character is tested. Perseverance is the commitment to keep moving forward, despite the difficulties, with faith and determination.

Remaining steadfast under trial is not about ignoring the pain or pretending everything is fine. It's about trusting that God is with us in our struggles, and believing that He is shaping us through these experiences. Each trial we face and overcome builds our resilience and deepens our faith.

Action Plan:

Identify a challenge you are currently facing. Instead of feeling overwhelmed, choose to see it as an opportunity to strengthen your perseverance. Write down one practical step you can take today to move forward. Reflect on God's promises and ask for His strength to endure.

Heavenly Father, give me the strength to persevere through life's challenges. Help me to remain steadfast in my faith, trusting that You are with me every step of the way. Strengthen my resolve and help me to see each trial as an opportunity for growth. In Jesus' name, Amen.

DAY 139

The Power of Faithfulness

"His master said to him, 'Well done, good and faithful servant. You have been faithful over a little; I will set you over much. Enter into the joy of your master.'" - Matthew 25:23 (ESV)

The power of faithfulness lies in its ability to transform the ordinary into the extraordinary. Being faithful in the small, everyday tasks demonstrates our commitment and trustworthiness. It's in these moments that we cultivate integrity and build character, proving ourselves ready for greater responsibilities and blessings.

Faithfulness isn't just about the big, noticeable acts. It's about showing up consistently, doing what's right even when no one is watching, and honoring our commitments. When we are faithful, we reflect God's unwavering faithfulness toward us.

Action Plan:

Today, focus on being faithful in one small area of your life. It could be showing up on time for work, keeping a promise to a friend, or dedicating a few minutes to prayer and Bible study. Consistently apply yourself in this area, recognizing that even the smallest acts of faithfulness are significant in God's eyes.

Lord, help me to be faithful in all areas of my life, both big and small. Grant me the strength to remain committed and trustworthy in my daily actions. May my faithfulness reflect Your love and bring glory to Your name. In Jesus' name, Amen.

DAY 140

Embracing God's Wisdom

"If any of you lacks wisdom, you should ask God, who gives generously to all without finding fault, and it will be given to you."
- James 1:5 (NIV)

Embracing God's wisdom is an invitation to lead a life guided by divine insight rather than mere human understanding. In a world overflowing with opinions and advice, the wisdom that comes from God stands unparalleled, offering clarity, direction, and peace.

God's wisdom transcends our limited perspectives, helping us navigate life's complexities with discernment and grace. It's available to us through prayer, the study of His Word, and the counsel of the Holy Spirit.

Action Plan:

Today, take a few moments to seek God's wisdom in a specific area of your life. Open your Bible and read a chapter from Proverbs, known for its insights on living wisely. As you read, ask God to illuminate His wisdom and how it applies to your current situation. Write down any insights or guidance you receive and commit to applying them in your daily life.

Heavenly Father, I seek Your wisdom today. Guide my thoughts, decisions, and actions so that they reflect Your will. Open my heart and mind to understand and embrace Your teachings. Grant me discernment and the courage to follow Your path. In Jesus' name, Amen.

DAY 141

The Importance of Discipline

"No discipline seems pleasant at the time, but painful. Later on, however, it produces a harvest of righteousness and peace for those who have been trained by it." - Hebrews 12:11 (NIV)

Discipline is the cornerstone of success in all aspects of life. It's the steadfast commitment to do what is necessary, even when it's difficult or uncomfortable. Just as an athlete trains diligently for victory, so too must we cultivate discipline in our spiritual, personal, and professional endeavors.

Discipline is not merely about self-control; it's about aligning our actions with our values and goals. It's about making intentional choices that lead to growth and fulfillment. While it may be challenging in the moment, the rewards of discipline are abundant and enduring.

Action Plan:

Today, identify an area in your life where you could use more discipline. It could be in your daily routine, your habits, or your relationships. Commit to implementing one small but meaningful change to exercise discipline in that area.

Gracious Father, grant me the strength and wisdom to embrace discipline in my life. Help me to cultivate habits that honor You and lead to growth and transformation. Guide me in making choices that align with Your will and bring glory to Your name. In Jesus' name, Amen.

DAY 142

Trusting God's Plan

"For I know the plans I have for you," declares the Lord, "plans to prosper you and not to harm you, plans to give you hope and a future." - Jeremiah 29:11 (NIV)

Trusting God's plan is an act of surrender and faith. It means releasing our grip on control and placing our trust in the One who knows the beginning from the end. Even when life's circumstances seem uncertain or challenging, we can find comfort in knowing that God's plans for us are filled with hope and purpose.

God's plan may not always align with our own desires or expectations, but it is always for our ultimate good. It's about believing that He is working all things together for our benefit, even when we can't see the bigger picture. When we trust in His plan, we experience a sense of peace that surpasses understanding, knowing that we are held in the palm of His hand.

Action Plan:

Today, take a moment to reflect on a situation in your life where you're struggling to trust God's plan. Surrender that situation to Him in prayer, acknowledging His sovereignty and wisdom. Choose to let go of worry and doubt, and instead, affirm your trust in His perfect plan for your life.

Heavenly Father, I thank You for the assurance that Your plans for me are good. Help me to trust in Your wisdom and timing, even when I can't see the way ahead. Strengthen my faith and grant me peace as I surrender my will to Yours. In Jesus' name, Amen.

DAY 143

The Role of Humility

"He has shown you, O mortal, what is good. And what does the LORD require of you? To act justly and to love mercy and to walk humbly with your God." - Micah 6:8 (NIV)

Humility is not weakness but strength under control. It's the acknowledgment that our talents, achievements, and even our very existence are gifts from a higher power. In a world that often glorifies self-promotion and pride, humility stands as a counter-cultural virtue, reminding us of our interconnectedness and dependence on something greater than ourselves.

True humility fosters empathy and compassion. It allows us to see the inherent worth and dignity of every individual, regardless of their status or background. When we humble ourselves before others, we create space for genuine relationships to flourish, free from the barriers of ego and superiority.

Action Plan:

Today, practice humility by actively listening to someone else without interrupting or interjecting your own opinions. Whether it's a colleague, friend, or family member, make a conscious effort to truly understand their perspective and validate their experiences.

Gracious God, teach me to walk humbly in Your presence. Help me to set aside my pride and ego, and to recognize the beauty and worth in every person I encounter. May humility guide my words and actions, reflecting Your love and grace to the world. In Your holy name, Amen.

DAY 144

The Power of Prayer

*"The prayer of a righteous person is powerful and effective." -
James 5:16b (NIV)*

Prayer is not merely a ritual; it's a powerful connection with the Almighty. It's our direct line to God, a channel through which we communicate our deepest hopes, fears, and gratitude. Through prayer, we tap into the infinite wisdom and strength of our Creator.

The power of prayer lies in its ability to transform hearts and circumstances. When we pray with sincerity and faith, we invite God's intervention into our lives. It's a reminder that we are not alone in our struggles but are held in the loving embrace of a compassionate Father.

Action Plan:

Today, set aside intentional time for prayer. Find a quiet place where you can be alone with God, free from distractions. Pour out your heart to Him, expressing your joys, concerns, and desires. Take a few moments to listen for His voice in the stillness. Write down any insights or impressions you receive during this time of communion.

Heavenly Father, thank You for the gift of prayer. Help me to approach You with faith and humility, knowing that You hear and answer my prayers. Grant me the wisdom to discern Your will and the courage to follow where You lead. In Jesus' name, Amen.

DAY 145

Embracing God's Presence

"The Lord is near to all who call on him, to all who call on him in truth." - Psalm 145:18 (NIV)

Embracing God's presence is about cultivating a deep awareness of His nearness in our daily lives. It's understanding that we are never alone, for God is with us every step of the way. His presence brings comfort, strength, and guidance, even in the midst of life's challenges.

When we embrace God's presence, we open ourselves to a profound relationship with Him. It's not merely about acknowledging His existence but actively seeking His companionship in our joys and sorrows. Through prayer, worship, and meditation on His Word, we can experience His presence in tangible ways, finding solace and reassurance in His love.

Action Plan:

Today, set aside time for intentional prayer and reflection. Find a quiet space where you can be alone with God. Invite Him into your thoughts and emotions, sharing your joys, concerns, and desires with Him. As you spend this time in His presence, listen for His voice and allow His peace to fill your heart.

Heavenly Father, thank You for the gift of Your presence. Help me to cultivate a deeper awareness of You in my life each day. May Your nearness be my constant source of strength and comfort. Guide me as I seek to walk closely with You. In Jesus' name, Amen.

DAY 146

The Importance of Reflection

"Let us examine our ways and test them, and let us return to the Lord." - Lamentations 3:40 (NIV)

Reflection is a powerful tool for spiritual growth and self-improvement. In the hustle and bustle of life, it's easy to get caught up in the daily grind without pausing to assess our actions, attitudes, and motives. Yet, taking time to reflect allows us to gain insight into our lives, fostering a deeper connection with God and a greater understanding of ourselves.

Through reflection, we can celebrate our victories and learn from our mistakes. It enables us to recognize areas where we've grown and areas where we still need to improve. When we reflect on our journey, we invite God into the process, seeking His guidance and wisdom to help us become the best version of ourselves.

Action Plan:

Today, set aside some quiet time for reflection. Find a peaceful place where you can be alone with your thoughts. Reflect on the events of the past week and consider how you've responded to challenges and opportunities. Write down any insights or lessons learned, and commit to applying them to your life moving forward.

Heavenly Father, thank You for the gift of reflection. Help me to embrace this practice as a means of deepening my relationship with You and growing in spiritual maturity. Guide me as I reflect on my life, and grant me the wisdom to discern Your will for my journey. In Jesus' name, Amen.

DAY 147

Trusting in God's Peace

"You will keep in perfect peace those whose minds are steadfast, because they trust in you." - Isaiah 26:3 (NIV)

Trusting in God's peace is a profound act of surrender and faith. In a world filled with chaos and uncertainty, God offers us a peace that surpasses all understanding. This peace isn't dependent on external circumstances but stems from a deep trust in God's sovereignty and goodness.

When we trust in God's peace, we acknowledge that He is in control, even when everything around us seems to be falling apart. It's about relinquishing our worries and anxieties to Him, knowing that He holds our future in His hands. This trust allows us to rest in His presence, finding solace and strength in the midst of life's storms.

Action Plan:

Today, take a moment to quiet your mind and heart. Reflect on any areas of your life where you are struggling to find peace. Surrender these concerns to God in prayer, trusting that He will provide the peace you need. As you go about your day, practice mindfulness, intentionally choosing to focus on God's promises rather than your worries.

Heavenly Father, thank You for the promise of Your perfect peace. Help me to trust in You wholeheartedly, even when circumstances are challenging. Grant me the strength to surrender my worries to You and to find peace in Your presence. In Jesus' name, Amen.

DAY 148

The Power of God's Promises

"For no matter how many promises God has made, they are 'Yes' in Christ. And so through him the 'Amen' is spoken by us to the glory of God." - 2 Corinthians 1:20 (NIV)

God's promises are not just empty words; they are declarations of His faithfulness and love toward us. Each promise in the Bible is a pledge of His unending care, provision, and guidance. When we hold onto these promises, we tap into a source of unshakable strength and hope.

The power of God's promises lies in their certainty. Unlike human promises that may fail or be forgotten, God's promises are steadfast and enduring. They serve as anchors in the storms of life, guiding us through every trial and challenge.

Action Plan:

Today, choose a promise from Scripture that speaks to your current situation or need. Write it down and meditate on it throughout the day. Whenever doubt or fear arises, remind yourself of this promise and declare it over your life. Allow the truth of God's word to permeate your heart and fill you with confidence and peace.

Heavenly Father, thank you for your unfailing promises that sustain and empower us. Help me to cling to your word and trust in your faithfulness, especially in times of uncertainty. May your promises be a guiding light in my life, leading me closer to you each day. In Jesus' name, Amen.

DAY 149

Living with Conviction

"But just as we have been approved by God to be entrusted with the gospel, so we speak, not to please man, but to please God who tests our hearts." - 1 Thessalonians 2:4 (ESV)

Living with conviction means aligning our actions and beliefs with the truth of God's Word, regardless of the opinions or pressures of the world around us. It's about standing firm in our faith and principles, even when faced with opposition or adversity.

When we live with conviction, we become beacons of light in a world filled with darkness. Our unwavering commitment to God's truth inspires others and glorifies Him. It's not always easy; there may be moments of doubt or fear, but through prayer and reliance on God's strength, we can persevere.

Action Plan:

Today, reflect on your convictions and how they influence your daily life. Are there areas where you compromise your beliefs to fit in or avoid conflict? Take a stand for one conviction that you hold dear, whether it's speaking up for justice, showing love to those in need, or sharing the gospel boldly. Trust in God's guidance and let your actions reflect His truth.

Heavenly Father, grant me the courage and strength to live with conviction in a world that often opposes Your truth. Help me to stand firm in my beliefs and to always seek Your will above all else. May my life be a testimony to Your faithfulness and love. In Jesus' name, Amen.

DAY 150

Embracing God's Guidance

"Trust in the Lord with all your heart and lean not on your own understanding; in all your ways submit to him, and he will make your paths straight." - Proverbs 3:5-6 (NIV)

Embracing God's guidance is about surrendering our will to His divine wisdom. In a world filled with noise and distractions, it's easy to rely solely on our own understanding. However, the Bible reminds us to trust in the Lord completely, acknowledging His sovereignty over our lives.

God's guidance may not always align with our plans or expectations, but it leads us to where we need to be. When we submit our ways to Him, we open ourselves to His direction, which often surpasses our human comprehension. His guidance brings clarity, peace, and purpose to our journey.

Action Plan:

Today, carve out some quiet time for prayer and reflection. Seek God's guidance on a specific decision or direction in your life. Listen attentively for His voice through Scripture, prayer, or inner promptings. Then, take a step of faith in obedience to His leading, even if it seems daunting or uncertain.

Gracious God, I humbly submit my life to Your guidance. Help me to trust in Your wisdom above my own understanding. Grant me clarity and discernment as I seek Your direction. May Your will be done in my life, and may I walk in obedience to Your leading. In Jesus' name, Amen.

DAY 151

The Importance of Faithfulness

"His master replied, 'Well done, good and faithful servant! You have been faithful with a few things; I will put you in charge of many things. Come and share your master's happiness!'" - Matthew 25:21 (NIV)

Faithfulness is a cornerstone of Christian living, embodying steadfastness, loyalty, and commitment. It's about being reliable in our relationships, responsibilities, and endeavors, even when faced with challenges or temptations to stray.

Being faithful in the small things cultivates a spirit of trustworthiness and excellence, preparing us for greater opportunities and blessings. It's not always easy to remain faithful, especially when the path is long or the rewards seem distant, but the rewards of faithfulness are eternal.

Action Plan:

Reflect on an area of your life where you can demonstrate greater faithfulness. It could be in your relationships, work, or spiritual disciplines. Commit to being consistent and reliable in this area, trusting that your faithfulness honors God and blesses those around you.

Heavenly Father, thank You for Your faithfulness to us. Help us to mirror Your faithfulness in our lives, remaining steadfast in our commitments and responsibilities. Give us the strength to be faithful even in the small things, knowing that You are pleased with our obedience. In Jesus' name, Amen.

DAY 152

Trusting God's Sovereignty

"The LORD has established his throne in heaven, and his kingdom rules over all." - Psalm 103:19 (NIV)

Trusting God's sovereignty means acknowledging His ultimate authority and control over all things. It's recognizing that even in the midst of uncertainty and chaos, God is still seated on His throne, orchestrating events according to His perfect will.

As men of faith, we are called to surrender our fears and anxieties to the sovereignty of God. This doesn't mean that life will always be easy or that we will understand His ways, but it does mean that we can find peace in knowing that God is in control. His plans for us are good, and His purposes will prevail.

Action Plan:

Today, take a moment to reflect on an area of your life where you struggle to trust God's sovereignty. It could be a situation at work, a health concern, or a relationship issue. Choose to release your grip on trying to control the outcome and instead surrender it to God. Write a prayer or a journal entry expressing your trust in His sovereignty and asking for His peace to fill your heart.

Heavenly Father, I acknowledge Your sovereignty over all things. Help me to trust in Your wisdom and goodness, even when life seems uncertain. Grant me the strength to surrender my worries and fears to You, knowing that Your plans for me are perfect. In Jesus' name, Amen.

DAY 153

The Role of Spiritual Strength

"I can do all things through him who strengthens me." -
Philippians 4:13 (ESV)

Spiritual strength is the cornerstone of our faith journey. It empowers us to navigate life's challenges with courage, resilience, and grace. Just as physical exercise builds our muscles, cultivating spiritual strength through prayer, meditation, and studying God's Word fortifies our inner being.

In a world where we face trials and temptations daily, spiritual strength equips us to stand firm in our convictions and resist the forces that seek to pull us away from God's path. It is not merely about our own willpower, but about tapping into the limitless power of God's spirit dwelling within us.

Action Plan:

Today, set aside time for spiritual exercise. Engage in prayer, reflecting on your strengths and weaknesses, and asking God to strengthen you in areas where you feel vulnerable. Spend time reading a passage of Scripture that speaks to the importance of spiritual strength, and meditate on its meaning for your life.

Heavenly Father, thank you for the gift of spiritual strength. As I face the challenges of today, I ask for Your power to strengthen me from within. Help me to rely on Your spirit to guide me and empower me to live according to Your will. May my actions reflect Your love and grace to those around me. In Jesus' name, Amen.

DAY 154

The Power of a Thankful Heart

"Give thanks in all circumstances; for this is God's will for you in Christ Jesus." - 1 Thessalonians 5:18 (NIV)

The power of a thankful heart is profound. It transforms our perspective, elevates our spirits, and draws us closer to God. Gratitude isn't just about recognizing blessings in times of abundance; it's about finding reasons to be thankful even in the midst of challenges.

When we cultivate a spirit of gratitude, we shift our focus from what we lack to what we have. Gratitude opens our eyes to the countless gifts and blessings that surround us daily, from the air we breathe to the relationships we cherish. It fosters contentment and joy, regardless of our circumstances.

Action Plan:

Today, take a few moments to reflect on three things you're grateful for. They could be simple pleasures, like a warm cup of coffee in the morning or a phone call from a friend. Throughout the day, consciously express gratitude for these blessings, thanking God for His goodness in your life.

Heavenly Father, thank You for the countless blessings You've bestowed upon me. Help me cultivate a heart of gratitude, even in the midst of challenges. May my thankfulness be a constant reminder of Your faithfulness and love. In Jesus' name, Amen.

DAY 155

Embracing God's Patience

"The Lord is not slow in keeping his promise, as some understand slowness. Instead, he is patient with you, not wanting anyone to perish, but everyone to come to repentance." - 2 Peter 3:9 (NIV)

Embracing God's patience is acknowledging His enduring love and mercy towards us. In a world where everything moves at a rapid pace, God's patience stands as a beacon of hope and assurance. He waits patiently for us to turn to Him, offering forgiveness and redemption to all who seek it.

God's patience is a reflection of His character. It's a reminder that His timing is perfect, even when we may feel impatient or uncertain. He patiently walks alongside us, guiding us through the ups and downs of life, never giving up on us.

Action Plan:

Today, practice patience in your interactions with others. Choose to respond with kindness and understanding, even in challenging situations. Take a moment to pause and reflect before reacting impulsively. Ask God to fill your heart with His patience and grace, allowing His love to shine through your actions.

Heavenly Father, thank You for Your infinite patience towards me. Help me to embody Your patience in my daily life, especially in moments of frustration or impatience. Fill me with Your love and compassion, that I may reflect Your character to those around me. In Jesus' name, Amen.

DAY 156

The Importance of Generosity

"A generous person will prosper; whoever refreshes others will be refreshed." - Proverbs 11:25 (NIV)

Generosity is a powerful virtue that reflects the heart of God. When we give freely and generously, we not only bless others but also experience profound joy and fulfillment ourselves. It's a reminder that we are stewards, not owners, of the blessings entrusted to us.

The importance of generosity lies not only in the tangible impact it has on those in need but also in the transformation it brings to our own lives. When we give sacrificially, we cultivate a spirit of gratitude and humility, recognizing that all we have comes from God's hand. Moreover, generosity fosters community and strengthens relationships, creating bonds of love and compassion that transcend material wealth.

Action Plan:

Today, look for an opportunity to be generous in a tangible way. It could be donating to a charity, volunteering your time to help someone in need, or simply offering a listening ear and words of encouragement to a friend. Take a moment to reflect on the blessings in your life and how you can share them with others.

Heavenly Father, thank you for your abundant blessings in my life. Help me to cultivate a spirit of generosity, that I may be a conduit of your love and grace to those around me. Show me opportunities to give freely and generously, and empower me to do so with joy and gratitude. In Jesus' name, Amen.

DAY 157

Trusting in God's Grace

"But he said to me, 'My grace is sufficient for you, for my power is made perfect in weakness.' Therefore I will boast all the more gladly about my weaknesses, so that Christ's power may rest on me." - 2 Corinthians 12:9 (NIV)

Trusting in God's grace is about acknowledgeng our own inadequacies and relying wholeheartedly on His unmerited favor and strength. It's recognizing that we are imperfect vessels, yet through His grace, we are made whole and empowered to fulfill His purpose for our lives.

God's grace is a gift freely given to us, not because of anything we have done to deserve it, but simply because of His boundless love for us. It's through His grace that we find forgiveness, redemption, and the courage to face life's challenges with faith and hope.

Action Plan:

Today, take a moment to reflect on areas in your life where you struggle or feel inadequate. Instead of dwelling on your weaknesses, surrender them to God and ask for His grace to fill those gaps. Choose to let go of self-reliance and trust in His sufficient grace to carry you through any situation.

Heavenly Father, thank You for Your abundant grace that sustains me in my weakness. Help me to trust in Your unfailing love and to rely on Your strength rather than my own. Fill me with Your grace, Lord, and guide me in walking confidently in Your will. In Jesus' name, Amen.

DAY 158

The Power of God's Love

"For I am convinced that neither death nor life, neither angels nor demons, neither the present nor the future, nor any powers, neither height nor depth, nor anything else in all creation, will be able to separate us from the love of God that is in Christ Jesus our Lord."
- Romans 8:38-39 (NIV)

The power of God's love is unmatched and unyielding. It transcends all boundaries, conquers all fears, and brings hope to the weary soul. This divine love is not conditional; it's freely given to each and every one of us, regardless of our past mistakes or present circumstances.

In a world often filled with hatred and division, God's love stands as a beacon of light, offering redemption and reconciliation to all who embrace it. It's a love that knows no limits, reaching down to the depths of our brokenness and lifting us up with its boundless grace.

Action Plan:

Today, meditate on the depth of God's love for you. Take a few moments to reflect on specific instances in your life where you have experienced His love in tangible ways. Reach out to them with a simple act of kindness, whether it's a word of encouragement, a gesture of support, or a listening ear.

Heavenly Father, thank You for the overwhelming power of Your love. Help me to fully comprehend the depth and breadth of Your love for me, and empower me to share that love with others. May Your love shine through me, bringing hope and healing to those in need. In Jesus' name, Amen.

DAY 159

Living with Integrity

"The integrity of the upright guides them, but the crookedness of the treacherous destroys them." - Proverbs 11:3 (ESV)

Living with integrity means aligning our actions with our beliefs and values, even when no one is watching. It's about being honest and truthful in all aspects of life, even when faced with temptation or adversity. When we live with integrity, we build a foundation of trust and respect with others, and we honor God with our lives.

Integrity is not just about avoiding wrongdoing; it's also about doing what is right, even when it's difficult. It's about being consistent in our character and principles, regardless of the circumstances we find ourselves in. In a world where moral compromises are often made for personal gain, living with integrity sets us apart as men of honor and integrity.

Action Plan:

Today, reflect on your actions and decisions. Are there areas in your life where you've compromised your integrity? Take the time to confess any wrongdoing to God and ask for His forgiveness. Then, commit to living with integrity in all aspects of your life, even if it means making difficult choices.

Heavenly Father, I confess any areas in my life where I have fallen short of living with integrity. Give me the strength and wisdom to make choices that honor You and align with Your will. Help me to be a man of integrity in all that I do, guided by Your truth and grace. In Jesus' name, Amen.

DAY 160

Embracing God's Truth

"Jesus answered, 'I am the way and the truth and the life. No one comes to the Father except through me.'" - John 14:6 (NIV)

Embracing God's truth is more than just acknowledging a set of beliefs; it's about aligning our lives with the eternal truths found in His Word. In a world filled with shifting perspectives and subjective truths, God's truth stands firm and unchanging, offering us a solid foundation on which to build our lives.

God's truth brings clarity and direction to our journey of faith. It reveals His character, His promises, and His will for our lives. When we embrace His truth, we find freedom from the lies and deceptions that seek to ensnare us. We discover the path to abundant life and lasting fulfillment.

Action Plan:

Today, spend time meditating on a specific truth from God's Word that resonates with you. It could be a promise, a commandment, or a revelation of His character. Reflect on how this truth applies to your life and write it down. Then, commit to living out this truth in your thoughts, words, and actions throughout the day.

Heavenly Father, thank You for revealing Your truth to us through Your Word. Help me to embrace Your truth wholeheartedly and to live in alignment with Your will. Guide me by Your Spirit as I seek to walk in Your ways and share Your truth with others. In Jesus' name, Amen.

DAY 161

The Importance of Forgiveness

"Be kind and compassionate to one another, forgiving each other, just as in Christ God forgave you." - Ephesians 4:32 (NIV)

Forgiveness holds immense power in our lives. It's not just an act of mercy; it's a transformative force that sets us free from the shackles of resentment and bitterness. When we forgive, we emulate the unconditional love and grace of our Savior, Jesus Christ.

Choosing forgiveness doesn't mean forgetting the hurt or excusing the wrong. It's a conscious decision to release the grip of anger and pain, allowing healing to take place. By extending forgiveness, we break the cycle of hurt and retaliation, paving the way for reconciliation and restoration.

Action Plan:

Today, reflect on someone in your life whom you need to forgive. It might be a friend, a family member, or even yourself. Take a moment to pray for the strength and courage to let go of any lingering resentment or bitterness. Write a letter to the person you need to forgive, expressing your willingness to release the hurt and extend grace. Even if you don't send the letter, the act of writing can

Gracious God, grant me the grace to forgive as You have forgiven me. Help me to let go of any bitterness or resentment in my heart and extend Your love and mercy to those who have wronged me. Strengthen me to walk in the path of forgiveness each day, reflecting Your unconditional love to the world. In Jesus' name, Amen.

]DAY 162

Trusting God's Faithfulness

"Know therefore that the Lord your God is God; he is the faithful God, keeping his covenant of love to a thousand generations of those who love him and keep his commandments." - Deuteronomy 7:9 (NIV)

Trusting in God's faithfulness is akin to anchoring our souls in the unshakable certainty of His promises. It's acknowledging that amidst life's uncertainties, God remains steadfast and true to His word. His faithfulness endures through every trial, every joy, and every season of our lives.

God's faithfulness is not contingent upon our circumstances or our performance; it is rooted in His unchanging character. Even when we falter, He remains faithful to His covenant of love, extending grace and mercy beyond measure.

Action Plan:

Today, take a moment to reflect on a time when you experienced God's faithfulness in your life. Write down this testimony and keep it somewhere visible as a reminder of His unwavering love and provision. Then, choose to share this testimony with someone who may need encouragement in their own journey of faith.

Gracious Father, thank You for Your unfailing faithfulness. Help me to trust in Your promises, knowing that You are always faithful to fulfill them. Strengthen my faith, Lord, and grant me the courage to testify to Your faithfulness in my life. In Jesus' name, Amen.

DAY 163

The Role of Spiritual Wisdom

"The fear of the Lord is the beginning of wisdom, and knowledge of the Holy One is understanding." - Proverbs 9:10 (NIV)

Spiritual wisdom is more than just knowledge; it's the deep understanding that comes from a close relationship with God. It's about seeing the world through His eyes and aligning our thoughts and actions with His will. In a world filled with distractions and noise, spiritual wisdom acts as a guiding light, leading us towards truth, righteousness, and fulfillment.

To cultivate spiritual wisdom, we must first humble ourselves before God, acknowledging His sovereignty and seeking His guidance in all aspects of our lives.

Action Plan:

Today, set aside time for quiet reflection and prayer. Ask God to grant you spiritual wisdom and understanding. Spend time reading a passage of Scripture and meditating on its meaning for your life. As you go about your day, practice listening to the promptings of the Holy Spirit, seeking His guidance in your decisions and interactions with others.

Heavenly Father, grant me the wisdom and understanding that comes from knowing You deeply. Help me to seek Your will in all things and to walk in alignment with Your purposes. Fill me with Your Spirit, that I may live a life that brings glory to Your name. In Jesus' name, Amen.

DAY 164

The Power of Hope

"May the God of hope fill you with all joy and peace as you trust in him, so that you may overflow with hope by the power of the Holy Spirit." - Romans 15:13 (NIV)

Hope is the anchor of our souls, the fuel that keeps us pressing forward even in the darkest of times. It's the confident expectation that God is faithful and that better days are ahead. In a world often fraught with uncertainty and despair, hope shines as a beacon of light, guiding us through the storms of life.

When we embrace the power of hope, we are infused with joy and peace that surpasses understanding. This hope isn't wishful thinking; it's a firm assurance rooted in the promises of God. It's knowing that no matter what challenges we face, God is with us, working all things together for our good.

Action Plan:

Today, take a moment to reflect on a situation in your life where you need hope. It could be a dream you're pursuing, a relationship in need of restoration, or a trial you're facing. Write down a specific prayer, asking God to fill you with hope and confidence in His plans. Then, choose to speak words of hope and encouragement to someone else who may be struggling.

Heavenly Father, thank You for being the God of hope. Fill me with Your joy and peace as I trust in You. Help me to anchor my heart in Your promises and to overflow with hope by the power of Your Spirit. In Jesus' name, Amen.

DAY 165

Embracing God's Righteousness

"But seek first his kingdom and his righteousness, and all these things will be given to you as well." - Matthew 6:33 (NIV)

Embracing God's righteousness is about aligning our lives with His perfect standards. It's recognizing that our own efforts fall short, but through His grace, we can strive to live in accordance with His will.

God's righteousness is not merely about following rules, but about embodying His love, mercy, and justice in all aspects of our lives. When we prioritize seeking His kingdom and righteousness above all else, we open ourselves to His transformative power.

Living in God's righteousness means pursuing justice and mercy, loving our neighbors as ourselves, and walking in integrity. It's a daily commitment to reflect His character in our thoughts, words, and actions.

Action Plan:

Today, take a moment to reflect on an area of your life where you may have strayed from God's righteousness. It could be in your relationships, your work, or your personal habits. Commit to making a change and ask God for His guidance and strength to live according to His righteousness.

Heavenly Father, thank you for your perfect righteousness. Help me to seek your kingdom above all else and to live in alignment with your will. Give me the grace to embody your love, mercy, and justice in all that I do. Guide me on the path of righteousness, and may my life be a reflection of your glory. In Jesus' name, Amen.

DAY 166

The Importance of Trust

"Trust in the LORD with all your heart and lean not on your own understanding; in all your ways submit to him, and he will make your paths straight." - Proverbs 3:5-6 (NIV)

In today's fast-paced and uncertain world, trust is a foundational pillar upon which all meaningful relationships are built. Trust fosters a sense of security, reliability, and confidence in both our interactions with others and our journey with the Divine. This deep trust enables us to navigate life's twists and turns with courage and resilience, knowing that God's plans for us are always for our good.

Trust is not merely a passive state of mind but an active choice we make daily. When we trust in God, we surrender our anxieties and uncertainties, allowing Him to guide us on the path of righteousness.

Action Plan:

Today, commit to surrendering your worries and fears to God. Choose to trust Him completely, knowing that He is faithful to fulfill His promises. Practice leaning on His understanding rather than relying solely on your own, and watch as He directs your steps with wisdom and clarity.

Heavenly Father, thank You for the gift of trust. Help us to surrender our doubts and fears to You, placing our full confidence in Your unfailing love and wisdom. Guide us on the path of righteousness, and may our lives be a testament to Your faithfulness. In Jesus' name, Amen.

DAY 167

Trusting in God's Strength

"I can do all this through him who gives me strength." -
Philippians 4:13 (NIV)

In the journey of life, there are moments when we feel overwhelmed, inadequate, and unsure of our abilities. His strength knows no bounds, and it is readily available to us when we place our trust in Him.

Trusting in God's strength means acknowledging our own limitations and surrendering them to Him. It means relying not on our own power or understanding, but on His infinite wisdom and might. When we trust in God's strength, we tap into a reservoir of courage, resilience, and perseverance that empowers us to overcome any obstacle that stands in our way.

Even in our weakest moments, God's strength is made perfect. It is in our times of greatest need that His power shines brightest, illuminating our path and guiding us through the storms of life.

Action Plan:

Today, make a conscious effort to surrender your worries and weaknesses to God. Choose to trust in His strength to carry you through difficult situations and empower you to accomplish His purposes.

Heavenly Father, thank You for the gift of Your strength. Grant us the courage and resilience to face whatever challenges come our way, confident in Your unwavering love and support. In Jesus' name, Amen.

DAY 168

The Power of God's Mercy

"But because of his great love for us, God, who is rich in mercy, made us alive with Christ even when we were dead in transgressions—it is by grace you have been saved." - Ephesians 2:4-5 (NIV)

God's mercy is a profound expression of His love and compassion toward humanity. It is the divine attribute that withholds the punishment we rightfully deserve and instead bestows upon us His unmerited favor and forgiveness. The power of God's mercy knows no bounds; it reaches into the depths of our brokenness and lifts us up, granting us new life and hope in Christ.

In our moments of weakness and sinfulness, it is God's mercy that offers us redemption and reconciliation. Through the sacrifice of Jesus Christ, we are made alive with Him, transformed by the overwhelming grace of God. His mercy is not a license to continue in sin but an invitation to turn away from it and embrace the abundant life He offers.

Action Plan:

Reflect on the depth of God's mercy in your life. Take time to meditate on His forgiveness and grace, and consider how you can extend that same mercy to others. Make a conscious effort to forgive those who have wronged you and seek reconciliation where needed.

Heavenly Father, thank You for Your boundless mercy and grace. Help us to fully comprehend the depth of Your love for us and to live in the freedom that comes from Your forgiveness. Empower us to extend mercy to others as You have shown mercy to us. In Jesus' name, Amen.

DAY 169

Living with Compassion

"Be kind and compassionate to one another, forgiving each other, just as in Christ God forgave you." - Ephesians 4:32 (NIV)

Living with compassion is a calling that transcends gender, age, and culture. It is the essence of Christ-like living, embodying love, kindness, and empathy towards others. Compassion compels us to see beyond ourselves, to recognize the struggles and pain of those around us, and to respond with grace and understanding.

In a world often marked by division and selfishness, living with compassion becomes a powerful testament to the transformative power of God's love. It opens doors for reconciliation, heals wounds, and builds bridges of understanding. When we live with compassion, we reflect the very heart of God, who loved us so deeply that He sent His Son to redeem us.

Action Plan:

Today, make a conscious effort to practice compassion in your interactions with others. Take a moment to truly listen to someone's story, offer a word of encouragement, or extend a helping hand to someone in need. Look for opportunities to show kindness and empathy, even in the midst of challenging circumstances.

Heavenly Father, thank You for the example of compassion You have set for us through Your Son, Jesus Christ. Empower us to live with open hearts and minds, seeking to love others as You have loved us. May Your compassion flow through us, bringing healing and hope to a broken world. In Jesus' name, Amen.

DAY 170

Embracing God's Peace

"Peace I leave with you; my peace I give you. I do not give to you as the world gives. Do not let your hearts be troubled and do not be afraid." - John 14:27 (NIV)

It is a peace that surpasses all understanding, offering solace to weary souls and strength to those who are overwhelmed. Embracing God's peace is not merely the absence of turmoil, but rather a deep-seated confidence in His sovereign control over every aspect of our lives.

God's peace is not contingent upon our circumstances but is rooted in our relationship with Him. When we surrender our worries and anxieties to God, His peace becomes a guard around our hearts and minds, shielding us from the storms of life. It is a peace that transcends human comprehension, bringing calm to the chaos and light to the darkness.

Action Plan:

Today, choose to actively embrace God's peace by spending time in prayer and meditation on His Word. Trust in His promises and surrender your fears and worries to Him. Allow His peace to reign in your heart, knowing that He is always in control.

Heavenly Father, thank You for the gift of Your peace. In the midst of life's trials and tribulations, help us to turn to You for comfort and strength. May Your peace reign in our hearts today and always. In Jesus' name, Amen.

DAY 171

The Importance of Prayer

"Rejoice always, pray continually, give thanks in all circumstances; for this is God's will for you in Christ Jesus." - 1 Thessalonians 5:16-18 (NIV)

In the hustle and bustle of life, it's easy to overlook the importance of prayer, but it is in these moments of communion with God that we find peace, clarity, and renewed strength. Prayer is not merely a religious ritual; it is a sacred conversation with our Creator, a channel through which we express our deepest desires, fears, and gratitude.

Through prayer, we invite God into every aspect of our lives, acknowledging our dependence on Him and trusting in His wisdom and provision. It is in the quiet moments of prayer that we find solace in the midst of chaos, and it is through prayer that we experience the transformative power of His love.

Action Plan:

Set aside a few minutes each day to commune with God, pouring out your heart to Him and listening for His still, small voice. Whether it's in the morning, during your lunch break, or before bed, make prayer a priority in your daily routine.

Heavenly Father, thank You for the gift of prayer. Help us to cultivate a spirit of continual communion with You, knowing that in Your presence, we find strength, peace, and direction. Guide us as we seek Your will and grant us the faith to trust in Your perfect plan for our lives. In Jesus' name, Amen.

DAY 172

Trusting God's Guidance

*"Commit your way to the LORD; trust in him, and he will act." -
Psalm 37:5 (ESV)*

Trusting God's guidance is akin to embarking on a journey with an all-knowing guide. When we trust in God's guidance, we acknowledge His sovereignty over our lives and surrender our need for control. It's an act of faith, believing that His ways are higher than ours, and His plans are always for our ultimate good.

God's guidance isn't always clear-cut or immediate, but it's always present for those who seek it earnestly. It may come in the form of a gentle whisper, a nudge in the right direction, or through the wise counsel of others. Trusting in His guidance requires patience, humility, and a willingness to let go of our own agenda.

Action Plan:

Today, take a moment to quiet your heart and listen for God's guidance. Reflect on an area of your life where you're seeking direction, and surrender it to Him in prayer. Trust that He will lead you in the right path, even if it's different from what you initially envisioned.

Heavenly Father, thank You for Your unwavering guidance in our lives. Give us the wisdom to trust in Your plans, even when they diverge from our own. May Your will be done in every aspect of our lives, as we surrender to Your loving guidance. In Jesus' name, Amen.

DAY 173

The Role of Spiritual Growth

"But grow in the grace and knowledge of our Lord and Savior Jesus Christ. To him be glory both now and forever! Amen." - 2 Peter 3:18 (NIV)

Just as physical exercise strengthens our bodies, nurturing our spiritual selves through prayer, study, and fellowship strengthens our souls. Spiritual growth is a dynamic process of deepening our relationship with God, gaining wisdom, and becoming more Christ-like in our thoughts, words, and actions.

As we commit to spiritual growth, we open ourselves to divine transformation. We become more attuned to God's voice, more compassionate toward others, and more resilient in the face of trials. Our faith becomes a source of strength and hope, guiding us through life's challenges with grace and courage.

Action Plan:

Today, make a deliberate effort to prioritize your spiritual growth. Set aside time each day for prayer and reflection, immerse yourself in Scripture, and seek opportunities for fellowship with other believers. Embrace the disciplines of the faith with enthusiasm and dedication, trusting that God will honor your commitment with abundant blessings.

Heavenly Father, thank You for the gift of spiritual growth. Help us to cultivate a deeper relationship with You, growing in grace and knowledge each day. May our lives be a reflection of Your love and truth, bringing glory to Your name. In Jesus' name, Amen.

DAY 174

The Power of God's Word

"For the word of God is alive and active. Sharper than any double-edged sword, it penetrates even to dividing soul and spirit, joints and marrow; it judges the thoughts and attitudes of the heart." - Hebrews 4:12 (NIV)

The Word of God is not merely a collection of ancient texts; it is a living, breathing entity with the power to transform lives. Its words carry divine authority, capable of piercing through the deepest recesses of our souls, revealing truth, and igniting change. When we immerse ourselves in Scripture, we invite God's presence into our lives, allowing His truth to penetrate our hearts and minds.

God's Word provides comfort in times of distress, guidance in moments of uncertainty, and strength in times of weakness. It is a source of wisdom and discernment, illuminating the path we are called to walk. Through the study and meditation of Scripture, we cultivate a deeper intimacy with God, aligning our thoughts and desires with His will.

Action Plan:

Dedicate time each day to immerse yourself in God's Word. Whether it's through reading a passage, listening to a sermon, or engaging in a Bible study, commit to allowing the transformative power of Scripture to shape your heart and mind.

Heavenly Father, thank You for the gift of Your Word. Help us to draw strength and wisdom from Scripture each day, that we may live according to Your will. In Jesus' name, Amen.

DAY 175

Embracing God's Love

"See what great love the Father has lavished on us, that we should be called children of God! And that is what we are!" - 1 John 3:1a (NIV)

Yet, Scripture reminds us time and again of the depth of His love—a love so immense that it transcends our understanding and labels us as His beloved children. Embracing God's love is not merely acknowledging it intellectually but allowing it to permeate every aspect of our being, transforming our self-perception and empowering us to live victoriously.

When we fully embrace God's love, we find acceptance, worth, and purpose beyond measure. His love becomes the foundation upon which we build our identities and navigate life's challenges with confidence and grace. It is through experiencing and embracing His love that we discover true fulfillment and joy.

Action Plan:

Today, make a conscious decision to embrace God's love for you. Remind yourself daily of His unconditional acceptance and unwavering affection. Spend time in prayer and meditation, allowing His love to penetrate your heart and renew your mind.

Heavenly Father, thank You for loving us with an incomprehensible love. Empower us to extend Your love to those around us, that Your light may shine brightly through us. In Jesus' name, Amen.

DAY 176

The Importance of Reflection

"Search me, God, and know my heart; test me and know my anxious thoughts. See if there is any offensive way in me, and lead me in the way everlasting." - Psalm 139:23-24 (NIV)

Reflection allows us to delve into the depths of our souls, examining our thoughts, motives, and actions in the light of God's truth. It provides an opportunity for self-awareness and introspection, enabling us to identify areas of strength and areas in need of improvement.

When we engage in reflection, we open ourselves up to the transformative work of the Holy Spirit, who convicts, corrects, and empowers us to live lives that honor God. Through reflection, we can cultivate a heart of humility, repentance, and gratitude, acknowledging our dependence on God's grace and mercy.

Action Plan:

Today, set aside intentional time for reflection. Find a quiet place free from distractions, and ask God to search your heart. Reflect on your thoughts, attitudes, and behaviors, inviting the Holy Spirit to reveal areas in need of growth and transformation.

Gracious God, thank You for the gift of reflection. Help us to carve out time in our busy lives to pause and ponder Your truths. Illuminate our hearts and minds, revealing any areas that need Your healing touch. May our reflections lead us closer to You and empower us to live lives that bring glory to Your name. In Jesus' name, Amen.

DAY 177

Trusting in God's Promises

"For no matter how many promises God has made, they are 'Yes' in Christ. And so through him the 'Amen' is spoken by us to the glory of God." - 2 Corinthians 1:20 (NIV)

Throughout the Scriptures, God has made countless promises to His children, and each one is a declaration of His commitment to us. When we trust in these promises, we align our hearts with His will and open ourselves to receive His blessings.

God's promises are like anchors in the storms of life, providing us with hope and assurance in times of uncertainty. They remind us that no matter what challenges we may face, God's word stands firm, and His plans for us are always good.

Action Plan:

Today, choose to meditate on one of God's promises that speaks directly to your current circumstances. Write it down, memorize it, and declare it over your life daily. Allow God's promise to permeate your heart and mind, anchoring you in His truth and giving you strength to persevere.

Heavenly Father, thank You for Your unending faithfulness and the promises You have given us in Your word. Help us to trust in Your promises wholeheartedly, knowing that You are always true to Your word. Strengthen our faith and guide us in Your ways, that we may walk in the fullness of Your blessings. In Jesus' name, Amen.

DAY 178

The Power of God's Grace

"But he said to me, 'My grace is sufficient for you, for my power is made perfect in weakness.' Therefore I will boast all the more gladly about my weaknesses, so that Christ's power may rest on me." - 2 Corinthians 12:9 (NIV)

God's grace is a boundless and unmerited gift, freely given to us despite our flaws and shortcomings. It is through His grace that we find forgiveness, redemption, and strength to overcome life's challenges. God's grace empowers us to rise above our weaknesses and walk in the fullness of His love and mercy.

In the face of our inadequacies, God's grace stands as a powerful reminder of His unconditional love for us. It is not our own efforts or achievements that earn us salvation, but rather the extravagant grace of our Heavenly Father. Through His grace, we are transformed and renewed, able to live lives that reflect His glory.

Action Plan:

Today, meditate on the depth of God's grace in your life. Reflect on the areas where you feel weak or inadequate, and surrender them to God. Embrace His grace as a source of strength and courage, trusting in His promise that His power is made perfect in your weakness.

Gracious God, thank You for Your overflowing grace that sustains us in our weakness. Help us to fully embrace Your grace and live each day in the light of Your love. May Your power be evident in our lives as we walk in obedience to Your will. In Jesus' name, Amen.

DAY 179

Living with Joy

"May the God of hope fill you with all joy and peace as you trust in him, so that you may overflow with hope by the power of the Holy Spirit." - Romans 15:13 (NIV)

Living with joy is not merely about fleeting moments of happiness but about embracing a deep sense of contentment and fulfillment that transcends circumstances. It's about finding joy in the journey, even amidst life's challenges and uncertainties.

True joy is not dependent on external factors but springs forth from an intimate relationship with our Creator. It is a choice we make each day to focus on the blessings rather than the burdens, to rejoice in the Lord always, regardless of our circumstances.

Action Plan:

Today, choose joy. Cultivate a spirit of gratitude by intentionally counting your blessings and acknowledging God's faithfulness in your life. Practice finding joy in the simple moments and in serving others with love and compassion. Let your joy be contagious, inspiring those around you to also embrace the abundant life God has promised.

Heavenly Father, thank You for the gift of joy that comes from knowing You. Fill our hearts with Your peace and joy, that we may radiate Your love to the world around us. Help us to find contentment in Your presence and to live each day with gratitude and purpose. In Jesus' name, Amen.

DAY 180

Embracing God's Patience

"But do not overlook this one fact, beloved, that with the Lord one day is as a thousand years, and a thousand years as one day. The Lord is not slow to fulfill his promise as some count slowness, but is patient toward you, not wishing that any should perish, but that all should reach repentance." - 2 Peter 3:8-9 (ESV)

His timing may not always align with our own, but His patience is a testament to His boundless love and mercy towards us. Embracing God's patience requires us to release our desire for immediate results and instead trust in His perfect timing.

God's patience is not a sign of indifference or delay, but rather a demonstration of His deep desire for our spiritual growth and redemption. Just as a master craftsman takes time to perfect his masterpiece, God works patiently within us, shaping us into vessels of His grace and love.

Action Plan:

Today, choose to surrender your timelines and expectations to God. Embrace His patience by trusting in His sovereignty and timing. Practice patience in your daily interactions and circumstances, knowing that God is working all things together for your good.

Heavenly Father, thank You for Your infinite patience and steadfast love. Help us to trust in Your perfect timing and surrender our desires to Your will. Grant us the strength to embrace Your patience in our lives, knowing that Your plans for us are always for our good. In Jesus' name, Amen.

DAY 181

The Importance of Humility

"Do nothing out of selfish ambition or vain conceit. Rather, in humility value others above yourselves, not looking to your own interests but each of you to the interests of the others." - Philippians 2:3-4 (NIV)

Humility is not about thinking less of ourselves but about thinking of ourselves less. It's a posture of gentleness, grace, and selflessness that opens doors to deeper connections and richer relationships. When we embrace humility, we acknowledge our dependence on God and recognize the inherent worth and dignity of every person we encounter.

It requires us to set aside our pride and ego, choosing instead to prioritize the needs and well-being of others above our own. In doing so, we reflect the very nature of Christ, who humbled Himself to the point of death on a cross for the sake of humanity.

Action Plan:

Today, seek opportunities to practice humility in your interactions with others. Whether it's through a kind word, a helping hand, or a listening ear, look for ways to serve and uplift those around you without seeking recognition or praise.

Gracious God, teach us the beauty of humility and the power of selfless love. Help us to set aside our pride and ego, and to value others above ourselves. May our lives be a reflection of Your grace and humility, as we seek to serve others with genuine love and compassion. In Jesus' name, Amen.

DAY 182

Trusting God's Wisdom

"For the foolishness of God is wiser than human wisdom, and the weakness of God is stronger than human strength." - 1 Corinthians 1:25 (NIV)

Often, we are tempted to rely on our own intellect and reasoning, believing that we have all the answers. However, the wisdom of God transcends human comprehension. It surpasses our logic and understanding, offering a higher perspective that leads to fulfillment and peace.

When we choose to trust in God's wisdom, we acknowledge His sovereignty over every aspect of our lives. We release the burden of trying to figure everything out on our own and instead lean on His understanding, knowing that His ways are higher than ours. In every decision and circumstance, God's wisdom provides guidance and direction, leading us along the path of righteousness.

Action Plan:

Today, make a conscious effort to seek God's wisdom in all areas of your life. Spend time in prayer and meditation, asking Him for clarity and insight. Trust that His wisdom will illuminate your path and empower you to make choices that honor Him.

Heavenly Father, thank You for Your infinite wisdom that surpasses human understanding. Help us to trust in Your guidance and lean not on our own understanding. Give us the courage to surrender our plans to You, knowing that Your wisdom will lead us to fulfillment and joy. In Jesus' name, Amen.

DAY 183

The Role of Spiritual Discipline

"But grow in the grace and knowledge of our Lord and Savior Jesus Christ." - 2 Peter 3:18a (NIV)

Just as an athlete trains diligently to excel in their sport, spiritual disciplines are the exercises that strengthen our spiritual muscles and equip us for the challenges of life. These disciplines include prayer, meditation, fasting, Bible study, worship, and service to others. Through consistent practice, we cultivate a heart that is attuned to the voice of God and a spirit that is sensitive to His leading.

Spiritual discipline is not about rigid rules or legalism but about creating space in our lives for God to work. It requires intentionality and commitment, as we prioritize time with God amidst the busyness of life. As we engage in spiritual disciplines, we open ourselves up to the transforming power of the Holy Spirit, allowing Him to mold us into the image of Christ.

Action Plan:

Today, choose one spiritual discipline to focus on and commit to practicing it daily for the next week. Whether it's spending extra time in prayer, diving deeper into Scripture, or serving others with a joyful heart, let your actions be guided by a desire to grow closer to God.

Heavenly Father, thank You for the gift of spiritual discipline. Help us to cultivate a heart that is hungry for Your presence and a spirit that is disciplined in seeking You. Empower us to grow in grace and knowledge, so that we may reflect Your love and truth to the world around us. In Jesus' name, Amen.

DAY 184

The Power of God's Presence

*"You make known to me the path of life; in your presence there is fullness of joy; at your right hand are pleasures forevermore." -
Psalm 16:11 (ESV)*

It's not merely a theological concept but a tangible reality that brings comfort, strength, and joy to our lives. In His presence, we find solace amidst chaos, clarity in confusion, and courage in times of fear. The power of God's presence is not limited by time or space; it is ever-present, always available to those who seek Him.

When we dwell in the presence of God, we experience a profound sense of peace and contentment that surpasses all understanding. His presence fills the voids in our hearts, satisfying our deepest longings and desires. In His presence, we discover our true identity and purpose, realizing that we are beloved children of the Most High.

Action Plan:

Today, make it a priority to cultivate intimacy with God through prayer, worship, and meditation on His Word. Set aside dedicated time each day to seek His presence and allow Him to speak to your heart. Practice being still before Him, listening attentively to His voice, and experiencing His love in a tangible way.

Heavenly Father, thank You for the gift of Your presence. Help us to be ever mindful of Your nearness and to seek You earnestly in every moment of our lives. Fill us with Your peace, joy, and strength as we abide in Your presence. In Jesus' name, Amen.

DAY 185

Embracing God's Plan

"For I know the plans I have for you," declares the LORD, "plans to prosper you and not to harm you, plans to give you hope and a future." - Jeremiah 29:11 (NIV)

In the hustle and bustle of life, it's easy to get caught up in our own plans and ambitions. However, God's plans for us far surpass anything we could ever imagine. Embracing God's plan means surrendering our own desires and trusting in His perfect timing and purpose for our lives.

When we embrace God's plan, we acknowledge that He knows what is best for us. Even when His plan seems unclear or different from what we had envisioned, we can rest assured that it is ultimately for our good. God's plan is filled with hope, purpose, and abundance, leading us towards a future filled with blessings beyond measure.

Action Plan:

Today, take a moment to surrender your plans to God. Trust in His wisdom and sovereignty, knowing that His plan for your life is far greater than anything you could ever imagine. Seek His guidance through prayer and meditation on His word, and be open to His leading in every area of your life.

Heavenly Father, thank You for the plans You have for us. Give us the strength and courage to embrace Your plan wholeheartedly, even when it may not align with our own desires. Help us to trust in Your perfect timing and purpose, knowing that Your plan is always for our good. In Jesus' name, Amen.

DAY 186

The Importance of Commitment

"Commit your way to the LORD; trust in him and he will do this." -
Psalm 37:5 (NIV)

Commitment is the bedrock of accomplishment. It is the unwavering dedication to a purpose or goal despite obstacles or setbacks. In our journey of faith, commitment is essential. It is the fuel that propels us forward, even when the path seems arduous or unclear.

True commitment requires sacrifice and perseverance. It means prioritizing our spiritual growth and relationship with God above all else. When we commit to seeking His will and following His ways, we open ourselves up to a life of purpose and fulfillment. Our commitment to God shapes every aspect of our lives, from our relationships to our careers, infusing each moment with meaning and significance.

Action Plan:

Today, make a conscious decision to recommit yourself to God. Reflect on areas of your life where you may have wavered in your commitment, and ask for His strength to help you stay steadfast. Set aside time each day for prayer, scripture reading, and quiet reflection, renewing your commitment to walk closely with Him.

Heavenly Father, thank You for Your faithfulness and love. Give us the courage and determination to fully commit our lives to You.. May our commitment to You be unwavering, and may it bear fruit in every aspect of our lives. In Jesus' name, Amen.

DAY 187

Trusting in God's Sovereignty

"For I know the plans I have for you," declares the LORD, "plans to prosper you and not to harm you, plans to give you hope and a future." - Jeremiah 29:11 (NIV)

Trusting in God's sovereignty means acknowledging His supreme authority and control over all things. It's recognizing that even in the midst of uncertainty and adversity, God is working out His perfect plan for our lives. When we surrender to His sovereignty, we find peace in knowing that He is orchestrating every detail according to His will.

In a world filled with chaos and unpredictability, our trust in God's sovereignty becomes an anchor for our souls. No matter what challenges we face, we can trust that God's plans for us are good and that He is working everything together for our ultimate good.

Action Plan:

Today, choose to surrender control to God and embrace His sovereignty over your life. Spend time in prayer, seeking His guidance and wisdom in every decision you make. Trust that He will lead you on the path He has laid out for you, even when it may seem uncertain.

Heavenly Father, thank You for Your sovereignty and faithfulness. Help us to trust in Your perfect plan for our lives, knowing that You are always working for our good. Give us the strength to surrender control to You and to follow Your leading with courage and obedience. In Jesus' name, Amen.

DAY 188

The Power of God's Spirit

*"But you will receive power when the Holy Spirit comes on you;
and you will be my witnesses in Jerusalem, and in all Judea and
Samaria, and to the ends of the earth." - Acts 1:8 (NIV)*

The power of God's Spirit is not just a distant concept; it's a dynamic force that transforms lives and empowers believers to fulfill their divine purpose. This divine presence within us enables us to overcome obstacles, break chains of bondage, and live victoriously in Christ.

The Spirit of God empowers us to be bold witnesses of His love and grace, both in our immediate communities and to the farthest corners of the earth. It's not by our own might or strength, but by the Spirit of God working within us, that we can impact lives and advance the Kingdom of God.

Action Plan:

Today, surrender to the leading of the Holy Spirit in every aspect of your life. Seek His guidance in decision-making, His strength in moments of weakness, and His boldness in sharing the gospel. Allow His power to flow through you, making you a vessel of His love and transformation.

*Heavenly Father, thank You for the precious gift of Your Spirit.
Fill us anew with Your power and presence, empowering us to be
bold witnesses of Your love and truth. Guide us by Your Spirit, and
use us to bring glory to Your name in all that we do. In Jesus'
name, Amen.*

DAY 189

Living with Conviction

"But Daniel resolved not to defile himself with the royal food and wine, and he asked the chief official for permission not to defile himself this way." - Daniel 1:8 (NIV)

Living with conviction means standing firm in your beliefs and values, even in the face of opposition or temptation. It's about having the courage to follow God's truth, no matter the circumstances. Daniel's resolve to honor God by refusing to compromise his principles serves as a powerful example for us today.

In a world that often pressures us to conform to its standards, living with conviction requires strength and determination. It means choosing righteousness over convenience, integrity over compromise. When we live with conviction, we become beacons of light in a dark world, shining forth God's truth and love.

Action Plan:

Today, make the decision to live with unwavering conviction. Choose to stand firm in your faith, regardless of the challenges you may face. Let your actions reflect your commitment to God's truth, inspiring others to do the same.

Heavenly Father, thank You for the example of Daniel, who lived with unwavering conviction in the midst of adversity. Give us the strength and courage to stand firm in our faith, even when it's difficult. May our lives be a testimony to Your truth and love. In Jesus' name, Amen.

DAY 190

Embracing God's Truth

"Jesus answered, 'I am the way and the truth and the life. No one comes to the Father except through me.'" - John 14:6 (NIV)

In a world filled with conflicting voices and ideologies, embracing God's truth is essential for finding direction, purpose, and fulfillment. God's truth, embodied in Jesus Christ, is not merely a set of principles or beliefs; it is a living, transformative power that illuminates our path and sets us free from the bondage of sin and deception.

Embracing God's truth requires a humble heart and a willingness to surrender our preconceived notions and desires. It means aligning our thoughts, words, and actions with His Word and allowing His truth to permeate every aspect of our lives. When we embrace God's truth, we experience freedom from the lies that entangle us and discover the abundant life He has promised us.

Action Plan:

Today, commit to spending time in God's Word daily. Set aside a specific time each day to read, meditate on, and apply His truth to your life. Allow the Holy Spirit to guide you into all truth and empower you to live according to His will.

Heavenly Father, thank You for the gift of Your truth revealed in Your Son, Jesus Christ. Help us to embrace Your truth wholeheartedly and to live lives that reflect Your glory. May Your Word be a lamp unto our feet and a light unto our path. In Jesus' name, Amen.

DAY 191

The Importance of Faithfulness

*"The one who is faithful in a very little is also faithful in much, and
the one who is dishonest in a very little is also dishonest in much."
- Luke 16:10 (ESV)*

Faithfulness is a virtue that speaks to the core of our character and
integrity. It is the steadfast commitment to uphold our
responsibilities and promises, whether big or small, even when
faced with challenges or temptations. Just as the Scripture tells us,
our faithfulness in the little things reflects our capacity for
trustworthiness in greater endeavors.

To cultivate faithfulness in our lives, let us start by honoring our
commitments, no matter how insignificant they may seem.
Whether it's showing up on time, fulfilling our duties at work, or
being faithful in our relationships, let us do so with unwavering
dedication and integrity.

Action Plan:

Today, commit to being faithful in the small tasks you encounter.
Choose to demonstrate reliability and consistency in your actions,
knowing that faithfulness in little things paves the way for greater
opportunities and blessings.

*Heavenly Father, thank You for Your faithfulness towards us.
Teach us to emulate Your example by being faithful in all areas of
our lives. May our faithfulness bring glory to Your name and
blessings to those around us. In Jesus' name, Amen.*

DAY 192

Trusting God's Timing

"For I know the plans I have for you," declares the LORD, "plans to prosper you and not to harm you, plans to give you hope and a future." - Jeremiah 29:11 (NIV)

Trusting God's timing can be one of the most challenging aspects of our faith journey. Often, we find ourselves impatient, wanting things to happen according to our own timetable. However, God's timing is perfect, and His plans for us are far greater than we can imagine. When we trust in His timing, we align ourselves with His purposes and experience His peace amidst life's uncertainties.

God sees the bigger picture, and He knows what is best for us. Even when circumstances seem bleak or our prayers go unanswered, we can trust that God is working behind the scenes, orchestrating events for our good. His timing is never too late nor too early; it is always just right.

Action Plan:

Today, surrender your desire for immediate results to God. Instead of trying to force outcomes according to your own schedule, practice patience and trust in God's perfect timing. Embrace each moment as an opportunity to grow in faith and dependence on Him.

Heavenly Father, thank You for Your perfect timing. Help us to trust in Your plans for our lives, even when they don't align with our own expectations. Give us the patience to wait on You and the faith to believe that Your timing is always best. In Jesus' name, Amen.

DAY 193

The Role of Spiritual Strength

"Be strong and courageous. Do not be afraid; do not be discouraged, for the Lord your God will be with you wherever you go." - Joshua 1:9 (NIV)

As men navigating the challenges of life, we often find ourselves confronted with trials that test our strength, both physically and spiritually. Yet, it is our spiritual strength that truly sustains us through the storms of life. Just as physical exercise strengthens our bodies, cultivating spiritual strength fortifies our souls, enabling us to withstand adversity with unwavering faith and courage.

Spiritual strength is not a passive attribute but an active pursuit. It involves deepening our relationship with God through prayer, meditation on His Word, and fellowship with other believers. When we prioritize our spiritual well-being, we tap into a reservoir of divine power that empowers us to overcome obstacles and live with purpose and conviction.

Action Plan:

Today, commit to strengthening your spiritual muscles through daily devotions and prayer. Set aside time each day to commune with God, seeking His guidance and wisdom. As you cultivate spiritual strength, trust in God's promise to be with you wherever you go, knowing that His presence will sustain you through every trial.

Prayer: Heavenly Father, thank You for the gift of spiritual strength. Help us to cultivate this strength daily, drawing near to You in prayer and meditation on Your Word. Grant us courage and faith to face the challenges before us, knowing that You are always by our side. In Jesus' name, Amen.

DAY 194

The Power of God's Love

"For I am convinced that neither death nor life, neither angels nor demons, neither the present nor the future, nor any powers, neither height nor depth, nor anything else in all creation, will be able to separate us from the love of God that is in Christ Jesus our Lord."
- Romans 8:38-39 (NIV)

God's love is an unstoppable force, transcending every boundary and overcoming every obstacle. It is a love that knows no limits, reaching out to embrace us in our darkest moments and lifting us up with its unwavering strength. In a world filled with uncertainty and pain, the power of God's love stands as a beacon of hope, reminding us that we are never alone.

His love heals our brokenness, restores our faith, and empowers us to live with purpose and passion. It is a love that conquers fear, dispels doubt, and brings light into the darkest corners of our hearts.

Action Plan:

Today, choose to meditate on the overwhelming love of God. Reflect on His faithfulness and goodness, allowing His love to fill you with peace and joy. Then, let that love overflow to those around you, demonstrating kindness, compassion, and grace to all you encounter.

Prayer: Gracious God, thank You for the incredible gift of Your love. Help us to fully comprehend the depth and breadth of Your love for us, that we may live each day in the fullness of Your grace. In Jesus' name, Amen.

DAY 195

Embracing God's Grace

"But he said to me, 'My grace is sufficient for you, for my power is made perfect in weakness.' Therefore I will boast all the more gladly about my weaknesses, so that Christ's power may rest on me." - 2 Corinthians 12:9 (NIV)

It's about recognizing that we are imperfect beings, flawed and prone to mistakes, yet loved unconditionally by a God whose grace knows no bounds. His grace is our lifeline in times of trial, our strength in moments of weakness, and our hope in the midst of despair.

When we embrace God's grace, we release the burden of perfectionism and self-reliance, acknowledging that it is through our weaknesses that His power is made perfect.

Action Plan:

Today, take a moment to reflect on areas in your life where you've been striving in your own strength. Surrender those areas to God, inviting His grace to work in and through you. Practice extending grace to yourself and others, knowing that we are all in need of God's mercy.

Heavenly Father, thank You for Your abundant grace that sustains us in every season of life. Teach us to embrace Your grace fully, allowing it to transform us from the inside out. Help us to extend grace to ourselves and others, just as You have graciously extended it to us. In Jesus' name, Amen.

DAY 196

The Importance of Reflection

"Search me, God, and know my heart; test me and know my anxious thoughts. See if there is any offensive way in me, and lead me in the way everlasting." - Psalm 139:23-24 (NIV)

Reflection is a powerful tool for spiritual growth and self-awareness. In the hustle and bustle of life, it's easy to get caught up in the busyness and lose sight of our innermost thoughts and feelings. Yet, taking the time to pause and reflect allows us to examine our hearts, confront our shortcomings, and align ourselves with God's will.

When we engage in reflection, we invite God into the depths of our souls, asking Him to reveal any areas of our lives that need His healing touch. It's a humbling process that requires honesty and vulnerability, but the rewards are immeasurable. Through reflection, we gain clarity and insight, enabling us to make better decisions and live more intentionally.

Action Plan:

Today, set aside some time for quiet reflection. Find a peaceful place where you can be alone with your thoughts and invite God to search your heart. Journaling can be a helpful tool to record your reflections and insights.

Prayer: Heavenly Father, thank You for the gift of reflection. Help us to quiet our hearts and minds so that we may hear Your gentle voice speaking to us. Show us any areas of our lives that need Your healing touch and give us the strength to make changes that honor You. In Jesus' name, Amen.

DAY 197

Trusting in God's Strength

"I can do all this through him who gives me strength." -
Philippians 4:13 (NIV)

In our own strength, we may falter and stumble, but when we lean on the Almighty, we tap into an infinite reservoir of power and resilience.

God's strength knows no bounds. It sustains us in our weakest moments and carries us through the darkest valleys. When we trust in His strength, we relinquish our need to control outcomes and instead place our confidence in His perfect plan for our lives.

Trusting in God's strength requires surrendering our pride and self-reliance. It means acknowledging our limitations and humbly accepting His provision. In doing so, we discover a newfound sense of freedom and peace, knowing that we are not alone in our struggles.

Action Plan:

Today, choose to trust in God's strength in every area of your life. When faced with challenges or uncertainties, pause and remind yourself of Philippians 4:13. Surrender your worries and fears to God, and allow His strength to flow through you.

Heavenly Father, thank You for being our source of strength and courage. Help us to trust in Your power, especially when we feel weak and overwhelmed. May Your strength sustain us and Your peace fill our hearts as we journey through life with You. In Jesus' name, Amen.

DAY 198

The Power of God's Mercy

"But because of his great love for us, God, who is rich in mercy, made us alive with Christ even when we were dead in transgressions—it is by grace you have been saved." - Ephesians 2:4-5 (NIV)

God's mercy is a profound expression of His unfailing love and compassion towards us, despite our shortcomings and failures. It is through His mercy that we find redemption and restoration, as He extends forgiveness and grace to all who seek Him.

It is not based on our merit or deservingness but flows from His boundless love for His creation. In His mercy, God offers us a second chance, a fresh start, and the opportunity to experience true transformation.

When we grasp the depth of God's mercy, it compels us to respond with gratitude and humility. We recognize our need for His mercy every day and are inspired to extend that same mercy to others.

Action Plan:

Today, meditate on God's mercy and reflect on areas in your life where you need His forgiveness and grace. Take time to confess any sins or mistakes, knowing that God is ready to forgive and cleanse you.

Heavenly Father, thank You for Your boundless mercy that knows no bounds. Empower us to extend mercy to others, reflecting Your love and compassion in all we do. In Jesus' name, Amen.

DAY 199

Living with Integrity

"The integrity of the upright guides them, but the unfaithful are destroyed by their duplicity." - Proverbs 11:3 (NIV)

Living with integrity means aligning our actions with our values and principles. It's about being honest, reliable, and true to ourselves and others, even when no one is watching. Integrity is the cornerstone of character, the bedrock upon which trust and respect are built.

When we live with integrity, we walk with confidence and purpose, knowing that our words and deeds are in harmony with our beliefs. It's a testament to our commitment to righteousness and moral excellence, even in the face of temptation or adversity.

Integrity is not always easy. It requires courage and conviction to stand firm in the face of opposition or temptation. Yet, the rewards of living with integrity are immeasurable. It brings peace of mind, inner strength, and the respect of others.

Action Plan:

Today, commit to living with integrity in all areas of your life. Take a moment to reflect on your values and principles, and identify any areas where your actions may not align with them. Make a conscious effort to make choices that honor your integrity, even if it's difficult or unpopular.

Heavenly Father, thank You for the example of integrity set forth in Your Word. Help us to walk in righteousness and truth, living lives that honor You in all that we do. Give us the strength and courage to stand firm in our convictions, even when faced with challenges. In Jesus' name, Amen.

DAY 200

Embracing God's Peace

"Peace I leave with you; my peace I give you. I do not give to you as the world gives. Do not let your hearts be troubled and do not be afraid." - John 14:27 (NIV)

In a world filled with chaos and uncertainty, God offers us a profound gift: His peace. This peace surpasses all understanding and transcends the challenges and trials we face in our daily lives. Embracing God's peace doesn't mean the absence of difficulties but rather a deep-seated confidence in His presence and provision.

When we embrace God's peace, we surrender our anxieties and fears, trusting in His perfect plan for our lives. This peace guards our hearts and minds, offering comfort and assurance even in the midst of life's storms.

Action Plan:

Today, make a conscious decision to embrace God's peace in every area of your life. When faced with challenges or uncertainties, choose to surrender them to God, trusting in His faithfulness and goodness. Practice mindfulness and prayer as ways to cultivate a sense of peace in your heart, and seek opportunities to share this peace with others who may be struggling.

Heavenly Father, thank You for the gift of Your peace that surpasses all understanding. Help us to embrace this peace in every aspect of our lives, trusting in Your sovereignty and goodness. Guard our hearts and minds, and lead us in the path of peace. In Jesus' name, Amen.

DAY 201

The Importance of Prayer

"Do not be anxious about anything, but in every situation, by prayer and petition, with thanksgiving, present your requests to God. And the peace of God, which transcends all understanding, will guard your hearts and your minds in Christ Jesus." - Philippians 4:6-7 (NIV)

Prayer is the lifeblood of our relationship with God. In a world filled with chaos and uncertainty, prayer offers us a sense of peace and reassurance, knowing that we serve a God who hears and answers our prayers according to His perfect will.

Through prayer, we not only express our needs and desires but also cultivate a deeper intimacy with God. It's a sacred dialogue where we align our hearts with His, surrendering our will to His divine plan. In times of joy, prayer allows us to express gratitude and praise.

Action Plan:

Today, commit to making prayer a priority in your life. Set aside dedicated time each day to commune with God, whether it's in the morning, during your lunch break, or before bed. Keep a prayer journal to track your requests and God's faithfulness in answering them.

Heavenly Father, thank You for the gift of prayer. Help us to cultivate a deeper intimacy with You through our time spent in prayer. May our prayers be a sweet fragrance unto You, bringing glory and honor to Your name. In Jesus' name, Amen.

DAY 202

Trusting God's Guidance

"Trust in the LORD with all your heart and lean not on your own understanding; in all your ways submit to him, and he will make your paths straight." - Proverbs 3:5-6 (NIV)

Trusting God's guidance is not always easy, especially when life throws unexpected challenges our way. Yet, when we surrender our will to His and place our trust in His unfailing wisdom, we open ourselves up to a journey of divine purpose and fulfillment. God's guidance is like a steady beacon in the midst of life's storms, leading us along the path He has ordained for us.

When we trust in God's guidance, we acknowledge His sovereignty over our lives and recognize that His plans are far greater than our own. Even when we cannot see the road ahead clearly, we can take comfort in knowing that God sees the bigger picture and is always working for our good.

Action Plan:

Today, make a conscious decision to surrender control to God and trust in His guidance. Spend time in prayer, seeking His direction for your life. As you go about your day, listen for His still, small voice prompting you in the right direction. Step out in faith, knowing that God is with you every step of the way.

Heavenly Father, thank You for Your constant guidance and love. Help us to trust in Your wisdom and submit to Your will for our lives. Give us the courage to follow where You lead, knowing that Your plans are always for our good. In Jesus' name, Amen.

DAY 203

The Role of Spiritual Wisdom

"The fear of the LORD is the beginning of wisdom, and knowledge of the Holy One is understanding." - Proverbs 9:10 (NIV)

Spiritual wisdom is not merely knowledge or intelligence; it is the deep understanding and application of divine truths in our everyday lives. When we seek spiritual wisdom, we open ourselves up to a higher perspective—one that transcends our limited human understanding and taps into the infinite wisdom of the Creator.

Through spiritual wisdom, we gain clarity in decision-making, discernment in navigating life's challenges, and insight into the mysteries of God's plan. It empowers us to live with purpose and intention, guiding us towards a life of fulfillment and significance.

Action Plan:

Today, commit to seeking spiritual wisdom through prayer, meditation, and the study of Scripture. Set aside time each day to commune with God and ask for His guidance. Be open to His leading and willing to follow wherever He may lead you. Practice applying spiritual principles to your daily life, trusting that God's wisdom will guide you in all things.

Heavenly Father, thank You for the gift of spiritual wisdom. Grant us the humility to seek Your guidance in all things and the discernment to recognize Your voice. Help us to walk in Your ways and to live our lives in accordance with Your divine will. In Jesus' name, Amen.

DAY 204

The Power of God's Word

"For the word of God is alive and active. Sharper than any double-edged sword, it penetrates even to dividing soul and spirit, joints and marrow; it judges the thoughts and attitudes of the heart." -
Hebrews 4:12 (NIV)

The Word of God is not merely a collection of ancient texts; it is a living and powerful force that has the ability to transform lives. In its pages, we find wisdom, guidance, and comfort for every season of life. The Word speaks directly to our hearts, revealing the truth about who we are and who God is.

When we immerse ourselves in God's Word, we open ourselves up to the transformative work of the Holy Spirit. The Word has the power to renew our minds, strengthen our faith, and equip us for every good work. It is a lamp to guide our steps and a light to illuminate the darkness around us.

Action Plan:

Commit to spending time in God's Word each day. Set aside a specific time and place where you can focus without distractions. Choose a passage of Scripture to meditate on and allow the Holy Spirit to speak to you through it. Consider journaling your reflections and insights to deepen your understanding.

Heavenly Father, thank You for the gift of Your Word. Help us to treasure it in our hearts and allow it to transform us from the inside out. May Your Word be a lamp to guide our feet and a light to illuminate our path. In Jesus' name, Amen.

DAY 205

Embracing God's Love

"See what great love the Father has lavished on us, that we should be called children of God! And that is what we are!" - 1 John 3:1a (NIV)

God's love is the very essence of our existence. It's a love that surpasses all understanding, a love that knows no bounds. Yet, so often, we struggle to fully embrace this love. We may feel unworthy or undeserving, allowing doubt and insecurity to cloud our perception of God's immense love for us.

But embracing God's love is not about our worthiness; it's about recognizing the depth of His grace and the magnitude of His affection for us. When we truly embrace God's love, we are transformed from the inside out. We no longer seek validation from the world because we know that we are unconditionally loved by the Creator of the universe.

Action Plan:

Today, take a moment to meditate on the overwhelming love of God. Reflect on all the ways He has shown His love for you throughout your life. Let go of any doubts or insecurities, and allow yourself to bask in the warmth of His love.

Heavenly Father, thank You for loving us so extravagantly. Help us to fully embrace Your love and to live our lives as beloved children of God. May Your love overflow from us, touching the lives of those around us and drawing them closer to You. In Jesus' name, Amen.

DAY 206

The Importance of Reflection

"Be still, and know that I am God; I will be exalted among the nations, I will be exalted in the earth." - Psalm 46:10 (NIV)

Reflection is not merely a luxury but a necessity for the soul. In the chaos of our daily lives, it's easy to lose sight of our purpose and direction. Yet, when we pause to reflect, we create space for God to speak to us, guiding us on the path He has set before us.

Through reflection, we gain insight into our thoughts, emotions, and actions. We uncover patterns and habits that may be hindering our spiritual growth. It's a time to evaluate our priorities, assess our relationships, and discern God's will for our lives.

Reflection also fosters gratitude and mindfulness. As we look back on our experiences, we recognize the countless blessings God has bestowed upon us.

Action Plan:

Today, carve out time for reflection in your schedule. Find a quiet space where you can be alone with God. Reflect on your day or week, asking Him to reveal any areas where you need His guidance or correction. Consider journaling your thoughts and prayers as a way to deepen your reflection.

Heavenly Father, thank You for the gift of reflection. Help us to be still before You, knowing that You are God. Speak to our hearts as we reflect on Your goodness and grace. Guide us in the way we should go, that we may walk in Your truth. In Jesus' name, Amen.

DAY 207

Trusting in God's Promises

"For no matter how many promises God has made, they are 'Yes' in Christ. And so through him the 'Amen' is spoken by us to the glory of God." - 2 Corinthians 1:20 (NIV)

Trusting in God's promises is not merely an act of faith; it is an affirmation of His unwavering love and faithfulness towards us. From the covenant with Abraham to the coming of the Messiah, God's promises are always fulfilled in His perfect timing and according to His divine plan.

In our own lives, trusting in God's promises means anchoring our faith in His character. It means believing that He is faithful to His word and that He will never leave us nor forsake us, no matter the circumstances we face. When we trust in God's promises, we can find peace in the midst of uncertainty, strength in times of weakness, and hope in moments of despair.

Action Plan:

Today, choose to meditate on one of God's promises found in Scripture. Reflect on its significance in your life and how it brings assurance and comfort. Write down this promise and keep it somewhere visible as a reminder of God's faithfulness.

Heavenly Father, thank You for Your faithful promises that sustain us through every season of life. Help us to trust in Your word wholeheartedly, knowing that You are always true to Your promises. Strengthen our faith and fill us with confidence as we walk in Your truth. In Jesus' name, Amen.

DAY 208

The Power of God's Grace

"But he said to me, 'My grace is sufficient for you, for my power is made perfect in weakness.' Therefore I will boast all the more gladly about my weaknesses, so that Christ's power may rest on me." - 2 Corinthians 12:9 (NIV)

God's grace is a transformative force that empowers us to overcome our weaknesses and live victoriously. It is His unmerited favor and divine assistance freely given to us, regardless of our flaws or failures. In our moments of deepest need, God's grace shines brightest, offering strength, hope, and redemption.

The power of God's grace is limitless and unfathomable. It sustains us through trials, comforts us in sorrow, and empowers us to fulfill our purpose. When we embrace His grace, we acknowledge our dependence on Him and invite His miraculous intervention into our lives.

Action Plan:

Today, meditate on the abundance of God's grace in your life. Reflect on the times when His grace has sustained you and carried you through difficult circumstances. Take a moment to thank God for His boundless love and mercy. Then, extend that grace to others by showing kindness, forgiveness, and compassion.

Heavenly Father, thank You for Your immeasurable grace that sustains us and strengthens us in our times of need. May we be vessels of Your love and mercy, extending grace to others as You have graciously extended it to us. In Jesus' name, Amen.

DAY 209

Living with Joy

"May the God of hope fill you with all joy and peace as you trust in him, so that you may overflow with hope by the power of the Holy Spirit." - Romans 15:13 (NIV)

Living with joy is not merely about experiencing fleeting moments of happiness but cultivating a deep and abiding sense of contentment that transcends circumstances. It's about finding fulfillment and purpose in the midst of life's challenges and uncertainties.

Joy stems from a heart that is rooted in faith and trust in God. When we surrender our worries and fears to Him, we open ourselves up to receiving His peace and joy that surpasses all understanding. It's a choice we make daily to focus on the blessings rather than the burdens, to embrace gratitude over complaint.

Action Plan:

Today, choose joy. Make a conscious effort to find joy in the little things, whether it's spending time with loved ones, pursuing a passion, or simply enjoying God's creation. Practice gratitude by keeping a journal of blessings and take time each day to reflect on the goodness of God in your life.

Heavenly Father, thank You for the gift of joy that comes from knowing You. Fill our hearts with Your peace and contentment, even in the midst of life's challenges. Help us to choose joy each day and to live our lives as a reflection of Your love and grace. In

DAY 210

Embracing God's Patience

"But do not forget this one thing, dear friends: With the Lord a day is like a thousand years, and a thousand years are like a day. The Lord is not slow in keeping his promise, as some understand slowness. Instead he is patient with you, not wanting anyone to perish, but everyone to come to repentance." - 2 Peter 3:8-9 (NIV)

Embracing God's patience is an essential aspect of our spiritual journey. In a world obsessed with instant gratification and immediate results, we often struggle to wait patiently for God's timing. However, God's perspective of time is vastly different from ours.

God's patience is not merely about waiting for His promises to be fulfilled but about the transformative process He takes us through during the waiting period. It's during these times of waiting that our faith is refined, our character is shaped, and our trust in God deepens.

Action Plan:

Today, practice embracing God's patience by surrendering your timeline to Him. When faced with delays or setbacks, choose to see them as opportunities for growth and allow God to work in and through you.

Heavenly Father, thank You for Your infinite patience with us. Give us the strength to wait patiently for Your promises to be fulfilled, knowing that You are always faithful. In Jesus' name, Amen.

DAY 211

The Importance of Humility

"Humble yourselves before the Lord, and he will lift you up." -
James 4:10 (NIV)

Humility is often misunderstood in today's culture that praises self-promotion and individualism. However, true humility is a virtue that lies at the core of a strong and noble character. It involves recognizing our own limitations, acknowledging the worth of others, and submitting ourselves to God's will with reverence and obedience.

When we embrace humility, we open ourselves to a deeper understanding of our place in the world and our relationship with God. Humility enables us to approach others with compassion and empathy, fostering genuine connections and building meaningful relationships.

Action Plan:

Today, practice humility by serving others with a genuine heart. Look for opportunities to put others' needs before your own and demonstrate kindness and generosity in your interactions. Remember that true greatness is found in serving others, just as Jesus modeled for us.

Heavenly Father, teach us the beauty of humility. Help us to cultivate a spirit of gentleness and grace in our hearts, that we may reflect Your love to those around us. Give us the strength to humble ourselves before You and trust in Your perfect plan for our lives. In Jesus' name, Amen.

DAY 212

Trusting God's Wisdom

"For my thoughts are not your thoughts, neither are your ways my ways," declares the LORD. "As the heavens are higher than the earth, so are my ways higher than your ways and my thoughts than your thoughts." - Isaiah 55:8-9 (NIV)

Trusting in God's wisdom is an act of surrender, acknowledging that His understanding surpasses our own finite minds. It's recognizing that while we may not always comprehend His plans, we can rest assured that they are always for our ultimate good. God's wisdom transcends human understanding, encompassing eternity and unfathomable depths of knowledge.

Trusting God's wisdom doesn't mean we won't face challenges or difficulties. Instead, it means we face them with the confidence that God is orchestrating every detail according to His perfect plan. Even in the midst of uncertainty, we can find peace knowing that God's wisdom will never lead us astray.

Action Plan:

Today, commit to surrendering your plans and desires to God's wisdom. Spend time in prayer, asking Him to guide your thoughts and decisions. Trust that His wisdom far surpasses your own, and allow Him to lead you in the paths He has prepared for you.

Heavenly Father, thank You for Your infinite wisdom that surpasses all understanding. Give us the faith to surrender our own desires and follow Your leading with confidence. In Jesus' name, Amen.

DAY 213

The Role of Spiritual Discipline

"But seek first his kingdom and his righteousness, and all these things will be given to you as well." - Matthew 6:33 (NIV)

Spiritual discipline is the cornerstone of a vibrant and fulfilling relationship with God. Just as an athlete trains diligently to excel in their sport, so too must we cultivate spiritual disciplines to grow in our faith and draw closer to the heart of God. These disciplines, such as prayer, fasting, meditation on Scripture, and worship, are not merely rituals but pathways to experiencing the presence and power of God in our lives.

By engaging in spiritual disciplines, we create space in our hearts and minds for God to work. Through discipline, we develop spiritual muscles that enable us to withstand the challenges and temptations of life, allowing us to live with purpose and passion.

Action Plan:

Today, commit to incorporating one spiritual discipline into your daily routine. Whether it's setting aside time for prayer and meditation, fasting from distractions that hinder your relationship with God, or immersing yourself in Scripture, choose one practice and commit to it faithfully.

Gracious God, thank You for the gift of spiritual disciplines. Grant us the strength and discipline to seek You first in all things and to grow in our love and devotion to You. May our lives be a reflection of Your glory as we commit ourselves to spiritual growth and transformation. In Jesus' name, Amen.

DAY 214

The Power of God's Presence

"The LORD replied, 'My Presence will go with you, and I will give you rest.'" - Exodus 33:14 (NIV)

The presence of God is an incomparable source of strength, comfort, and peace. In a world filled with chaos and uncertainty, knowing that God is with us brings reassurance like no other. His presence is not merely a concept or an abstract idea but a tangible reality that we can experience daily.

When we acknowledge and embrace the power of God's presence, we invite Him into every aspect of our lives. His presence brings clarity to confusion, hope to despair, and light to darkness. In His presence, we find refuge from life's storms and strength to face whatever challenges may come our way.

Action Plan:

Today, make a conscious effort to cultivate awareness of God's presence in your life. Take moments throughout the day to pause and acknowledge His presence with you. Whether through prayer, meditation, or simply quiet reflection, invite God to walk beside you in every moment. Trust that His presence will bring you peace and rest, even in the midst of life's trials.

Heavenly Father, thank You for the gift of Your presence. Help us to be ever mindful of Your nearness and to find strength and comfort in Your presence. Guide us through each day, knowing that You are with us always. In Jesus' name, Amen.

DAY 215

Embracing God's Plan

"For I know the plans I have for you," declares the LORD, "plans to prosper you and not to harm you, plans to give you hope and a future." - Jeremiah 29:11 (NIV)

Embracing God's plan for our lives is an act of faith and surrender. It requires us to trust in His wisdom and goodness, even when His plans seem unclear or challenging. God's plan for us is always for our ultimate good, leading us toward a future filled with hope and purpose.

When we surrender our own plans and desires to God, we open ourselves up to His divine guidance and direction. We acknowledge that He knows what is best for us and that His ways are higher than our ways. Embracing God's plan involves letting go of our need for control and allowing Him to work in and through us according to His perfect timing.

Action Plan:

Today, take a moment to surrender your plans to God. Reflect on areas of your life where you may be resisting His guidance or trying to control outcomes. Release your grip on these areas and trust that God's plan for you is far greater than anything you could imagine.

Heavenly Father, thank You for the assurance that Your plans for us are good and filled with hope. Help us to trust in Your wisdom and embrace Your plan for our lives, even when it feels difficult or uncertain. Give us the courage to surrender our own desires and follow You wholeheartedly. In Jesus' name, Amen.

DAY 216

The Importance of Commitment

"Commit your way to the LORD; trust in him and he will do this:
He will make your righteous reward shine like the dawn, your
vindication like the noonday sun." - Psalm 37:5-6 (NIV)

Commitment is the cornerstone of success in every aspect of life. Whether it's in our relationships, careers, or spiritual journeys, wholehearted dedication and perseverance are essential. When we commit ourselves to a cause or a goal, we demonstrate our unwavering faith and determination.

Commitment is not merely a fleeting emotion or a half-hearted effort; it's a conscious decision to stay the course, no matter the obstacles or challenges we may face. It requires sacrifice, discipline, and a willingness to prioritize what truly matters in life.

Action Plan:

Today, identify an area of your life where you may have been lacking commitment. It could be a relationship, a project, or a spiritual discipline. Set specific goals and create a plan of action to ensure that you stay committed, even when faced with adversity.

Heavenly Father, thank You for Your faithfulness and steadfast love. Help us to cultivate a spirit of commitment in every area of our lives, trusting in Your guiding hand to lead us on the path of righteousness. Give us the strength and perseverance to stay committed, even when the journey gets tough. In Jesus' name, Amen.

DAY 217

Trusting in God's Sovereignty

"I am the Alpha and the Omega," says the Lord God, "who is, and who was, and who is to come, the Almighty." - Revelation 1:8 (NIV)

Trusting in God's sovereignty is surrendering to His ultimate authority and acknowledging His complete control over all aspects of our lives. It's recognizing that He is the Alpha and the Omega, the beginning and the end, and that His plans for us are perfect and purposeful, even when we can't see the bigger picture.

When we trust in God's sovereignty, we relinquish our need for control and place our faith in His wisdom and goodness. It's a journey of surrendering our fears and doubts, knowing that He is faithful to fulfill His promises and lead us on the path of righteousness.

Action Plan:

Today, choose to surrender control to God and trust in His sovereignty. Spend time in prayer, surrendering your fears and anxieties to Him, and ask Him to give you the strength to trust in His perfect plan for your life.

Heavenly Father, thank You for Your sovereignty and Your perfect plan for our lives. Help us to trust in Your wisdom and goodness, knowing that You are always in control. Give us the strength to surrender our fears and anxieties to You and to walk in faith, knowing that You are faithful to fulfill Your promises. In Jesus' name, Amen.

DAY 218

The Power of God's Spirit

"But you will receive power when the Holy Spirit comes on you;
and you will be my witnesses in Jerusalem, and in all Judea and
Samaria, and to the ends of the earth." - Acts 1:8 (NIV)

The power of God's Spirit is a force beyond human comprehension. It is the divine energy that empowers believers to live victoriously and fulfill their purpose on earth. Just as the disciples experienced on the day of Pentecost, when the Holy Spirit descended upon them like tongues of fire, igniting their hearts with boldness and zeal, so too does God's Spirit empower us today.

When we allow the Holy Spirit to dwell within us, we tap into a reservoir of strength, wisdom, and supernatural ability. It is through the Spirit that we are transformed from the inside out, becoming more like Christ in character and conduct.

Action Plan:

Today, invite the Holy Spirit to fill you afresh. Take time to pray and seek His presence, surrendering your will and desires to His leading. As you go about your day, remain sensitive to His promptings and guidance. Step out in faith, knowing that you have the power of God's Spirit dwelling within you.

Heavenly Father, thank You for the precious gift of Your Spirit. Fill us anew with Your power and presence, that we may live as bold witnesses for Christ in this world. Help us to yield to Your leading and rely on Your strength in all that we do. In Jesus' name, Amen.

DAY 219

Living with Conviction

"But Daniel resolved not to defile himself with the royal food and wine, and he asked the chief official for permission not to defile himself this way." - Daniel 1:8 (NIV)

Living with conviction means standing firm in our beliefs and values, even in the face of opposition or adversity. It requires courage, strength, and unwavering faith in God. Just as Daniel refused to compromise his convictions in the Babylonian court, we too are called to uphold our principles in every aspect of our lives.

Living with conviction also means being willing to endure hardship and persecution for the sake of righteousness. It may not always be easy, but the rewards of staying true to our faith far outweigh the temporary trials we may face.

Action Plan:

Today, identify one area of your life where you have been tempted to compromise your convictions. Take a stand for what you believe in, even if it means facing opposition or ridicule. Trust in God's strength to sustain you and remain steadfast in your commitment to live with conviction.

Heavenly Father, give us the courage and strength to live with conviction in a world that often challenges our faith. Help us to stand firm in our beliefs and honor You in all that we do. Grant us the wisdom to discern Your will and the courage to follow it, no matter the cost. In Jesus' name, Amen.

DAY 220

Embracing God's Truth

"Jesus said to the people who believed in him, 'You are truly my disciples if you remain faithful to my teachings. And you will know the truth, and the truth will set you free.'" - John 8:31-32 (NLT)

Embracing God's truth is not merely about acknowledging it intellectually but allowing it to permeate every aspect of our lives. It's about aligning our thoughts, words, and actions with His Word, which is the ultimate source of wisdom and guidance. When we wholeheartedly embrace God's truth, we experience a profound sense of freedom and fulfillment.

God's truth serves as a beacon of light in the midst of darkness, providing clarity and direction in a world filled with confusion and uncertainty. Embracing God's truth empowers us to live with purpose and passion, knowing that we are walking in alignment with His divine plan for our lives.

Action Plan:

Today, commit to immersing yourself in God's Word. Set aside time each day to read and meditate on Scripture, allowing its truths to sink deep into your heart. As you encounter God's truth, ask Him to reveal areas of your life where you may be resisting His guidance.

Heavenly Father, thank You for the gift of Your truth. Help us to embrace it wholeheartedly and allow it to transform our lives. Give us the strength and courage to live faithfully according to Your Word, trusting in Your promises and following Your guidance. In Jesus' name, Amen.

DAY 221

The Importance of Faithfulness

"Let love and faithfulness never leave you; bind them around your neck, write them on the tablet of your heart." - Proverbs 3:3 (NIV)

Faithfulness is a virtue that stands the test of time. It's the unwavering commitment to uphold our promises, honor our commitments, and remain steadfast in our relationships.

When we are faithful, we mirror the character of our Heavenly Father, who remains faithful to us even in our unfaithfulness. Living a life of faithfulness requires discipline and perseverance. It means choosing to honor our word even when it's inconvenient, staying true to our commitments even when the going gets tough, and remaining loyal to those we love even in the face of temptation or adversity.

Action Plan:

Today, commit to practicing faithfulness in every area of your life. Be intentional about keeping your promises, honoring your commitments, and staying true to your relationships. Remember that every act of faithfulness is an opportunity to reflect the character of God to the world around you.

Heavenly Father, thank You for Your unfailing faithfulness. Teach us to be faithful in all things, just as You are faithful to us. Give us the strength and courage to honor our commitments and remain steadfast in our relationships. May our lives be a testament to Your faithfulness and love. In Jesus' name, Amen.

DAY 222

Trusting God's Timing

"For still the vision awaits its appointed time; it hastens to the end—it will not lie. If it seems slow, wait for it; it will surely come; it will not delay." - Habakkuk 2:3 (ESV)

Trusting God's timings can be challenging in a world that often demands instant gratification. Yet, throughout Scripture, we see countless examples of God's perfect timing unfolding in the lives of His people. From Abraham and Sarah waiting for the birth of Isaac to Joseph enduring years of hardship before being elevated to a position of power, God's timing is always impeccable.

When we trust in God's timings, we relinquish our need for control and surrender to His sovereign plan for our lives. While His timings may not always align with our desires or expectations, we can rest assured that they are always for our ultimate good and His glory.

Action Plan:

Today, practice patience and surrender by letting go of the need to control the timing of events in your life. Instead, commit to trusting God's perfect timing, knowing that He is always working behind the scenes for your benefit.

Heavenly Father, thank You for Your perfect timing in our lives. Help us to trust in Your sovereign plan, even when we cannot see the road ahead. Give us patience and faith to wait for Your appointed time, knowing that Your ways are always higher than our own. In Jesus' name, Amen.

DAY 223

The Role of Spiritual Strength

"Finally, be strong in the Lord and in his mighty power." -
Ephesians 6:10 (NIV)

Spiritual strength is the cornerstone of a resilient and purposeful life. It's not about relying solely on our own abilities, but rather tapping into the infinite power of God that resides within us. When we are strong in the Lord, we can face life's challenges with courage, knowing that we are not alone.

Developing spiritual strength requires intentional effort and a deepening relationship with God. It involves nurturing our faith through prayer, studying His Word, and surrounding ourselves with a supportive community of believers. As we cultivate this strength, we become more attuned to God's voice and His guiding presence in our lives.

Action Plan:

Today, commit to strengthening your spiritual muscles through daily practices of prayer and meditation. Set aside dedicated time each day to connect with God and seek His wisdom and guidance. Engage in Bible study and fellowship with other believers to encourage and uplift one another on your spiritual journey.

Heavenly Father, thank You for the gift of spiritual strength. Help us to lean on You in times of weakness and to draw upon Your mighty power to overcome any obstacles we may face. Guide us as we seek to deepen our relationship with You and empower us to live lives that honor and glorify Your name. In Jesus' name, Amen.

DAY 224

The Power of God's Favor

"For you bless the righteous, O LORD; you cover him with favor as with a shield." - Psalm 5:12 (ESV)

God's favor is a force that transcends human understanding. It is His divine grace and kindness bestowed upon those who seek Him and walk in righteousness.

The power of God's favor is not limited by circumstances or human limitations. It opens doors that seem closed, makes a way where there seems to be no way, and brings about opportunities beyond our wildest dreams. God's favor goes before us, paving the path for success and prosperity in every aspect of our lives.

When we live in the awareness of God's favor, we walk with confidence and assurance, knowing that He is working all things together for our good. His favor is not based on our own merits or achievements but on His unchanging love and faithfulness towards us.

Action Plan:

Today, choose to walk in the confidence of God's favor. Start your day by declaring His promises over your life and thanking Him for His abundant blessings. Throughout the day, remain mindful of His presence and trust in His favor to guide you through every situation.

Heavenly Father, thank You for Your unending favor and grace towards us. Help us to walk in the awareness of Your favor, trusting in Your provision and guidance in all things. In Jesus' name, Amen.

DAY 225

Embracing God's Mercies

"The steadfast love of the LORD never ceases; his mercies never come to an end; they are new every morning; great is your faithfulness." - Lamentations 3:22-23 (ESV)

God's mercies are a gift freely given to us each day, a testament to His unfailing love and faithfulness. Despite our flaws and failures, His compassion knows no bounds. Embracing God's mercies means recognizing our need for His grace and allowing it to transform our lives.

In our journey with God, it's essential to understand that His mercies are not limited by our past mistakes or shortcomings. They are renewed each morning, offering us a fresh start and the opportunity to experience His love in a profound way. When we embrace God's mercies, we release the burden of guilt and shame, knowing that His forgiveness is abundant and unconditional.

Action Plan:

Today, choose to embrace God's mercies fully. Take a moment to reflect on His faithfulness and goodness in your life. Surrender any feelings of unworthiness or inadequacy to Him, and receive His grace with open arms.

Gracious God, thank You for Your boundless mercies that are new every morning. Help us to embrace Your love and forgiveness wholeheartedly, knowing that Your compassion knows no bounds. Give us the strength to extend Your mercy to others and live lives that honor You. In Jesus' name, Amen.

DAY 226

The Importance of Affirmation

"Death and life are in the power of the tongue, and those who love it will eat its fruits." - Proverbs 18:21 (ESV)

Affirmation holds immense power in shaping our thoughts, attitudes, and ultimately, our destinies. The words we speak to ourselves and others have the potential to breathe life into dreams, build confidence, and instill hope. Conversely, negative self-talk and criticism can erode our sense of worth and hinder our progress.

When we choose to affirm ourselves and others, we are aligning our words with God's truth and speaking life into existence. Affirmation reminds us of our inherent value as beloved children of God and empowers us to step into our full potential. It's a reminder that we are capable, worthy, and deserving of love and success.

Action Plan:

Today, make a conscious effort to speak words of affirmation to yourself and others. Start by identifying one positive trait or accomplishment in yourself and affirming it aloud. Encourage those around you with sincere compliments and words of appreciation. Choose to focus on the good in yourself and others, knowing that your words have the power to uplift and inspire.

Heavenly Father, thank You for the gift of affirmation. Help us to use our words to build up and encourage those around us, reflecting Your love and truth in all that we say. May our words be a source of strength and inspiration to others, guiding them toward their purpose and destiny. In Jesus' name, Amen.

DAY 227

Trusting in God's Promises

"For no matter how many promises God has made, they are 'Yes' in Christ. And so through him the 'Amen' is spoken by us to the glory of God." - 2 Corinthians 1:20 (NIV)

Trusting in God's promises is not merely an act of faith but a declaration of our unwavering confidence in His unfailing love and sovereignty. Throughout the Bible, God has made countless promises to His children, and each one is a testament to His faithfulness and commitment to our well-being.

When we trust in God's promises, we are anchoring our souls to the unshakable foundation of His Word. Even in the face of uncertainty and adversity, we can stand firm knowing that God's promises are true and His plans for us are good. Our faith is not based on wishful thinking but on the solid assurance that God keeps His word.

Action Plan:

Today, choose to meditate on one of God's promises found in Scripture. Write it down and carry it with you throughout the day as a reminder of His faithfulness. Whenever doubt or fear creeps in, declare God's promise aloud and reaffirm your trust in His provision.

Heavenly Father, thank You for the abundance of promises found in Your Word. Help us to trust in Your faithfulness and cling to Your promises, knowing that You are always true to Your word. Strengthen our faith, Lord, and lead us into a deeper relationship with You. In Jesus' name, Amen.

DAY 228

The Power of God's Mercy

"But because of his great love for us, God, who is rich in mercy, made us alive with Christ even when we were dead in transgressions—it is by grace you have been saved." - Ephesians 2:4-5 (NIV)

God's mercy is a profound expression of His boundless love and compassion toward us, His children. It is through His mercy that we find forgiveness, redemption, and new life in Christ. Despite our flaws and failures, God extends His mercy to us freely, inviting us to experience His grace and restoration.

The power of God's mercy is transformative. It transcends our shortcomings and offers us the opportunity for a fresh start. When we accept God's mercy, we are released from the burden of guilt and shame, and we are empowered to live in freedom and victory.

Action Plan:

Today, meditate on the depth of God's mercy toward you. Reflect on the ways in which His mercy has transformed your life and brought you closer to Him. Take a moment to express gratitude for His unfailing love and forgiveness, and commit to extending that same mercy to others.

Heavenly Father, thank You for Your boundless mercy and grace. Give us the strength to extend that same mercy to others, showing compassion and forgiveness as You have shown to us. In Jesus' name, Amen.

DAY 229

Living with Integrity

"The integrity of the upright guides them, but the unfaithful are destroyed by their duplicity." - Proverbs 11:3 (NIV)

Living with integrity means aligning our actions with our values and principles, even when no one is watching. It's about being true to ourselves and to God, striving to do what is right and honorable in all circumstances. Integrity is the foundation of trust and respect in our relationships, both with others and with God.

When we live with integrity, we cultivate a sense of inner peace and confidence, knowing that we are walking in alignment with God's will. Our words and deeds become a reflection of His love and truth, inspiring others to do the same. Integrity is not always easy, and it may require sacrifice and self-discipline, but the rewards far outweigh the challenges.

Action Plan:

Today, commit to living with unwavering integrity in every area of your life. Take inventory of your values and principles, and identify areas where you may need to make adjustments to align more closely with God's standards.

Heavenly Father, thank You for the gift of integrity. Help us to live with honesty and integrity in all that we do, honoring You with our words and deeds. May our lives be a shining example of Your truth and love to the world. In Jesus' name, Amen.

DAY 230

Embracing God's Peace

"Peace I leave with you; my peace I give you. I do not give to you as the world gives. Do not let your hearts be troubled and do not be afraid." - John 14:27 (NIV)

In a world filled with chaos, stress, and uncertainty, embracing God's peace is essential for our well-being and spiritual growth. Unlike the fleeting peace that the world offers, God's peace transcends all understanding and remains steadfast in the midst of life's storms.

Embracing God's peace involves surrendering our anxieties, fears, and worries to Him, trusting in His sovereignty and provision. It's a conscious choice to dwell in His presence, allowing His peace to guard our hearts and minds. When we embrace God's peace, we experience a profound sense of calm and serenity, knowing that He is in control and will never leave us nor forsake us.

Action Plan:

Today, take a moment to pause and invite God's peace into your life. Spend time in prayer and meditation, releasing any burdens or concerns to Him. Choose to dwell on His promises and meditate on His Word, allowing His peace to permeate every area of your life.

Heavenly Father, thank You for the gift of Your peace that surpasses all understanding. Help us to surrender our worries and fears to You, trusting in Your unfailing love and provision. May Your peace guard our hearts and minds, guiding us through life's challenges with confidence and grace. In Jesus' name, Amen.

DAY 231

The Importance of Prayer

"Do not be anxious about anything, but in every situation, by prayer and petition, with thanksgiving, present your requests to God." - Philippians 4:6 (NIV)

Prayer is the lifeline of the soul, the bridge that connects us to the heart of God. It's not merely a religious ritual but a profound expression of our relationship with the Creator of the universe. Through prayer, we open ourselves up to divine guidance, comfort, and transformation.

It reminds us that we are never alone, that God is always listening, ready to respond to our needs with love and compassion. Prayer is where we find refuge in times of trouble, strength in moments of weakness, and hope in the face of adversity.

Action Plan:

Today, carve out a dedicated time for prayer in your daily routine. Set aside distractions and create a sacred space where you can commune with God. Begin by expressing gratitude for His blessings, then pour out your heart with honesty and sincerity. Share your joys, fears, hopes, and dreams, knowing that God hears every word.

Gracious God, thank You for the gift of prayer. Help us to cultivate a deeper intimacy with You through our conversations. May our prayers be a source of strength, guidance, and comfort, drawing us closer to Your heart with each passing moment. In Jesus' name, Amen.

DAY 232

Trusting God's Lead

"Trust in the Lord with all your heart and lean not on your own understanding; in all your ways submit to him, and he will make your paths straight." - Proverbs 3:5-6 (NIV)

Trusting God's lead is an act of faith that requires surrendering our own plans and desires to His divine guidance. It's about relinquishing control and placing our confidence in His wisdom and sovereignty, even when we cannot see the full picture.

In the journey of life, there will be moments of uncertainty and doubt, but trusting God's lead enables us to navigate through the storms with unwavering faith. It's a constant reminder that we are not alone, for God is with us every step of the way, guiding us along the path of righteousness.

Action Plan:

Today, take a moment to surrender your plans and worries to God. Choose to trust His lead, even when it seems counterintuitive or challenging. Spend time in prayer and reflection, seeking His guidance and wisdom for the decisions you need to make. Then, step out in faith, knowing that God is faithful to fulfill His promises.

Heavenly Father, thank You for Your unwavering love and guidance. Help us to trust Your lead in all areas of our lives, knowing that Your plans for us are good. Give us the courage to surrender our own agendas and follow wherever You may lead us. In Jesus' name, Amen.

DAY 233

The Role of Spiritual Wisdom

"The fear of the LORD is the beginning of wisdom, and knowledge of the Holy One is understanding." - Proverbs 9:10 (NIV)

Spiritual wisdom is the guiding light that illuminates our path in life. It transcends mere knowledge or intelligence, offering profound insights into the mysteries of God's will and purpose. When we seek spiritual wisdom, we align ourselves with divine truth, gaining clarity and discernment to navigate life's challenges with grace and strength.

It involves deepening our relationship with God through prayer, meditation, and the study of His Word. As we open our hearts to His guidance, He imparts wisdom that surpasses human understanding, equipping us to make wise decisions and live with purpose.

Action Plan:

Today, commit to spending time in prayer and meditation, seeking God's wisdom for your life. Set aside a few moments to reflect on a passage of Scripture and ask the Holy Spirit to reveal its deeper meaning to you.

Heavenly Father, thank You for the gift of spiritual wisdom. Grant us the humility to seek Your guidance in all areas of our lives, trusting in Your infinite wisdom to lead us on the path of righteousness. May we grow in wisdom and understanding, becoming vessels of Your love and truth in the world. In Jesus' name, Amen.

DAY 234

The Power of God's Word

"For the word of God is alive and active. Sharper than any double-edged sword, it penetrates even to dividing soul and spirit, joints and marrow; it judges the thoughts and attitudes of the heart." - Hebrews 4:12 (NIV)

The Word of God is not merely a collection of ancient texts; it is a living, breathing entity that holds transformative power. When we immerse ourselves in Scripture, we invite the Holy Spirit to work in our hearts, illuminating truth and revealing God's purpose for our lives.

God's Word has the power to penetrate the deepest recesses of our being, exposing our thoughts, desires, and motivations. It convicts, challenges, and ultimately leads us to a place of surrender and obedience. Through Scripture, we find strength in times of weakness, comfort in times of sorrow, and hope in times of despair.

Action Plan:

Commit to spending regular time in God's Word each day. Start small if necessary, but be consistent. Choose a passage of Scripture to meditate on and ask God to speak to you through His Word.

Heavenly Father, thank You for the gift of Your Word. Help us to approach it with reverence and humility, recognizing its power to transform our lives. Open our hearts and minds to receive Your truth, and empower us to live according to Your will. In Jesus' name, Amen.

DAY 235

Embracing God's Love

"See what great love the Father has lavished on us, that we should be called children of God! And that is what we are!" - 1 John 3:1a (NIV)

Embracing God's love is perhaps one of the most transformative experiences we can have as believers. It's not merely an intellectual understanding but a deep, heartfelt realization of the profound love that the Creator of the universe has for each one of us. God's love is unconditional, unwavering, and unfathomable. It surpasses all human understanding and transcends our failures and shortcomings.

We are no longer defined by our past mistakes or present circumstances but by the overwhelming love and grace of our Heavenly Father. This realization fills us with a sense of purpose, belonging, and security, knowing that we are deeply cherished and valued by the One who created us.

Action Plan:

Today, take a moment to meditate on the depth of God's love for you. Reflect on His faithfulness, mercy, and grace in your life. Choose to accept and embrace His love wholeheartedly, allowing it to transform your thoughts, attitudes, and actions. Share this love with others through acts of kindness, compassion, and forgiveness.

Gracious Father, thank You for loving us with an everlasting love. Empower us to share Your love with those around us, reflecting Your light in a world that desperately needs it. In Jesus' name, Amen.

DAY 236

The Importance of Reflection

"But be doers of the word, and not hearers only, deceiving
yourselves. For if anyone is a hearer of the word and not a doer,
he is like a man who looks intently at his natural face in a mirror.
For he looks at himself and goes away and at once forgets what he
was like. But the one who looks into the perfect law, the law of
liberty, and perseveres, being no hearer who forgets but a doer
who acts, he will be blessed in his doing." - James 1:22-25 (ESV)

Reflection is like holding up a mirror to our souls, allowing us to see ourselves more clearly. It's a time to pause, ponder, and evaluate our thoughts, actions, and motives. In the midst of life's chaos, reflection provides a sacred space for introspection and growth. It enables us to recognize areas for improvement, celebrate our successes, and realign our hearts with God's will.

Through reflection, we gain insight into our strengths and weaknesses, discern God's voice amidst the noise of the world, and cultivate a deeper intimacy with Him. It's a transformative practice that empowers us to live with intentionality and purpose.

Action Plan:

Take a few moments each day for reflection. Find a quiet place free from distractions, and ask God to guide your thoughts. Reflect on your experiences, emotions, and interactions with others. Consider how you can apply God's truth to your life and strive to live more fully in alignment with His will.

Heavenly Father, thank You for the gift of reflection. Help us to embrace this sacred practice as a means of drawing closer to You and becoming more like Your Son, Jesus Christ. Grant us wisdom and discernment as we reflect on our lives, and empower us to live with purpose and passion for Your glory. In Jesus' name, Amen.

DAY 237

Trusting in God's Promises

"For no matter how many promises God has made, they are 'Yes' in Christ. And so through him the 'Amen' is spoken by us to the glory of God." - 2 Corinthians 1:20 (NIV)

Trusting in God's promises is foundational to our faith journey. Throughout the Bible, God has made countless promises to His people, and He is faithful to fulfill every single one of them. These promises serve as a source of hope and assurance, guiding us through life's challenges and uncertainties.

When we trust in God's promises, we are declaring our confidence in His character and His ability to fulfill what He has spoken. Even when circumstances may seem bleak, we can hold fast to the promises of God, knowing that He is always working for our good.

Action Plan:

Today, meditate on one promise of God that resonates with you. Write it down and carry it with you as a reminder of His faithfulness. Whenever doubt or fear creeps in, declare this promise aloud, affirming your trust in God's unfailing love and provision.

Heavenly Father, thank You for Your unending faithfulness and the promises You have given us in Your Word. Strengthen our faith, Lord, and guide us as we walk in obedience to Your will. In Jesus' name, Amen.

DAY 238

The Power of God's Grace

"But he said to me, 'My grace is sufficient for you, for my power is made perfect in weakness.' Therefore I will boast all the more gladly about my weaknesses, so that Christ's power may rest on me." - 2 Corinthians 12:9 (NIV)

God's grace is a transformative force that transcends our human understanding. It's the unmerited favor and love that He lavishes upon us, regardless of our flaws and shortcomings. In our moments of weakness, His grace shines brightest, offering strength, redemption, and hope.

Understanding the power of God's grace is essential for our spiritual journey. It reminds us that we don't have to rely solely on our own strength or merit to experience His blessings. Instead, we can rest in the assurance that His grace is more than sufficient to sustain us through every trial and challenge.

Action Plan:

Meditate on the ways in which His grace has transformed your circumstances and empowered you to overcome adversity. Then, extend that same grace to yourself and others. Practice forgiveness, compassion, and empathy, recognizing that we are all recipients of God's unending grace.

Heavenly Father, thank You for Your boundless grace that sustains us through every season of life. May Your grace empower us to live lives of gratitude, humility, and love, reflecting Your goodness to the world. In Jesus' name, Amen.

DAY 239

Living with Joy

"You make known to me the path of life; in your presence there is fullness of joy; at your right hand are pleasures forevermore." - Psalm 16:11 (ESV)

Living with joy is not merely about experiencing fleeting moments of happiness, but rather embracing a deep-seated sense of contentment and fulfillment that transcends circumstances. It is a state of being that flows from a heart rooted in gratitude, faith, and trust in God's promises.

True joy is found in the presence of the Lord, where we discover an abundance that surpasses anything the world can offer. It is a choice we make daily to rejoice in the goodness of God, regardless of our circumstances. Even in the midst of trials and challenges, we can find joy knowing that God is with us, guiding us, and working all things together for our good.

Action Plan:

Today, choose to cultivate joy in your life by practicing gratitude. Take a moment each day to reflect on the blessings in your life and thank God for His faithfulness. Choose to focus on the positive aspects of your circumstances and trust that God is at work, even in the difficult seasons.

Heavenly Father, thank You for the gift of joy that comes from knowing You. May Your joy be our strength as we navigate life's ups and downs, trusting in Your unfailing love and faithfulness. In Jesus' name, Amen.

DAY 240

Embracing God's Patience

"But do not overlook this one fact, beloved, that with the Lord one day is as a thousand years, and a thousand years as one day. The Lord is not slow to fulfill his promise as some count slowness, but is patient toward you, not wishing that any should perish, but that all should reach repentance." - 2 Peter 3:8-9 (ESV)

God's timing is not bound by our human limitations; His patience is a reflection of His boundless love and mercy toward us. He patiently waits for us to turn to Him, to grow in faith, and to fulfill His purposes in our lives.

When we embrace God's patience, we surrender our need for control and trust in His perfect timing. We learn to wait with hopeful anticipation, knowing that God's plans for us are far greater than anything we could imagine. In the waiting, we are refined, strengthened, and prepared for the blessings He has in store for us.

Action Plan:

Today, practice patience in one area of your life where you have been feeling anxious or restless. Use this waiting period as an opportunity to deepen your relationship with Him through prayer, meditation, and reflection on His Word.

Gracious God, thank You for Your infinite patience and love toward us. Help us to embrace Your timing, knowing that Your plans are always for our good. Give us the strength to wait patiently and the faith to trust in Your unfailing promises. In Jesus' name, Amen.

DAY 241

The Importance of Humility

"Do nothing out of selfish ambition or vain conceit. Rather, in humility value others above yourselves." - Philippians 2:3 (NIV)

Humility is a virtue often misunderstood in today's world that exalts self-promotion and pride. Yet, true humility is not about thinking less of oneself but about esteeming others above oneself. It's an acknowledgment of our limitations and imperfections, coupled with a deep reverence for the worth and dignity of every individual.

When we embrace humility, we open ourselves to learning and growth. It allows us to recognize that we don't have all the answers and that we can benefit from the wisdom and perspectives of others.

Action Plan:

Today, practice humility by actively seeking opportunities to serve others without seeking recognition or praise. Look for ways to put the needs of others before your own and to listen with an open heart to their perspectives and experiences. Choose to approach each interaction with humility and grace, knowing that true greatness lies in acts of service and selflessness.

Gracious God, teach us the way of humility and selflessness. Help us to set aside our pride and ego, and to value others above ourselves. May our words and actions reflect Your love and grace, as we seek to serve and uplift those around us. In Jesus' name, Amen.

DAY 242

Trusting God's Wisdom

"Trust in the Lord with all your heart, and do not lean on your own understanding. In all your ways acknowledge him, and he will make straight your paths." - Proverbs 3:5-6 (ESV)

Trusting in God's wisdom is an act of surrender and faith. It requires letting go of our own limited understanding and placing our full confidence in His divine guidance. While our human intellect may falter, God's wisdom is perfect and unfailing. When we trust in Him completely, we can rest assured that He will lead us on the path of righteousness and fulfillment.

God's wisdom surpasses our comprehension, encompassing not only our present circumstances but also the intricacies of our past and the possibilities of our future. Trusting in His wisdom enables us to release our anxieties and embrace His peace, knowing that He is working all things together for our good.

Action Plan:

Today, choose to surrender your doubts and uncertainties to God. Spend time in prayer, acknowledging His sovereignty over your life and asking for His wisdom to guide your decisions. Seek His will in all that you do, trusting that He will lead you in the right direction.

Heavenly Father, thank You for Your infinite wisdom. Help us to trust in Your guidance, knowing that Your plans for us are good and perfect. Give us the strength to surrender our doubts and fears to You, and lead us on the path of righteousness. In Jesus' name, Amen.

DAY 243

The Role of Spiritual Warfare

"For our struggle is not against flesh and blood, but against the rulers, against the authorities, against the powers of this dark world and against the spiritual forces of evil in the heavenly realms." - Ephesians 6:12 (NIV)

Spiritual warfare is a reality that every believer faces in their journey of faith. It's a battle not fought with physical weapons, but with spiritual armor and the power of prayer. Our enemy, though unseen, is real, and his tactics are aimed at undermining our faith, stealing our joy, and destroying our relationships.

Understanding the role of spiritual warfare is essential for men who desire to live victoriously in Christ. It requires vigilance, discernment, and unwavering faith in God's promises. As we engage in spiritual warfare, we must arm ourselves with the truth of God's Word, the shield of faith, and the sword of the Spirit.

Action Plan:

Today, take time to assess areas of your life where spiritual warfare may be at play. Identify any thoughts, habits, or relationships that are hindering your spiritual growth and commit them to prayer.

Heavenly Father, thank You for the victory we have in Christ Jesus. Help us to recognize the reality of spiritual warfare and equip us with the spiritual armor needed to stand firm against the enemy's schemes. Give us wisdom and discernment to see beyond the physical realm and fight the good fight of faith. In Jesus' name, Amen.

DAY 244

The Power of God's Voice

"As soon as Jesus was baptized, he went up out of the water. At that moment heaven was opened, and he saw the Spirit of God descending like a dove and alighting on him. And a voice from heaven said, 'This is my Son, whom I love; with him I am well pleased.'" - Matthew 3:16-17 (NIV)

The power of God's voice is incomparable. In the Bible, we see countless instances where God's voice brings forth creation, speaks life into existence, and declares His love for His people. When we listen to God's voice, we tap into a source of wisdom, guidance, and reassurance that transcends human understanding.

God's voice has the power to transform lives, heal brokenness, and bring clarity to confusion. It cuts through the noise of the world, reminding us of our identity as His beloved children and the purpose He has for each of us. When we tune our ears to His voice, we open ourselves up to divine direction and supernatural breakthroughs.

Action Plan:

Today, take time to quiet your heart and mind in God's presence. Spend a few moments in prayer, asking God to speak to you. Listen intently for His voice, whether it comes through Scripture, a gentle whisper in your spirit, or the wise counsel of others.

Heavenly Father, thank You for the power of Your voice. Give us the courage to obey Your voice and trust Your guidance, knowing that You always lead us in the paths of righteousness. In Jesus' name, Amen.

DAY 245

Embracing God's Plan

"For I know the plans I have for you," declares the LORD, "plans to prosper you and not to harm you, plans to give you hope and a future." - Jeremiah 29:11 (NIV)

Embracing God's plan is an act of surrender and trust. It's about relinquishing our own agendas and desires, and aligning our hearts with His perfect will. God's plan for our lives is far greater and more magnificent than anything we could ever imagine. It's a plan filled with purpose, hope, and abundance.

When we embrace God's plan, we let go of the need to control every aspect of our lives. We trust that He knows what's best for us and that His timing is always perfect. Embracing God's plan requires faith and obedience, even when the path ahead seems uncertain or challenging.

Action Plan:

Today, surrender your plans and desires to God. Spend time in prayer, seeking His guidance and wisdom for your life. Be open to His leading and trust that He will direct your steps according to His perfect plan. Surrendering doesn't mean giving up; it means allowing God to work His miracles in your life.

Heavenly Father, thank You for the promise of Your perfect plan for our lives. Give us the strength and courage to surrender our own agendas and embrace Your will wholeheartedly. In Jesus' name, Amen.

DAY 246

The Importance of Giving

"Each of you should give what you have decided in your heart to give, not reluctantly or under compulsion, for God loves a cheerful giver." - 2 Corinthians 9:7 (NIV)

Giving is not merely an act of charity but a profound expression of love and gratitude. When we give freely and generously, we reflect the character of God, who is the ultimate giver of all good things. Whether it's our time, talents, or resources, giving allows us to participate in God's work of blessing others and advancing His kingdom on earth.

When we give with a joyful heart, we acknowledge God's abundant provision in our lives and demonstrate our trust in His faithfulness. It's an act of worship that transcends material wealth, enriching our souls and deepening our connection with the Divine. Moreover, giving opens the door for God's blessings to flow into our lives, as He promises to bless those who give cheerfully and abundantly.

Action Plan:

Today, look for opportunities to give generously to those in need. It could be a financial donation to a charitable organization, volunteering your time to serve others, or simply offering a kind word of encouragement to someone who is struggling.

Heavenly Father, thank You for the privilege of giving. Teach us to be cheerful givers, freely sharing the blessings You have bestowed upon us with others. In Jesus' name, Amen.

DAY 247

Trusting in God's Sovereignty

"For I know the plans I have for you," declares the LORD, "plans to prosper you and not to harm you, plans to give you hope and a future." - Jeremiah 29:11 (NIV)

Trusting in God's sovereignty means surrendering to His divine plan, even when we don't fully understand it. It's about acknowledging that God is in control of all things and that His ways are higher than ours. When we trust in His sovereignty, we find peace in knowing that He is working all things together for our good, according to His perfect will.

God's sovereignty doesn't mean that we won't face challenges or hardships, but it does mean that we can trust Him to see us through every trial. It's a reminder that nothing happens outside of His knowledge and authority, and that He is always faithful to His promises.

Action Plan:

Today, surrender your fears and uncertainties to God's sovereignty. Choose to trust in His wisdom and goodness, even when circumstances seem bleak. Spend time in prayer, asking God to help you relinquish control and to strengthen your faith in His sovereign plan for your life.

Heavenly Father, thank You for Your sovereignty and faithfulness. Help us to trust in Your perfect plan, even when we don't understand it. In Jesus' name, Amen.

DAY 248

The Power of God's Hand

"The LORD your God is with you, the Mighty Warrior who saves. He will take great delight in you; in his love he will no longer rebuke you, but will rejoice over you with singing." - Zephaniah 3:17 (NIV)

Throughout Scripture, we see countless examples of God's mighty hand at work, from parting the Red Sea to healing the sick and raising the dead. His hand is not limited by human understanding or constraints but is capable of accomplishing the impossible.

When we recognize the power of God's hand in our lives, we are filled with awe and reverence for His majesty. It reminds us that we serve a God who is greater than any obstacle or challenge we may face. His hand is always at work, guiding, protecting, and providing for us in ways we may not even realize.

Action Plan:

Today, surrender your fears and worries to God's mighty hand. Trust in His power to overcome any obstacle or adversity you may encounter. Take a moment to reflect on past experiences where you have seen God's hand at work in your life, and thank Him for His faithfulness.

Heavenly Father, thank You for the power of Your hand at work in our lives. Help us to trust in Your sovereignty and to rest in the assurance of Your unfailing love. May we always remember that Your hand is mighty to save and that nothing is impossible for You. In Jesus' name, Amen.

DAY 249

Living with Conviction

"Therefore, my dear brothers and sisters, stand firm. Let nothing move you. Always give yourselves fully to the work of the Lord, because you know that your labor in the Lord is not in vain." - 1 Corinthians 15:58 (NIV)

Living with conviction means anchoring your life on unwavering principles and values, regardless of external pressures or circumstances. It's about boldly standing for what you believe in and staying true to your faith, even when faced with opposition or adversity.

As men of conviction, we are called to lead lives of integrity and courage, grounded in our faith and guided by our convictions. This means making decisions that align with our values, even when it's not the popular choice, and persevering in the face of challenges.

Action Plan:

Today, reflect on your core values and beliefs. Identify one area of your life where you may be compromising your convictions, whether it's in your relationships, work, or personal habits. Commit to taking a stand for what you believe in, and ask God for the strength and wisdom to live with unwavering conviction.

Heavenly Father, thank You for the gift of conviction. Help us to stand firm in our faith and live lives that honor You in all that we do. Give us the courage to uphold our convictions, even in the face of adversity, knowing that You are with us every step of the way. In Jesus' name, Amen.

DAY 250

Embracing God's Truth

"Jesus said to him, 'I am the way, and the truth, and the life. No one comes to the Father except through me.'" - John 14:6 (ESV)

Embracing God's truth is the cornerstone of a fulfilling and purposeful life. In a world filled with conflicting messages and shifting values, God's truth remains unwavering and eternal. It is the light that guides us through the darkness, the compass that directs our steps on the path of righteousness.

When we embrace God's truth, we align our hearts and minds with His divine wisdom and promises. We acknowledge that His ways are higher than our ways and His thoughts higher than our thoughts. God's truth provides clarity in the midst of confusion, strength in times of weakness, and hope in the face of despair.

Action Plan:

Today, commit to immersing yourself in God's Word daily. Set aside time to read and meditate on Scripture, allowing His truth to penetrate your heart and renew your mind. Choose one key truth from Scripture that resonates with you and meditate on it throughout the day. Reflect on how you can apply that truth to your thoughts, words, and actions.

Heavenly Father, thank You for the gift of Your truth. Help us to embrace Your Word with open hearts and minds, allowing it to transform us from the inside out. May Your truth be a lamp unto our feet and a light unto our path, guiding us closer to You each day. In Jesus' name, Amen.

DAY 251

The Importance of Faithfulness

"The LORD passed before him and proclaimed, 'The LORD, the LORD, a God merciful and gracious, slow to anger, and abounding in steadfast love and faithfulness.'" - Exodus 34:6 (ESV)

Faithfulness is a cornerstone of character, rooted in the unchanging nature of God Himself. It embodies reliability, loyalty, and unwavering commitment. Just as God remains faithful to His promises, calling us to emulate His example, our faithfulness in relationships, responsibilities, and endeavors reflects His enduring love and integrity.

It fortifies marriages, cultivates trust in friendships, and sustains us through the trials of life. Moreover, faithfulness extends beyond human interactions; it encompasses our fidelity to God, demonstrating our devotion and trust in His providence.

Action Plan:

Today, commit to living a life of faithfulness in every aspect. Honor your commitments, remain loyal to those entrusted to your care, and uphold your word with integrity. In moments of doubt or temptation, remember the faithfulness of God and draw strength from His example to persevere.

Heavenly Father, thank You for Your unfailing faithfulness. Teach us to walk in Your footsteps, demonstrating steadfast love and commitment in all our relationships and endeavors. In Jesus' name, Amen.

DAY 252

Trusting God's Protection

"The LORD is my rock, my fortress, and my deliverer; my God is my rock, in whom I take refuge, my shield and the horn of my salvation, my stronghold." - Psalm 18:2 (NIV)

Trusting in God's protection is an act of faith that anchors us in the midst of life's storms. It's a recognition of His sovereignty and a surrender of our fears into His capable hands. Just as a fortress provides security and shelter from external threats, so does God shield us from harm and danger.

When we trust in God's protection, we release our anxieties and worries, knowing that He is always watching over us. It doesn't mean we won't face trials or difficulties, but it does mean that we can face them with courage and confidence, knowing that God is with us every step of the way.

Action Plan:

Today, choose to trust in God's protection by meditating on His promises of safety and security. Take time to reflect on instances in your life where God has proven Himself faithful in protecting you. Whenever fear or doubt creeps in, remind yourself of God's steadfast love and commit to placing your trust in Him.

Heavenly Father, thank You for being our ultimate protector and stronghold. Help us to trust in Your unfailing protection, knowing that You are always watching over us. Strengthen our faith and grant us the courage to face life's challenges with confidence, knowing that You are by our side. In Jesus' name, Amen.

DAY 253

The Role of Spiritual Awakening

"Therefore, if anyone is in Christ, the new creation has come: The old has gone, the new is here!" - 2 Corinthians 5:17 (NIV)

Spiritual awakening is a profound transformation of the heart and soul, a divine encounter that awakens us to the truth of who we are and our purpose in God's plan. It's a journey of self-discovery and enlightenment, where we are liberated from the chains of our past and embraced by the boundless love of our Creator.

In our spiritual awakening, we come to realize that we are not defined by our past mistakes or present circumstances. Instead, we are beloved children of God, called to live lives of purpose, joy, and abundance. This awakening opens our eyes to the beauty of God's creation and the limitless possibilities that await us when we surrender our lives to His will.

Action Plan:

Today, take a moment to quiet your mind and open your heart to God's presence. Reflect on areas of your life where you may be feeling spiritually stagnant or disconnected. Ask God to reveal Himself to you in a fresh and powerful way, igniting a fire within you to pursue Him wholeheartedly.

Heavenly Father, thank You for the gift of spiritual awakening. Open our eyes to see Your truth and our hearts to receive Your love. May our lives be transformed by Your grace, and may we walk in the fullness of Your purpose for us. In Jesus' name, Amen.

DAY 254

The Power of God's Love

"For I am convinced that neither death nor life, neither angels nor demons, neither the present nor the future, nor any powers, neither height nor depth, nor anything else in all creation, will be able to separate us from the love of God that is in Christ Jesus our Lord."
- Romans 8:38-39 (NIV)

The love of God is a force beyond measure, transcending all boundaries and limitations. It is a love that knows no end, no condition, and no limit. God's love is unconditional, unwavering, and steadfast, even in the face of our failures and shortcomings.

In a world filled with uncertainty and turmoil, the power of God's love serves as an anchor for our souls. It is a love that heals the brokenhearted, restores the lost, and transforms lives from the inside out. When we embrace the depth of God's love for us, we find peace amidst the storms of life and strength to overcome every obstacle.

Action Plan:

Today, meditate on the vastness of God's love for you. Reflect on the ways His love has sustained you and carried you through difficult times. Take a moment to express gratitude for His unfailing love and commit to sharing that love with others through acts of kindness and compassion.

Heavenly Father, thank You for the incomprehensible depth of Your love for us. May Your love be a guiding force in our lives, leading us closer to You and to one another. In Jesus' name, Amen.

DAY 255

Embracing God's Grace

"But he said to me, 'My grace is sufficient for you, for my power is made perfect in weakness.' Therefore I will boast all the more gladly about my weaknesses, so that Christ's power may rest on me." - 2 Corinthians 12:9 (NIV)

Embracing God's grace is an acknowledgment of our humanity and our need for His unmerited favor. It's a recognition that we are flawed and imperfect, yet deeply loved and valued by our Creator. God's grace is a gift freely given, not because of anything we have done to earn it, but because of His boundless love and mercy.

We surrender our pride and self-sufficiency, allowing His grace to fill our lives with forgiveness, peace, and hope. It's through our weaknesses and struggles that God's power is most evident, as His grace enables us to overcome obstacles and grow stronger in our faith.

Action Plan:

Today, reflect on areas of your life where you may be striving in your own strength. Surrender those areas to God and ask Him to fill you with His grace and strength. Practice extending grace to yourself and others, forgiving mistakes and embracing imperfections with love and compassion.

Prayer: Heavenly Father, thank You for Your abundant grace that covers us in our weakness. Fill us with Your love and mercy, and empower us to extend grace to ourselves and others. In Jesus' name, Amen.

DAY 256

The Importance of Meditation

"Be still, and know that I am God; I will be exalted among the nations, I will be exalted in the earth." - Psalm 46:10 (NIV)

Meditation is a powerful spiritual discipline that allows us to quiet our minds and connect deeply with God. In the midst of life's chaos and noise, taking time to meditate enables us to cultivate inner peace, clarity, and intimacy with the Divine. It's a sacred practice of tuning out the distractions of the world and tuning into the presence of God.

It's a time of reflection, contemplation, and listening, where we can surrender our worries and anxieties and trust in God's perfect plan for our lives. As we meditate on His Word and His promises, we are strengthened in our faith and empowered to live with purpose and intentionality.

Action Plan:

Today, commit to setting aside a specific time each day for meditation. Find a quiet place where you can be alone with God, free from distractions. Begin by taking deep breaths and clearing your mind. Then, meditate on a verse of Scripture or a spiritual truth, allowing God's presence to fill you with peace and wisdom.

Heavenly Father, thank You for the gift of meditation. Teach us to be still in Your presence, that we may know You more intimately and hear Your voice clearly. May our time of meditation be a source of strength and renewal, empowering us to live each day in alignment with Your will. In Jesus' name, Amen.

DAY 257

Embracing God's Strength

*"Fear not, for I am with you; be not dismayed, for I am your God;
I will strengthen you, I will help you, I will uphold you with my
righteous right hand." - Isaiah 41:10 (ESV)*

In the journey of life, especially as men facing the responsibilities
and challenges of daily living, it's easy to feel overwhelmed and
inadequate. God promises His unwavering presence and strength.
Embracing God's strength is about recognizing our own limitations
and allowing His power to work through us.

Embracing God's strength means leaning on Him when we feel
weak, trusting in His power when we feel powerless, and walking
in faith when the path ahead seems uncertain. It's about finding our
courage not in our own abilities, but in His boundless love and
support. This divine strength transforms our fears into confidence,
our worries into peace, and our struggles into victories.

Action Plan:

Today, begin by acknowledging any areas in your life where you
feel weak or overwhelmed. Write them down as a prayer to God,
inviting Him to take control. Make it a habit to start each day with
this practice of surrender and reliance on His strength.

*Almighty God, thank You for Your promise to be with us and to
strengthen us. Fill us with Your peace and empower us to face
each day with confidence and faith. In Jesus' name, Amen.*

DAY 258

The Power of God's Mercy

"But because of His great love for us, God, who is rich in mercy, made us alive with Christ even when we were dead in transgressions—it is by grace you have been saved." - Ephesians 2:4-5 (NIV)

The power of God's mercy is a transformative force that changes lives, restores hope, and breathes new life into weary souls. As men, we often carry the weight of our mistakes, our failures, and our shortcomings, believing that we must bear these burdens alone.

God's mercy is not just a one-time gift but a daily reality. It is through His mercy that we are not consumed by our sins but are given the opportunity to rise, grow, and become the men He has called us to be. His mercy reminds us that we are not defined by our past but by His love and grace. This understanding frees us from guilt and shame, empowering us to live boldly and courageously.

Action Plan:

Today, take time to reflect on God's mercy in your life. Let this be a reminder that His mercy is always available to you. Commit to extending the same mercy to others, forgiving those who have wronged you, and showing compassion to those in need.

Merciful Father, thank You for the boundless mercy You extend to us each day. Teach us to forgive as we have been forgiven and to show compassion to those around us. May Your mercy be a constant source of strength and renewal in our lives. In Jesus' name, Amen.

DAY 259

Living with Integrity

"The integrity of the upright guides them, but the unfaithful are destroyed by their duplicity." - Proverbs 11:3 (NIV)

For men, integrity is the foundation of a life that honors God and impacts those around us positively. It's about being trustworthy, honest, and consistent in all aspects of our lives—whether at work, at home, or in our personal time. Integrity is not just about doing the right thing but being the right person, one whose character reflects the heart of God.

However, the reward is a life of genuine peace and respect, both from others and within ourselves. Integrity builds trust and respect, fostering deeper and more authentic relationships. It also ensures that our actions match our words, making us reliable and true to our commitments.

Action Plan:

Reflect on areas of your life where your actions may not fully align with your values. Identify specific situations where you might be tempted to compromise your integrity, and create a plan to address them. This could include setting boundaries, seeking accountability from a trusted friend, or praying for strength and guidance.

Heavenly Father, we come before You with a desire to live lives of integrity. Give us the strength to resist temptations that lead us away from integrity and the courage to stand firm in our convictions. May our lives reflect Your character and bring glory to Your name. In Jesus' name, Amen.

DAY 260

Embracing God's Peace

"Peace I leave with you; my peace I give you. I do not give to you as the world gives. Do not let your hearts be troubled and do not be afraid." - John 14:27 (NIV)

In the hustle and bustle of life, filled with responsibilities, challenges, and uncertainties, finding peace can seem impossible. Embracing God's peace means allowing His calm to settle in our hearts, even amidst the chaos. It's about trusting that He is in control and letting go of the anxieties that weigh us down.

God's peace is not the absence of trouble but the assurance of His presence in the midst of it. This peace guards our hearts and minds, enabling us to face life's challenges with serenity and confidence. By embracing God's peace, we find the strength to navigate life's storms with grace and resilience.

Action Plan:

Today, make a conscious effort to seek God's peace. Begin by identifying sources of stress or anxiety in your life and bring them to God in prayer, asking for His peace to fill your heart. Spend time in His Word, focusing on passages that speak of His peace and faithfulness.

Heavenly Father, thank You for the precious gift of Your peace. We come before You with hearts burdened by the worries and stresses of life, seeking the tranquility only You can provide. May Your peace guard our hearts and minds, filling us with calm and confidence as we walk through each day. In Jesus' name, Amen.

DAY 261

The Importance of Praise

"I will bless the Lord at all times; his praise shall continually be in my mouth." - Psalm 34:1 (ESV)

Praise is a powerful act of worship that connects us directly with the heart of God. For men, who often bear the weight of responsibility and the pressure to remain strong, praise becomes a lifeline—a way to realign our hearts with God's truth and to draw on His limitless power.

When we make praise a daily practice, we invite God's presence into every area of our lives. Praise changes our perspective, lifting us above our challenges and reminding us of God's sovereignty and love. Moreover, praise is not just about what God can do for us, but about acknowledging and celebrating who He is—our Creator, Sustainer, and Redeemer.

Action Plan:

Today, commit to beginning and ending your day with praise. Choose a favorite worship song or a psalm and sing or recite it aloud. Throughout your day, make it a point to pause and thank God for His blessings, no matter how small.

Heavenly Father, we come before You with hearts full of gratitude and praise. Thank You for Your constant presence and unfailing love. May our praises bring us closer to You and remind us of Your greatness and power. Fill us with joy and strengthen our faith as we lift Your name on high. In Jesus' name, Amen.

DAY 262

Trusting God's Guidance

"Trust in the Lord with all your heart, and do not lean on your own understanding. In all your ways acknowledge Him, and He will make straight your paths." - Proverbs 3:5-6 (ESV)

As men, we are frequently called to lead—whether in our families, workplaces, or communities—yet the weight of these responsibilities can be overwhelming. In these moments, the call to trust in God's guidance becomes paramount. Trusting God's guidance means surrendering our plans and desires to His greater wisdom.

God's guidance is not always immediately clear, and it requires a faith that goes beyond our own understanding. It's about placing our confidence in His infinite wisdom, even when the road ahead is uncertain.

Action Plan:

Today, take time to reflect on areas of your life where you need guidance. Write these areas down and bring them before God in prayer, asking for His wisdom and direction. Make a commitment to start each day by acknowledging God in all your decisions, big or small.

Heavenly Father, thank You for Your promise to guide us when we trust in You. As we face decisions and challenges, remind us to seek Your guidance in all things. Lead us on the path You have prepared for us, and give us the courage to follow it faithfully. In Jesus' name, Amen.

DAY 263

The Role of Spiritual Wisdom

"For the Lord gives wisdom; from his mouth come knowledge and understanding." - Proverbs 2:6 (NIV)

This divine wisdom transcends mere human intellect and provides us with insight, discernment, and clarity in all aspects of our lives. As men, whether we're making decisions at work, leading our families, or navigating personal challenges, we need this spiritual wisdom to align our actions with God's will and purpose.

Spiritual wisdom is about seeking God's perspective and understanding beyond our limited human view. It's a humble acknowledgment that true knowledge and understanding come from the Lord. When we embrace this wisdom, we are equipped to handle life's complexities with grace and strength.

Action Plan:

Today, commit to seeking God's wisdom in all your decisions. Start your day with a prayer asking for His guidance and insight. Spend time in His Word, meditating on passages that speak to wisdom and understanding. Consider keeping a journal to document the ways God's wisdom manifests in your daily life.

Heavenly Father, we thank You for the gift of Your wisdom. We acknowledge our need for Your guidance and understanding in every area of our lives. Fill us with discernment and clarity, that we may live in a way that honors You and reflects Your love. In Jesus' name, Amen.

DAY 264

The Power of Worship

"Come, let us bow down in worship, let us kneel before the Lord our Maker; for he is our God and we are the people of his pasture, the flock under his care." - Psalm 95:6-7 (NIV)

Worship is a profound and powerful act that transcends the mere singing of songs or the recitation of prayers. It is the very heart of our relationship with God, a moment where we recognize His greatness, His love, and His sovereignty over our lives.

The power of worship lies in its ability to shift our focus from our struggles and weaknesses to God's majesty and power. It realigns our hearts with His, reminding us that we are not alone, that we are deeply loved, and that we have a purpose in His grand design. Worship is not just an activity; it is a lifestyle of honoring God in everything we do, allowing His presence to permeate our daily lives.

Action Plan:

Today, make a conscious effort to incorporate worship into your daily routine. Start your morning with a worship song that speaks to your heart or spend a few minutes in quiet reverence, acknowledging God's presence.

Heavenly Father, we come before You with hearts full of gratitude and awe. We acknowledge Your greatness and surrender our lives to Your will. Let Your presence fill our hearts, transforming our fears into faith and our worries into worship. May our lives be a testament to Your glory and love. In Jesus' name, Amen.

DAY 265

Embracing God's Love

"For God so loved the world, that he gave his only Son, that whoever believes in him should not perish but have eternal life." - John 3:16 (ESV)

God's love is the cornerstone of our faith, the foundation upon which we build our lives. It's a love so vast and deep that it surpasses human understanding, a love that knows no bounds and reaches to the depths of our souls. Embracing God's love is about recognizing our worth in His eyes, understanding that we are cherished beyond measure, and allowing His love to transform us from the inside out.

It's a love that sees us at our best and at our worst, yet never wavers. When we embrace God's love, we are set free from the chains of insecurity, fear, and self-doubt. We can live with confidence, knowing that we are deeply loved and accepted just as we are.

Action Plan:

Today, take a moment to reflect on God's love for you. Consider the ways in which His love has transformed your life and the blessings it has brought. Write down a few key verses about God's love and meditate on them throughout the day.

Heavenly Father, thank You for Your unconditional love that knows no bounds. May Your love be a guiding light in our lives, leading us closer to You and empowering us to love others as You have loved us. In Jesus' name, Amen.

DAY 266

The Importance of Positive Thinking

"Finally, brothers and sisters, whatever is true, whatever is noble, whatever is right, whatever is pure, whatever is lovely, whatever is admirable—if anything is excellent or praiseworthy—think about such things." - Philippians 4:8 (NIV)

Positive thinking is not about denying reality or ignoring challenges; rather, it's about choosing to focus on the good, the beautiful, and the hopeful aspects of life. Love, on the other hand, is the foundation of our relationships—with God and with others. It's a powerful force that heals, strengthens, and transforms.

The importance of positive thinking and love cannot be overstated, especially in the context of daily living as men. In a world filled with negativity, cynicism, and division, cultivating a positive mindset and a heart full of love becomes a radical act of resistance.

Action Plan:

Today, commit to being intentional about your thoughts and your words. Start by practicing gratitude—take a few moments each morning and evening to reflect on the things you're thankful for. Throughout your day, catch yourself whenever negative thoughts arise and consciously replace them with positive affirmations.

Gracious God, thank You for the gift of positive thinking and love. Teach us to see the beauty in every situation, to speak words of life and encouragement, and to love others as You have loved us. May our lives be a testament to Your goodness and grace. In Jesus' name, Amen.

DAY 267

Trusting in God's Promises

"For I know the plans I have for you," declares the Lord, "plans to prosper you and not to harm you, plans to give you hope and a future." - Jeremiah 29:11 (NIV)

Trusting in God's promises is an act of faith that transcends our circumstances and anchors our souls in the unchanging truth of His word. In a world filled with uncertainty and doubt, God's promises stand as pillars of hope, guiding us through life's storms and illuminating the path ahead.

As men, we often strive to control our destinies, relying on our own strength and wisdom to navigate life's challenges. Yet, true peace and fulfillment can only be found in surrendering to God's plans and trusting in His promises.

Action Plan:

Today, take a moment to reflect on God's promises found in Scripture. Write down a few that resonate with you personally, and meditate on them throughout the day. Finally, commit to prayer, asking God to deepen your trust in His promises and to guide you in living out His plans for your life.

Gracious Father, thank You for the abundance of Your promises that give us hope and assurance. Help us to trust in Your unfailing love and to hold fast to Your word, even in the midst of uncertainty. May Your promises be a source of comfort and inspiration, guiding us through every season of life. In Jesus' name, Amen.

DAY 268

The Power of God's Grace

"For it is by grace you have been saved, through faith—and this is not from yourselves, it is the gift of God." - Ephesians 2:8 (NIV)

The power of God's grace is not just a theological concept; it's a living reality that transforms lives. As men navigating the complexities of life, understanding and embracing God's grace is essential for our spiritual growth and well-being.

God's grace is boundless and unconditional. It's the divine force that reaches into the depths of our brokenness and lifts us up, offering forgiveness, redemption, and new life. It's through grace that we are saved, not by our own efforts or righteousness, but by the sacrificial love of Jesus Christ.

Action Plan:

Today, take a moment to reflect on the magnitude of God's grace in your life. Consider the ways in which His grace has rescued you, forgiven you, and transformed you. Journal your thoughts and feelings as a personal expression of gratitude to God.

Heavenly Father, we thank You for the immeasurable gift of Your grace. Help us to fully grasp the depth of Your love and the magnitude of Your mercy. Fill us with Your Holy Spirit, that we may be vessels of Your grace in a world in need of Your redeeming love. In Jesus' name, Amen.

DAY 269

Living with Joy

"May the God of hope fill you with all joy and peace as you trust in him, so that you may overflow with hope by the power of the Holy Spirit." - Romans 15:13 (NIV)

Joy is not just an emotion; it's a state of being rooted in our faith and trust in God. Living with joy is about finding contentment and gratitude in every circumstance, knowing that our hope is secure in Him. It's a deep-seated assurance that no matter what challenges we face, we can still experience joy because of the abiding presence of God in our lives.

When we live with joy, we radiate God's light and love to those around us. Our joy becomes contagious, uplifting others and pointing them towards the source of true happiness. It's a powerful testimony of our faith in God's goodness, even amidst life's struggles and hardships.

Action Plan:

Today, choose joy as a deliberate act of faith. Begin by counting your blessings and expressing gratitude to God for His goodness in your life. Make a conscious effort to focus on the positive aspects of your day, even amidst difficulties. Engage in activities that bring you joy and remind you of God's presence.

Gracious Father, thank You for the gift of joy that comes from knowing You. May our lives be a reflection of Your joy to the world around us, drawing others closer to You. In Jesus' name, Amen.

DAY 270

Embracing God's Patience

"For the Lord is good; his steadfast love endures forever, and his faithfulness to all generations." - Psalm 100:5 (ESV)

Patience is not merely the ability to wait; it's a virtue cultivated through trust in God's timing and faithfulness. As men navigating the complexities of life, we're called to embody this patience, understanding that God's plans unfold according to His perfect will and timing.

Embracing God's patience means relinquishing our desire for immediate gratification and surrendering to His sovereign timing. It's trusting that even in the midst of delays, setbacks, and uncertainties, God is still at work, orchestrating His purposes for our lives.

Action Plan:

Today, take a moment to reflect on areas of your life where impatience may be hindering your growth or causing unnecessary stress. Identify specific situations or circumstances where you struggle to trust God's timing. Surrender these concerns to Him in prayer, asking for His grace to cultivate patience in your heart.

Gracious Father, thank You for Your enduring patience and steadfast love. Forgive us for the times we've rushed ahead of Your plans or doubted Your faithfulness. May Your patience be reflected in our words, actions, and attitudes, bringing glory to Your name. In Jesus' name, Amen.

DAY 271

The Importance of Humility

"God opposes the proud but shows favor to the humble." - James 4:6 (NIV)

Humility is not weakness; rather, it's a posture of the heart that acknowledges our dependence on God and our interconnectedness with others. It's an attitude of selflessness, gentleness, and genuine concern for the well-being of others.

The importance of humility lies in its ability to foster authentic relationships, foster growth, and deepen our intimacy with God. When we humble ourselves before God, we open ourselves up to His grace and wisdom, allowing Him to work in and through us.

Action Plan:

Today, commit to cultivating humility in your daily life. Start by examining your thoughts, words, and actions, and ask yourself if they reflect a spirit of humility or pride. Spend time in prayer, asking God to reveal any areas of pride in your life and to help you cultivate a humble heart.

Gracious Father, forgive us for the times when we have exalted ourselves above others and neglected to walk in humility. Teach us the true value of humility and help us to follow the example of Your Son, Jesus Christ, who humbled Himself for our sake. In Jesus' name, Amen.

DAY 272

Trusting God's Wisdom

"The fear of the Lord is the beginning of wisdom, and knowledge of the Holy One is understanding." - Proverbs 9:10 (NIV)

Trusting God's wisdom is an act of faith that transcends our human understanding. In a world filled with uncertainty and complexity, leaning on God's wisdom offers us clarity, direction, and peace. It's acknowledging that His ways are higher than ours, and His plans are beyond our comprehension.

God's wisdom is not just about making the right decisions or avoiding mistakes; it's about living with purpose and alignment with His will. When we trust in His wisdom, we release the burden of trying to figure everything out on our own.

Action Plan:

Begin by reflecting on areas of your life where you struggle to trust God's wisdom. Is there a decision you're grappling with or a situation causing you anxiety? Take some time to pray and seek God's guidance, inviting Him to reveal His wisdom to you.

Heavenly Father, we come before You humbly, acknowledging Your infinite wisdom and sovereignty. Help us to trust in Your wisdom, even when we can't see the path ahead. May Your wisdom be our compass, guiding us in every decision and step we take. In Jesus' name, Amen.

DAY 273

The Role of Spiritual Discipline

"Train yourself in godliness, for, while bodily training is of some value, godliness is of value in every way, as it holds promise for the present life and also for the life to come." - 1 Timothy 4:7-8 (ESV)

Spiritual discipline is the cornerstone of a strong and vibrant faith. Just as an athlete trains diligently to excel in their sport, so too must we train ourselves in godliness to grow in our relationship with God. Spiritual disciplines such as prayer, fasting, meditation, and study of Scripture are not mere rituals, but powerful means by which we deepen our connection with the Divine and cultivate a Christ-like character.

Engaging in spiritual disciplines enables us to align our hearts with God's will, renew our minds with His truth, and strengthen our spirits for the journey ahead. Through consistent practice, we develop a greater sensitivity to the Holy Spirit's leading and a deeper intimacy with our Heavenly Father.

Action Plan:

Today, commit to incorporating spiritual disciplines into your daily routine. Begin by setting aside dedicated time each day for prayer and meditation, seeking God's presence and guidance.

Heavenly Father, thank You for the gift of spiritual disciplines that draw us closer to You and shape us into the image of Your Son, Jesus Christ. Empower us to walk in godliness and live out our faith boldly each day. In Jesus' name, Amen.

DAY 274

The Power of God's Presence

"Surely I am with you always, to the very end of the age." -
Matthew 28:20b (NIV)

The power of God's presence is a force unlike any other. It's the assurance that in every moment, in every circumstance, He is with us. His presence brings comfort in times of distress, strength in times of weakness, and joy in times of sorrow. It's a tangible reminder of His love and faithfulness, a beacon of hope guiding us through life's trials and triumphs.

We no longer walk alone but journey hand in hand with the Creator of the universe. His presence goes before us, paving the way for miracles and breakthroughs. It surrounds us, protecting us from harm and leading us into paths of righteousness. And it dwells within us, empowering us to live boldly and fulfill our purpose.

Action Plan:

Today, commit to cultivating a deeper awareness of God's presence in your life. Start by setting aside intentional time for prayer and meditation, inviting Him to draw near to you. Throughout your day, practice mindfulness, consciously acknowledging His presence in every moment.

Heavenly Father, thank You for the gift of Your presence. Open our eyes to see You, our ears to hear You, and our hearts to feel You in every aspect of our lives. Fill us with Your Spirit and use us to bring glory to Your name. In Jesus' name, Amen.

DAY 275

Embracing God's Plan

"Trust in the Lord with all your heart and lean not on your own understanding; in all your ways submit to him, and he will make your paths straight." - Proverbs 3:5-6 (NIV)

God's plan for our lives is often beyond our comprehension. It's easy to get caught up in our own desires, ambitions, and expectations, but true fulfillment comes from surrendering to His divine will. It's about releasing our need for control and allowing His guidance to lead us down the path He has designed specifically for us.

God's plan is not always easy or comfortable. It may involve challenges, setbacks, and periods of waiting. By aligning our hearts with His will, we open ourselves up to experiences, opportunities, and blessings beyond anything we could imagine.

Action Plan:

Today, take a moment to reflect on areas of your life where you may be resisting God's plan. Surrender those areas to Him in prayer, asking for His guidance and wisdom. Commit to seeking His will above your own desires, even when it requires sacrifice or stepping out of your comfort zone.

Heavenly Father, thank You for the assurance that Your plans for us are good and perfect. Help us to trust in Your wisdom and to submit to Your will in all things. May Your guidance lead us to a life filled with purpose, joy, and fulfillment. In Jesus' name, Amen.

DAY 276

The Importance of Consecration

"Present yourselves as a living sacrifice, holy and acceptable to God, which is your spiritual worship." - Romans 12:1 (ESV)

Consecration is a powerful act of devotion, a surrender of our whole selves to God. It's about setting ourselves apart for His purposes, dedicating our lives to His service, and living in accordance with His will. It invites us to lay down our own desires and ambitions at the feet of our Creator, trusting that His plans for us are greater than anything we could imagine.

Consecration is not a one-time event but a continuous journey of transformation. It's a process of purification, as God refines our hearts and molds us into vessels fit for His use. And it's a privilege, as we partner with God in His redemptive work in the world.

Action Plan:

Today, take time to reflect on areas of your life that may need consecration. Are there any habits, attitudes, or relationships that are hindering your walk with God? Surrender them to Him in prayer, asking for His grace to transform you from the inside out.

Heavenly Father, we come before You with humble hearts, acknowledging our need for Your grace and guidance. Help us to offer ourselves as living sacrifices, holy and pleasing to You. Lead us on the path of consecration, that we may walk in obedience and surrender to Your will. In Jesus' name, Amen.

DAY 277

Trusting in God's Sovereignty

"For I know the plans I have for you," declares the Lord, "plans to prosper you and not to harm you, plans to give you hope and a future." - Jeremiah 29:11 (NIV)

Trusting in God's sovereignty is to acknowledge His absolute authority and control over all things. It's understanding that even in the midst of uncertainty, God's plans for us are good, purposeful, and filled with hope. In a world marked by chaos and unpredictability, anchoring our faith in God's sovereignty brings peace to our souls and clarity to our minds.

When we trust in God's sovereignty, we release the burden of trying to control every aspect of our lives. This trust allows us to navigate life's storms with confidence, knowing that God is always with us, guiding us through every trial and triumph.

Action Plan:

Today, take a moment to reflect on areas of your life where you struggle to trust in God's sovereignty. Surrender those areas to Him in prayer, asking for His peace and assurance. Seek out Scripture passages that speak to God's sovereignty and meditate on them daily.

Heavenly Father, thank You for Your sovereignty and Your perfect plans for our lives. Help us to trust in Your wisdom and timing, even when we cannot see the way forward. May we surrender our will to Yours and walk confidently in Your promises. In Jesus' name, Amen.

DAY 278

The Power of God's Spirit

"The Spirit of God has made me, and the breath of the Almighty gives me life." - Job 33:4 (NIV)

The Power of God's Spirit is not merely a theological concept but a living reality that can transform every aspect of our lives. Just as the Spirit breathed life into creation, He continues to breathe life into us today, infusing us with divine energy, purpose, and direction. As men, we are called to tap into this incredible power, allowing it to guide us, empower us, and shape us into the men God created us to be.

The Spirit of God empowers us to overcome our weaknesses, conquer our fears, and step boldly into the plans and purposes that God has ordained for us. When we yield to His Spirit, He equips us with everything we need to live a life of courage, integrity, and impact.

Action Plan:

Today, take a moment to reflect on areas in your life where you need the power of God's Spirit. Write them down and lift them up to God in prayer, inviting His Spirit to work in and through you. Throughout your day, be intentional about listening to His voice and following His leading, even in the small things.

Heavenly Father, thank You for the gift of Your Spirit, who gives us life and power. Help us to be sensitive to Your Spirit's leading in our lives, guiding us into all truth and empowering us to live according to Your will. In Jesus' name, Amen.

DAY 279

Living with Conviction

"Be on your guard; stand firm in the faith; be courageous; be strong." - 1 Corinthians 16:13 (NIV)

Living with conviction is about embracing our beliefs and values with unwavering courage and strength, even in the face of opposition or adversity. In a world that often challenges and contradicts what we hold dear, living with conviction requires boldness, perseverance, and integrity.

When we live with conviction, we become beacons of light in the darkness, shining God's truth and love wherever we go. But living with conviction isn't just about what we believe; it's also about how we live out those beliefs in our daily lives, in our relationships, and in our communities.

Action Plan:

Today, take some time to reflect on your core beliefs and values. Write them down and meditate on how they influence your thoughts, words, and actions. Identify areas where you may be compromising your convictions or where you could be more intentional about living them out.

Gracious Father, thank You for the gift of faith and the convictions You have placed in our hearts. Help us to live with integrity and authenticity, being true to who You have called us to be. May our lives be a testimony to Your goodness and grace, drawing others closer to You. In Jesus' name, Amen.

DAY 280

Embracing God's Truth

"Jesus said to the Jews who had believed him, 'If you abide in my word, you are truly my disciples, and you will know the truth, and the truth will set you free.'" - John 8:31-32 (ESV)

His truth isn't just a set of principles or doctrines; it's a transformative force that penetrates the depths of our souls, revealing who we truly are and setting us free from the chains of falsehood and deception.

Embracing God's truth means anchoring our lives on the unshakable foundation of His Word. His truth is not always easy to accept, for it often challenges our preconceived notions and comforts, but it leads us to a life of authenticity, purpose, and freedom.

Action Plan:

Today, commit to immersing yourself in God's Word. Set aside time each day for reading and studying Scripture, allowing its truth to penetrate your heart and mind. As you encounter God's truth, reflect on how it applies to your life and circumstances. Journal your insights and revelations, and seek to live them out in practical ways.

Gracious God, thank You for the gift of Your truth, which sets us free from the bondage of lies and deception. Open our hearts and minds to receive Your truth, even when it challenges us. Empower us to walk in authenticity and freedom, reflecting Your love and grace to the world around us. In Jesus' name, Amen.

DAY 281

The Importance of Faithfulness

"Let love and faithfulness never leave you; bind them around your neck, write them on the tablet of your heart." - Proverbs 3:3 (NIV)

Faithfulness is a cornerstone of character, a virtue that defines the essence of who we are as men of God. It's the unwavering commitment to our beliefs, values, and relationships, even when faced with challenges or temptations. In a world that often prioritizes instant gratification and self-interest, faithfulness stands as a beacon of integrity and honor.

It's about staying true to His Word, trusting in His promises, and remaining steadfast in our devotion to Him. When we are faithful to God, we experience His faithfulness in return, as He showers us with His love, grace, and blessings.

Action Plan:

Today, take a moment to reflect on the areas of your life where faithfulness is needed. Is it in your relationships, your work, your spiritual journey, or all of the above? Surround yourself with accountability partners who can support you in your journey towards faithfulness, and be willing to hold others accountable as well.

Heavenly Father, we thank You for Your faithfulness that never wavers, even when we falter. Strengthen us to remain steadfast in our commitments, knowing that You are always faithful to fulfill Your promises. In Jesus' name, Amen.

DAY 282

Trusting God's Timing

"Yet those who wait for the Lord will gain new strength; they will mount up with wings like eagles, they will run and not get tired, they will walk and not become weary." - Isaiah 40:31 (NASB)

Trusting God's timing is an exercise in faith and patience. It's a recognition that His plans are far greater than our own, and His timing is always perfect. As men navigating the complexities of life, we often find ourselves striving for control and instant results.

God's timing is purposeful and intentional. He knows the desires of our hearts and the paths He has laid out for us. Trusting in His timing requires us to let go of our own agendas and surrender to His wisdom and guidance.

Action Plan:

Begin by reflecting on areas of your life where you may be struggling with impatience or doubt. Write down any desires or goals you're holding onto tightly and surrender them to God. Surround yourself with supportive community who can encourage you in faith and remind you of God's faithfulness in His timing.

Heavenly Father, teach us to trust in Your perfect timing. Help us to surrender our desires and plans to You, knowing that Your ways are higher than ours. Strengthen us with Your presence and fill us with hope as we trust in Your sovereign will. In Jesus' name, Amen.

DAY 283

The Role of Spiritual Strength

"Finally, be strong in the Lord and in his mighty power." -
Ephesians 6:10 (NIV)

In the hustle and bustle of modern life, the concept of strength often conjures images of physical prowess or mental fortitude. This strength isn't measured by the size of our muscles or the sharpness of our minds, but by the depth of our connection with the Divine.

Spiritual strength empowers us to weather life's storms with resilience and grace. It's the inner fortitude that sustains us when external circumstances threaten to overwhelm us. And it's the courage to stand firm in our convictions, even when faced with opposition or adversity.

Action Plan:

Today, take a moment to assess your spiritual strength. Reflect on areas of your life where you feel spiritually depleted or disconnected from God. Commit to nurturing your spiritual well-being through daily practices such as prayer, meditation, and studying Scripture. Surround yourself with a community of fellow believers who can encourage and support you on your journey.

Heavenly Father, we thank You for the gift of spiritual strength.
Help us to be strong in You and in Your mighty power. Grant us
the wisdom to recognize our need for You in every area of our lives
and the courage to surrender to Your will. In Jesus' name, Amen.

DAY 284

The Power of God's Love

"For I am convinced that neither death nor life, neither angels nor demons, neither the present nor the future, nor any powers, neither height nor depth, nor anything else in all creation, will be able to separate us from the love of God that is in Christ Jesus our Lord."
- Romans 8:38-39 (NIV)

In the depths of our struggles and the heights of our joys, there exists a love that surpasses all understanding - the love of God. This love is not fleeting or conditional; it is eternal and unconditional. It is a love that knows no bounds, reaching us in every circumstance and embracing us in every season of life.

As men, we are called to embrace the power of God's love in our lives. It means extending that same love to others, demonstrating compassion, forgiveness, and kindness in our relationships. It means living with confidence and assurance, knowing that nothing can separate us from the love of our Heavenly Father.

Action Plan:

Today, take a moment to reflect on the depth of God's love for you. Meditate on Romans 8:38-39 and allow its truth to penetrate your heart. Make a conscious effort to love yourself as God loves you - unconditionally and without reservation.

Heavenly Father, thank You for the incomprehensible gift of Your love. Fill us with Your love, that we may overflow with compassion and grace toward others. May Your love be our guiding light and our source of strength in all things. In Jesus' name, Amen.

DAY 285

Embracing God's Wisdom

"For the Lord gives wisdom; from his mouth come knowledge and understanding." - Proverbs 2:6 (NIV)

Embracing God's wisdom means acknowledging our own limitations and humbly submitting to His infinite understanding. It's a journey of growth and transformation, where we allow His Word to illuminate our paths and guide our decisions.

God's wisdom transcends human understanding. It surpasses worldly knowledge and offers us divine insights into every aspect of life - from relationships and work to personal growth and spiritual well-being.

Action Plan:

Begin by prioritizing time each day to engage with God's Word. Dedicate moments for reflection and meditation on passages that speak to wisdom and understanding. As you encounter challenges or decisions, pause and pray for God's guidance, trusting in His promise to provide wisdom generously to those who ask.

Heavenly Father, we thank You for the gift of Your wisdom, which surpasses all understanding. Help us to seek Your guidance in all areas of our lives, trusting in Your perfect knowledge and understanding. May Your wisdom be our guiding light, illuminating our path and shaping our hearts according to Your will. In Jesus' name, Amen.

DAY 286

The Importance of Fasting

"Yet even now," declares the Lord, "return to me with all your heart, with fasting, with weeping, and with mourning." - Joel 2:12 (ESV)

Fasting serves as a powerful reminder of our dependence on God and redirects our focus from worldly desires to heavenly pursuits. It's a time of self-denial that opens our hearts to hear God's voice more clearly and align our will with His.

The importance of fasting lies in its ability to deepen our intimacy with God, purify our motives, and strengthen our spiritual resolve. By denying ourselves physically, we make space for God to work in us spiritually. Fasting is a catalyst for spiritual breakthroughs, bringing clarity, wisdom, and renewed passion for God's kingdom.

Action Plan:

Start by prayerfully considering a specific area in your life where you need breakthrough or guidance. Dedicate a day or a mealtime for fasting, surrendering that area to God. Engage in spiritual practices such as reading Scripture, worship, and meditation to enrich your fasting experience.

Gracious God, we humbly come before You with hearts open to Your leading. Teach us the importance of fasting as a means of drawing closer to You. Grant us strength and perseverance as we seek Your face through fasting, knowing that You are faithful to meet us in our hunger and thirst for righteousness. In Jesus' name, Amen.

DAY 287

Trusting in God

"Trust in the Lord with all your heart, and do not lean on your own understanding. In all your ways acknowledge him, and he will make straight your paths." - Proverbs 3:5-6 (ESV)

Trusting in God is not just a passive belief, but an active surrender of our will and desires to His perfect plan. It's a journey of faith where we relinquish control and place our confidence in His wisdom, goodness, and faithfulness.

When we trust in God, we acknowledge that His ways are higher than our ways, and His thoughts are higher than our thoughts. Trusting in God requires humility, vulnerability, and a willingness to let go of our own agendas in favor of His divine purpose for our lives.

Action Plan:

Today, take a moment to examine areas in your life where you may be relying on your own understanding rather than trusting in God. Surrender those areas to Him in prayer, asking for His guidance and wisdom. Practice trust by intentionally stepping out in faith, even when circumstances seem daunting or uncertain.

Heavenly Father, we thank You for Your faithfulness and steadfast love. Help us to trust in You with all our hearts, leaning not on our own understanding but acknowledging You in all our ways. May our trust in You deepen each day, as we experience Your goodness and faithfulness in our lives. In Jesus' name, Amen.

DAY 288

The Power of God's Mercy

"Let us then approach God's throne of grace with confidence, so that we may receive mercy and find grace to help us in our time of need." - Hebrews 4:16 (NIV)

The power of God's mercy is a profound expression of His unconditional love and compassion towards us, His beloved children. Mercy is not merely an abstract concept; it's a tangible manifestation of God's character and His desire to reconcile us to Himself. In our brokenness and sinfulness, God extends His mercy as a lifeline, offering forgiveness, redemption, and restoration.

It humbles us, reminding us of our own shortcomings and the incomprehensible grace extended to us through Christ's sacrifice. It fills us with gratitude, knowing that we don't deserve such mercy, yet it is freely given to us out of God's boundless love.

Action Plan:

Today, take a moment to reflect on the ways God has shown His mercy in your life. Ask God to help you release any bitterness, resentment, or self-condemnation, and to fill your heart with His mercy and compassion.

Heavenly Father, we thank You for Your abundant mercy that knows no bounds. Help us to grasp the depth of Your love and forgiveness, and to extend that same mercy to others. May Your mercy flow through us, transforming lives and bringing glory to Your name. In Jesus' name, Amen.

DAY 289

Living with Integrity

"The integrity of the upright guides them, but the unfaithful are destroyed by their duplicity." - Proverbs 11:3 (NIV)

Living with integrity is about aligning our actions with our values, principles, and beliefs. It's about being true to ourselves and to God, even when no one is watching. Integrity is the foundation of character, the bedrock upon which trust is built, and the mark of a life well-lived.

We strive to do what is right, even when it's difficult or unpopular. Our words and actions are consistent, reflecting the inner integrity of our hearts. Integrity enables us to stand firm in the face of temptation, to resist compromise, and to pursue excellence in all that we do.

Action Plan:

Today, take time to reflect on your own values and principles. What matters most to you? What kind of person do you want to be? Write down your core values and commit to living them out each day. Identify areas in your life where you may be compromising your integrity, whether it's in your relationships, work, or personal habits.

Heavenly Father, we thank You for the gift of integrity and the example of Christ, who lived a life of perfect integrity. Give us the strength to resist compromise and to stand firm in our values, even when faced with challenges or temptations. In Jesus' name, Amen.

DAY 290

Embracing God's Peace

"The Lord gives strength to his people; the Lord blesses his people with peace." - Psalm 29:11 (NIV)

Embracing God's peace is not merely the absence of turmoil or conflict in our lives; it is a profound state of tranquility and assurance that transcends our circumstances. This peace is not dependent on external factors but flows from our intimate relationship with God, who is the source of all peace.

In a world filled with stress, anxiety, and busyness, embracing God's peace becomes a radical act of faith. As men, we may be tempted to rely on our own strength and abilities to navigate life's challenges, but true peace is found in surrendering to God's will and resting in His promises.

Action Plan:

Today, take a moment to assess the areas of your life where you lack peace. Are there worries or fears that are weighing heavy on your heart? Write them down and offer them up to God in prayer, asking Him to replace your anxiety with His peace.

Heavenly Father, we thank You for the peace that surpasses all understanding, which You freely offer to us. Help us to release our worries and fears into Your loving hands, trusting in Your sovereignty and goodness. May Your peace guard our hearts and minds, enabling us to walk in confidence and faith each day. In Jesus' name, Amen.

DAY 291

The Importance of Prayer

"Rejoice always, pray continually, give thanks in all circumstances; for this is God's will for you in Christ Jesus." - 1 Thessalonians 5:16-18 (NIV)

Prayer is not just a religious duty; it's a divine invitation into a relationship with our Creator. It's the channel through which we communicate with God, pouring out our hearts, expressing our gratitude, seeking His guidance, and finding solace in His presence.

It's through prayer that we find healing for our wounds, comfort for our sorrows, and wisdom for our decisions. And it's through prayer that we experience the transformative power of God's love, shaping us into men of faith, courage, and compassion.

Action Plan:

Today, commit to cultivating a lifestyle of prayer. Set aside dedicated time each day to commune with God, whether it's in the morning before the day begins, during your lunch break, or in the quiet moments before bed. Create a sacred space where you can pray without distractions, allowing yourself to fully focus on God's presence.

Gracious Father, we thank You for the gift of prayer, which allows us to draw near to You and experience Your presence in our lives. May our prayers be a fragrant offering to You, pleasing and acceptable in Your sight. And may we always find refuge and strength in Your presence. In Jesus' name, Amen.

DAY 292

Trusting God's Guidance

"The LORD will guide you always; he will satisfy your needs in a sun-scorched land and will strengthen your frame. You will be like a well-watered garden, like a spring whose waters never fail." - Isaiah 58:11 (NIV)

In a world filled with uncertainty and confusion, God offers us the assurance that He will lead us on the path of righteousness and provide for our every need. His guidance is like a steady beacon of light in the darkness, illuminating the way forward and giving us hope and direction.

When we trust in God's guidance, we are invited into a deeper relationship with Him. It requires us to let go of our own plans and desires, and to instead align our hearts with His will. It's about seeking His wisdom through prayer, meditation on His Word, and listening for His still, small voice in the midst of life's chaos.

Action Plan:

Today, commit to entrusting every aspect of your life to God's guidance. Start by spending time in prayer, asking Him to reveal His will for you and to give you the courage to follow where He leads. Then, seek guidance through Scripture, meditating on passages that speak to your current circumstances or decisions.

Heavenly Father, we thank You for Your promise to guide us always. May we be like well-watered gardens, flourishing in Your presence and bearing fruit for Your kingdom. In Jesus' name, Amen.

DAY 293

The Role of Spiritual Awareness

"Be still, and know that I am God; I will be exalted among the nations, I will be exalted in the earth." - Psalm 46:10 (NIV)

Spiritual awareness is the key that unlocks the door to a deeper connection with God and a more meaningful life. It's about tuning our hearts and minds to the whispers of the Holy Spirit, discerning His guidance amidst the noise of the world.

We recognize His handiwork in the beauty of creation, His voice in the stillness of prayer, and His guidance in the moments of decision-making. Spiritual awareness enables us to see beyond the surface level of our existence and perceive the deeper truths and purposes that God has for us.

Action Plan:

Today, set aside time for quiet reflection and prayer. Find a peaceful place where you can be alone with God, free from distractions. Begin by simply being still, allowing your mind to settle and your heart to open to God's presence. Throughout your day, practice mindfulness, paying attention to the small moments of grace and guidance that God sends your way.

Gracious God, thank You for the gift of spiritual awareness. Open our eyes and our hearts to Your presence in our lives, that we may walk in step with Your Spirit and live according to Your will. May our spiritual awareness deepen our relationship with You and empower us to live as faithful disciples. In Jesus' name, Amen.

DAY 294

The Power of God's Word

"Your word is a lamp for my feet, a light on my path." - Psalm 119:105 (NIV)

Scripture is not merely a collection of words on a page; it is living and active, penetrating to the deepest parts of our souls. God speaks to us through His Word, revealing His character, His will, and His promises. It serves as a light in the darkness, illuminating the path before us and showing us the way to walk in righteousness.

When we immerse ourselves in God's Word, we are nourished and strengthened spiritually. The Word of God is a powerful weapon against the enemy's lies and temptations, enabling us to stand firm in the face of adversity.

Action Plan:

Today, commit to prioritizing time in God's Word. Set aside a specific time each day for Bible reading and meditation, even if it's just a few minutes. Choose a passage of Scripture to focus on and ask God to speak to you through His Word.

Heavenly Father, thank You for the gift of Your Word, which is a lamp to our feet and a light to our path. Help us to approach Scripture with reverence and humility, eager to hear Your voice and be transformed by Your truth. May Your Word dwell richly in us, guiding us in righteousness and empowering us to live lives that bring glory to Your name. In Jesus' name, Amen.

DAY 295

Embracing God's Spirit

"But the Advocate, the Holy Spirit, whom the Father will send in my name, will teach you all things and will remind you of everything I have said to you." - John 14:26 (NIV)

Embracing God's Spirit is an invitation to experience the transformative power of the Holy Spirit in our lives. As men seeking to live according to God's will, we are not left to navigate this journey alone. The Holy Spirit, our Advocate and Guide, dwells within us, empowering us to live with purpose, wisdom, and courage.

He convicts us of sin and empowers us to live victoriously over temptation. He comforts us in times of sorrow and strengthens us in times of weakness. The Holy Spirit is not a distant force but a personal presence, dwelling within us and working through us to accomplish God's purposes on earth.

Action Plan:

Today, begin by acknowledging the presence of the Holy Spirit in your life. Take time to quiet your heart and listen for His voice. Commit to studying God's Word regularly, inviting the Holy Spirit to illuminate its truths and apply them to your life.

Gracious God, thank You for the precious gift of Your Holy Spirit. Teach us to embrace His presence in our lives, that we may walk in step with Your will and purpose. May we be vessels of Your love and grace, shining brightly in a world that desperately needs Your light. In Jesus' name, Amen.

DAY 296

The Importance of Giving

"Each of you should give what you have decided in your heart to give, not reluctantly or under compulsion, for God loves a cheerful giver." - 2 Corinthians 9:7 (NIV)

From the beginning of creation, we see God's generosity displayed in His provision for His people. As men of faith, we are called to reflect this same spirit of generosity in our own lives. Giving is not merely an obligation or a duty, but a joyful act of worship and obedience.

When we give, whether it's our time, talents, or resources, we participate in God's work of blessing others and advancing His kingdom. Giving also cultivates a spirit of humility and selflessness within us, as we learn to prioritize the needs of others above our own desires.

Action Plan:

Today, take some time to prayerfully consider how you can be more intentional about giving in your life. Reflect on your financial resources, your skills and abilities, and your available time, and ask God to show you how you can use them to bless others.

Heavenly Father, thank You for the countless blessings You have bestowed upon us. Teach us to be generous and cheerful givers, reflecting Your love and generosity in all that we do. May our giving be a source of joy and worship to You, bringing glory to Your name. In Jesus' name, Amen.

DAY 297

Holiness unto God

"As obedient children, do not conform to the evil desires you had when you lived in ignorance. But just as he who called you is holy, so be holy in all you do; for it is written: 'Be holy, because I am holy.'" - 1 Peter 1:14-16 (NIV)

Holiness unto God is not merely a call to religious rituals or outward appearances; it's a profound invitation to live a life that reflects the character and nature of our Creator. God, who is holy, calls us to embrace holiness in every aspect of our lives, transforming us from the inside out.

Living a life of holiness means making intentional choices to honor God in all we do. As men of God, we are called to be set apart from the ways of the world, to be a light in the darkness, and to reflect the love and purity of Christ to those around us.

Action Plan:

Today, take inventory of your life and identify areas where you may be compromising your commitment to holiness. This could include habits, attitudes, or relationships that are not in line with God's standards. Confess these areas to God and ask for His forgiveness and strength to overcome them.

Holy God, we acknowledge that You alone are worthy of our devotion and praise. Forgive us for the times when we have fallen short of Your standards of holiness. May our thoughts, words, and actions be a reflection of Your holiness, drawing others closer to You. In Jesus' name, Amen.

DAY 298

The Power of Sacrifice

"For whoever wants to save their life will lose it, but whoever loses their life for me will find it." - Matthew 16:25 (NIV)

The power of sacrifice is woven into the very fabric of our faith journey. It's a concept that challenges our natural inclinations and invites us to emulate the ultimate act of sacrificial love demonstrated by Jesus Christ on the cross. Sacrifice is not merely about giving up something tangible; it's about surrendering our will, desires, and ambitions to God's higher purpose.

Sacrifice calls us to step outside of our comfort zones, to embrace discomfort and uncertainty, knowing that God honors and rewards those who are willing to give of themselves wholeheartedly.

Action Plan:

Today, take time to reflect on areas of your life where God may be calling you to sacrificial action. It could be in your relationships, your career, your finances, or your time. Ask God to reveal any areas where you may be holding back or clinging too tightly to your own desires.

Gracious Lord, thank You for the example of sacrificial love set forth by Your Son, Jesus Christ. Give us the strength and courage to follow His example, to lay down our lives for the sake of others and for Your kingdom. May our acts of sacrifice bring glory to Your name and draw others closer to You. In Jesus' name, Amen.

DAY 299

Living with Joy

"May the God of hope fill you with all joy and peace as you trust in him, so that you may overflow with hope by the power of the Holy Spirit." - Romans 15:13 (NIV)

Living with joy is not just a fleeting emotion dependent on circumstances; it's a deep-rooted sense of contentment and delight that comes from knowing and trusting in God. It's a choice we make every day to focus on the blessings in our lives rather than the challenges, to find joy in the midst of trials, and to cultivate an attitude of gratitude regardless of our circumstances.

True joy is found in our relationship with God, in knowing that we are deeply loved and cherished by Him. It's a fruit of the Spirit that flourishes when we surrender our worries and fears to Him, trusting in His goodness and faithfulness.

Action Plan:

Today, take a moment to reflect on the blessings in your life and give thanks to God for His goodness. Write down three things you are grateful for, no matter how big or small. Then, identify any areas where you are struggling to find joy and surrender them to God in prayer.

Gracious God, thank You for the gift of joy that You freely offer to us. Fill us with Your Spirit and overflow our hearts with joy and peace as we trust in You. May our lives be a testimony to Your goodness and faithfulness, spreading joy and hope to those around us. In Jesus' name, Amen.

DAY 300

Embracing God's Patience

"For the Lord is good; his steadfast love endures forever, and his faithfulness to all generations." - Psalm 100:5 (ESV)

In a world that often demands instant results and immediate gratification, God's patience stands as a beacon of hope and reassurance. His patience extends beyond our understanding of time, waiting patiently for us to turn to Him, to grow in faith, and to become the people He created us to be.

It reminds us that God's timing is perfect, even when it doesn't align with our own desires or expectations. His patience gives us the space to learn and grow, to make mistakes and to try again, knowing that His grace covers us every step of the way. And it invites us into a deeper relationship with Him, where we can rest in the assurance of His unfailing love and provision.

Action Plan:

Today, reflect on areas of your life where you struggle with impatience or where you feel discouraged by the pace of your progress. Take these concerns to God in prayer, asking Him to help you trust in His timing and to surrender your plans and desires to His will.

Gracious God, we thank You for Your boundless patience and steadfast love towards us. Give us the strength to persevere through challenges with grace and humility, knowing that Your faithfulness endures forever. In Jesus' name, Amen.

DAY 301

The Importance of Assembly

"Let us not neglect meeting together, as some have made a habit, but let us encourage one another, and all the more as you see the Day approaching." - Hebrews 10:25 (NIV)

In gathering with fellow believers, we find strength, encouragement, and support for our spiritual journey. It's a time to worship God together, to study His Word, and to lift each other up in prayer. As men, we are not meant to walk this path alone; we are designed for fellowship, accountability, and mutual edification.

We are reminded that we are part of something much larger than ourselves, a body of believers united in purpose and love. Through assembly, we are challenged to grow in our relationship with God and to live out our faith authentically in the world.

Action Plan:

Today, commit to prioritizing regular attendance at your local church or a small group of believers. Additionally, consider ways you can extend the spirit of assembly beyond the church walls by reaching out to other men in your community for fellowship and accountability.

Gracious God, thank You for the gift of assembly, for the opportunity to come together as brothers in Christ to worship You and encourage one another. May our gatherings be filled with Your presence and Your love, drawing us closer to You and to each other. In Jesus' name, Amen.

DAY 302

Divine Healing

"Heal me, Lord, and I will be healed; save me and I will be saved, for you are the one I praise." - Jeremiah 17:14 (NIV)

Throughout Scripture, we witness miraculous healings performed by Jesus Christ, demonstrating His authority over sickness and disease. Today, as men seeking spiritual nourishment, we are reminded that divine healing is not confined to the pages of ancient texts; it is a present reality, available to us through faith and prayer.

Whether we are battling physical ailments, emotional wounds, or spiritual struggles, God's healing touch has the power to bring about transformation and restoration. It is a reminder that no matter how broken or hopeless we may feel, God is able to bring beauty from ashes and turn our mourning into dancing.

Action Plan:

Today, begin by identifying areas in your life where you are in need of healing. It could be physical sickness, emotional pain, spiritual doubt, or any other form of brokenness. Spend time in prayer, surrendering these areas to God and asking Him to bring healing and restoration.

Gracious Father, we come before You with humble hearts, acknowledging our need for Your healing touch. May Your healing touch bring glory to Your name and testify to Your unfailing love. In Jesus' name, Amen.

DAY 303

The Role of Fathers in Community

"As for me and my household, we will serve the Lord." - Joshua 24:15b (NIV)

As fathers, we are entrusted with the responsibility of not only nurturing and providing for our families but also of being pillars of strength, wisdom, and love in our communities. Just as Joshua declared his commitment to serve the Lord with his household, so too are we called to lead our families in faith and righteousness.

Fathers play a crucial role in shaping the moral fabric of society. Our words, actions, and examples have a profound impact on the lives of our children and those around us. When we prioritize our relationship with God and model integrity, kindness, and compassion, we leave a legacy that extends far beyond our own households, influencing the next generation and shaping the future of our communities.

Action Plan:

Today, reflect on the example you are setting for your family and community. Are you leading with humility, courage, and love? Take time to evaluate your priorities and make any necessary adjustments to align them with God's will.

Heavenly Father, thank You for the privilege and responsibility of fatherhood. Give us the strength and courage to stand firm in our convictions and to serve You faithfully in all that we do. In Jesus' name, Amen.

DAY 304

The Power of Unity in Family

"Behold, how good and pleasant it is when brothers dwell in unity!" - Psalm 133:1 (ESV)

When we come together in harmony and solidarity, we experience the richness of God's blessings and the strength that comes from mutual support and love. Unity doesn't mean uniformity; rather, it's the beautiful tapestry of diverse individuals joined together with a common purpose and shared values.

In the family, unity fosters a sense of belonging, security, and belongingness. It creates a safe space where each member feels valued, understood, and accepted.

Action Plan:

Today, reflect on the state of unity within your family and community. Seek out opportunities to strengthen your bonds with family members through intentional communication, acts of kindness, and quality time spent together. Additionally, look for ways to contribute to the unity of your community, whether it's through volunteering, participating in community events, or reaching out to neighbors in need.

Heavenly Father, we thank You for the gift of family and community. Help us to cultivate unity in our relationships, both within our homes and in the world around us. May Your Spirit guide us in building strong, loving bonds with one another, that we may reflect Your love and bring glory to Your name. In Jesus' name, Amen.

DAY 305

Loving The Family

"Behold, how good and pleasant it is when brothers dwell in unity!" - Psalm 133:1 (ESV)

Loving the family within the context of community is about recognizing the importance of connection and belonging, both within our own households and within the broader community of believers. It's about fostering a culture of unity, respect, and encouragement, where each member is valued and empowered to thrive.

Our homes become havens of love and acceptance, where each member feels safe to be themselves and to grow in their faith. And beyond our own families, we extend that love and care to those around us, reaching out to support and uplift others in their journey.

Action Plan:

Today, take intentional steps to nurture love and unity within your family and community. Start by spending quality time with your loved ones, engaging in meaningful conversations and activities that strengthen your bond.

Heavenly Father, thank You for the gift of family and community. Teach us to love one another deeply, just as You have loved us. May our homes be beacons of Your love and grace, and may our communities be transformed by the power of Your Spirit working through us. In Jesus' name, Amen.

DAY 306

The Importance of Commitment Family and Community

"Love one another with brotherly affection. Outdo one another in showing honor." - Romans 12:10 (ESV)

In a world where individualism often reigns supreme, committing to our families and communities demonstrates our willingness to prioritize the well-being and growth of others above ourselves. It's about cultivating a sense of belonging, unity, and support that withstands the tests of time and adversity.

Commitment in family means being present for each other through the highs and lows of life, showing up consistently, and investing time and effort into nurturing familial bonds. It's about actively listening, empathizing, and offering encouragement and support when needed.

Action Plan:

Today, reflect on the level of commitment you have towards your family and community. Consider areas where you can deepen your commitment and invest more intentionally in nurturing relationships.

Gracious God, thank You for the gift of family and community. Help us to understand the importance of commitment in nurturing strong, healthy relationships. May our commitment to our families and communities reflect Your heart of compassion and unity, bringing glory to Your name. In Jesus' name, Amen.

DAY 307

God's Guidance

"Trust in the Lord with all your heart and lean not on your own understanding; in all your ways submit to him, and he will make your paths straight." - Proverbs 3:5-6 (NIV)

God's guidance is like a beacon of light in the darkness, leading us along the path of righteousness and fulfillment. As men navigating the complexities of life, we often encounter crossroads where decisions must be made, challenges must be overcome, and directions must be chosen.

God's guidance is not always revealed in grand gestures or thunderous voices from the heavens. Instead, it often comes in whispers, nudges, and gentle tugs on our hearts. When we submit our ways to Him, He promises to direct our steps, aligning them with His divine purpose for our lives.

Action Plan:

Today, take time to quiet your heart and mind before God, seeking His guidance in prayer. Reflect on areas of your life where you're in need of direction, whether it's in your career, relationships, or personal growth.

Gracious Father, we thank You for the promise of Your guidance in our lives. Give us ears to hear Your voice and hearts willing to obey Your leading. May Your guidance be a light unto our feet, illuminating the way forward as we walk in faith and obedience. In Jesus' name, Amen.

DAY 308

The Power of the Holy Spirit

"When the Spirit of truth comes, he will guide you into all truth. He will not speak on his own but will tell you what he has heard. He will tell you about the future." - John 16:13 (NLT)

The power of the Holy Spirit is not just a theological concept; it's a dynamic reality that transforms lives. The Holy Spirit is the presence of God within us, empowering us, guiding us, and equipping us for the journey of faith. He is our comforter in times of distress, our counselor in times of confusion, and our source of strength in times of weakness.

Understanding the power of the Holy Spirit means recognizing His active role in our lives. He convicts us of sin, leading us to repentance and renewal. He illuminates the truth of God's Word, helping us to understand and apply it to our lives.

Action Plan:

Today, take time to cultivate a deeper relationship with the Holy Spirit. Begin by setting aside a few moments for prayer and meditation, inviting the Holy Spirit to speak to your heart and reveal His presence to you.

Holy Spirit, we thank You for Your presence in our lives and Your power at work within us. Open our hearts to receive Your guidance and Your wisdom, that we may walk in step with Your will. May Your power be evident in all that we do, bringing glory to Your name. In Jesus' name, Amen.

DAY 309

Living with Christ

*"For to me, to live is Christ and to die is gain." - Philippians 1:21
(NIV)*

When we choose to center our lives around Christ, we are choosing a life of profound meaning and fulfillment. It means surrendering our own desires and ambitions to His will, allowing His love and truth to permeate every aspect of our being.

Living with Christ means walking in His footsteps, emulating His character, and reflecting His love to the world. It means seeking His guidance in every decision, finding our strength in His presence, and finding our identity in Him alone. It's a life marked by faith, obedience, and unwavering trust in His promises.

Action Plan:

Today, commit to living with Christ as your center. Start by setting aside time each day for prayer and meditation on God's Word, allowing His truth to shape your thoughts and actions. Identify areas in your life where you have been living for yourself rather than for Christ, and ask Him to help you surrender those areas to Him.

Gracious Father, we thank You for the gift of life and for the privilege of living it with You at the center. May our lives be a reflection of Your love and grace, drawing others into relationship with You. Guide us, Lord, in every step we take, that we may walk closely with You all the days of our lives. In Jesus' name, Amen.

DAY 310

Embracing God's Truth

*"Sanctify them by the truth; your word is truth." - John 17:17
(NIV)*

Embracing God's truth is not just about acknowledging facts or beliefs; it's about allowing the profound wisdom and guidance found in His Word to permeate every aspect of our lives. God's truth is a beacon of light in a world filled with darkness and confusion. It offers clarity amidst chaos, hope amidst despair, and direction amidst uncertainty.

God's truth also has the power to transform us from the inside out. As we meditate on His Word and allow it to dwell richly within us, we are renewed in mind and spirit. Lies and falsehoods that once held us captive are replaced by the liberating truth of who we are in Christ.

Action Plan:

Today, commit to immersing yourself in God's truth. Set aside time each day to read and study Scripture, allowing God to speak to you through His Word. Choose a specific passage or theme to focus on for the week, and journal about how it applies to your life.

Heavenly Father, Your Word is a lamp unto our feet and a light unto our path. Sanctify us by Your truth, Lord, and empower us to walk in obedience to Your Word. Help us to embrace Your truth wholeheartedly, that we may experience the abundant life You have promised us. In Jesus' name, Amen.

DAY 311

The Importance of Faithfulness

"His master said to him, 'Well done, good and faithful servant. You have been faithful over a little; I will set you over much. Enter into the joy of your master.'" - Matthew 25:21 (ESV)

As men seeking to live lives of purpose and significance, faithfulness is paramount. It's about honoring our commitments, fulfilling our responsibilities, and staying true to our values, even in the face of adversity.

When we embrace the importance of faithfulness, we reflect the character of God Himself, who is steadfast and unwavering in His love and promises towards us. Our faithfulness in the small things prepares us for greater opportunities and blessings in the future.

Action Plan:

Today, take inventory of your commitments and responsibilities. Are there areas where you've been neglecting to be faithful? Are there relationships or tasks where you can demonstrate greater reliability and dedication? Ask God to reveal any areas of your life where you need to grow in faithfulness, and commit to making changes accordingly.

Gracious God, we thank You for Your faithfulness towards us, even when we fall short. Teach us to walk in faithfulness, Lord, both in our relationship with You and with others. May our lives be a testimony to Your faithfulness, bringing glory to Your name. In Jesus' name, Amen.

DAY 312

Victory Over Fear

"When I am afraid, I put my trust in you." - Psalm 56:3 (NIV)

Fear is a powerful force that can grip our hearts and paralyze us, preventing us from living the full and abundant life that God intends for us. It can manifest in various forms – fear of failure, fear of rejection, fear of the unknown – but regardless of its source, fear is ultimately a tool of the enemy to hinder our faith and rob us of joy.

Victory over fear is not about denying its existence or pretending to be fearless; rather, it's about choosing to trust in God's promises and His power to overcome every obstacle. It's about shifting our focus from our circumstances to the One who is greater than any challenge we may face. When we place our trust in God, fear loses its grip on us, and we are set free to live boldly and courageously.

Action Plan:

Today, identify one specific fear that has been holding you back or causing you anxiety. Write it down and take it to God in prayer, surrendering it to Him and asking for His strength to overcome it. Then, meditate on Psalm 56:3 and other Scriptures that remind you of God's faithfulness and protection.

Heavenly Father, we confess our fears and anxieties to You, knowing that You are our refuge and strength. Give us the courage to trust in Your promises and to face our fears with confidence, knowing that You are with us every step of the way. and minds in Christ Jesus. In His name, we pray, Amen.

DAY 313

The Role of the Husband

"However, let each one of you love his wife as himself, and let the wife see that she respects her husband." - Ephesians 5:33 (ESV)

The role of the husband is a sacred calling, one that is deeply rooted in love, sacrificial leadership, and servant-heartedness. As husbands, we are called to emulate the love that Christ has for His church, laying down our lives for our wives and families.

Being a husband is not merely about providing for material needs or exerting authority, but about cultivating a relationship of mutual respect, trust, and support with our wives. It's about being a source of strength and encouragement, a faithful partner in both joys and trials, and a humble servant-leader who leads with integrity and humility.

Action Plan:

Today, take time to reflect on your role as a husband. Consider areas where you can grow in your love and leadership within your marriage. Ask your wife for her perspective on how you can better fulfill your role as her husband.

Heavenly Father, thank You for the gift of marriage and for entrusting us with the role of husband. Help us to love our wives as You have loved us, with sacrificial, selfless love. May our marriages be a reflection of Your love and faithfulness, bringing glory to Your name. In Jesus' name, Amen.

DAY 314

The Power Amen

"Truly I tell you, whatever you bind on earth will be bound in heaven, and whatever you loose on earth will be loosed in heaven. Again, truly I tell you, if two of you on earth agree about anything they ask for, it will be done for them by my Father in heaven. For where two or three gather in my name, there am I with them." - Matthew 18:18-20 (NIV)

The power of "Amen" is not just a mere conclusion to a prayer; it's a declaration of faith and agreement with God's promises. When we say "Amen," we affirm our trust in God's sovereignty and His ability to answer our prayers according to His will.

In the biblical context, "Amen" means "so be it" or "let it be done." It signifies our submission to God's plans and purposes, acknowledging His wisdom and authority over our lives. When we pray in agreement with others, our collective "Amens" amplify the potency of our petitions, as Jesus Himself promised to be present where two or three are gathered in His name.

Action Plan:

Today, intentionally incorporate the power of "Amen" into your prayer life. As you pray, let your "Amen" be heartfelt and unwavering, trusting in God's faithfulness to answer according to His perfect timing and wisdom.

Heavenly Father, we thank You for the privilege of prayer and the power of "Amen." May our "Amens" be declarations of unwavering belief in Your ability to work all things for our good. Let Your will be done on earth as it is in heaven. In Jesus' name, Amen.

DAY 315

Embracing Peace

"Peace I leave with you; my peace I give you. I do not give to you as the world gives. Do not let your hearts be troubled and do not be afraid." - John 14:27 (NIV)

In a world filled with chaos, stress, and uncertainty, peace becomes a precious gift from God, a refuge for our weary souls. It's a peace that surpasses understanding, rooted in our trust and reliance on God's promises and presence.

When we embrace peace, we surrender our anxieties and worries to God, trusting in His sovereignty and goodness. We allow His peace to guard our hearts and minds, keeping us grounded in His truth and free from fear.

Action Plan:

Today, take a moment to identify areas in your life where you are struggling to find peace. It could be in your relationships, your work, or even within yourself. Write down these concerns and lift them up to God in prayer, asking Him to replace your fears and anxieties with His peace.

Gracious God, thank You for the gift of Your peace that surpasses all understanding. In the midst of life's challenges and uncertainties, help us to find our rest in You. May Your peace reign in our hearts and overflow into the lives of those around us. In Jesus' name, Amen.

DAY 316

The Importance of Sanctification

"For this is the will of God, your sanctification: that you abstain from sexual immorality; that each one of you know how to control his own body in holiness and honor." - 1 Thessalonians 4:3-4 (ESV)

The importance of sanctification is rooted in God's desire for His children to be set apart for His purposes and to reflect His holiness in every aspect of their lives. Sanctification is not just a one-time event but a lifelong process of becoming more like Christ, growing in spiritual maturity, and purifying our hearts and minds from the influences of sin.

As men seeking to live lives that honor God, sanctification calls us to intentionally pursue righteousness and resist the temptations of the world. It requires discipline, self-control, and a commitment to surrendering our will to God's will.

Action Plan:

Today, take time to examine your life in light of God's call to sanctification. Identify areas where you may be compromising with the values of the world or struggling with habitual sin. Confess these areas to God and ask for His strength to help you overcome them.

Gracious Father, thank You for calling us to a life of sanctification and holiness. May our lives be a reflection of Your holiness, bringing glory to Your name. In Jesus' name, Amen.

DAY 317

God's Divine Touch

"And all the crowd sought to touch him, for power came out from him and healed them all." - Luke 6:19 (ESV)

The Bible is replete with stories of Jesus touching the lives of those who sought Him, offering a glimpse into the profound impact of His divine intervention. When we experience God's touch, it revitalizes our spirit, infuses us with hope, and assures us of His constant presence and unwavering love.

God's divine touch is not limited to the pages of Scripture; it is available to us today. In our busy and often challenging lives, we may find ourselves yearning for a tangible sign of His presence. Whether through a comforting word, a moment of peace, or a miraculous healing, God reaches out to us, inviting us to draw near and experience His transformative power.

Action Plan:

Today, make it a priority to seek God's divine touch in your life. Set aside a specific time for prayer and reflection, inviting God to reveal His presence in a tangible way. Be open and honest with Him about your struggles, needs, and desires.

Gracious God, we come before You with open hearts, longing for Your divine touch. Help us to recognize and cherish the moments when You touch our hearts, and empower us to extend that same touch to those around us. May Your divine presence be our source of strength and hope each day. In Jesus' name, Amen.

DAY 318

The Power of God's Mercy

"Because of the Lord's great love we are not consumed, for his compassions never fail. They are new every morning; great is your faithfulness." - Lamentations 3:22-23 (NIV)

The power of God's mercy is an unfathomable gift that renews our souls and gives us hope each day. His mercy is a reflection of His infinite love and compassion towards us, despite our imperfections and failures.

Understanding the power of God's mercy changes how we view ourselves and others. It reminds us that no mistake is too great for God's forgiveness and that His love is steadfast and unwavering. This divine mercy is what sustains us in our weakest moments and lifts us when we feel unworthy.

Action Plan:

Today, take a moment to meditate on Lamentations 3:22-23. Reflect on how God's mercy has impacted your life and thank Him for His endless compassion. Write down any burdens, mistakes, or regrets you have been carrying and bring them to God in prayer, asking for His mercy and forgiveness.

Merciful Father, thank You for Your unfailing compassion and the new mercies You grant us each morning. We are humbled and grateful for Your love that never wavers, despite our shortcomings. May Your mercy renew us daily and draw us closer to You. In Jesus' name, Amen.

DAY 319

Victory Over Depression

"The Lord is close to the brokenhearted and saves those who are crushed in spirit." - Psalm 34:18 (NIV)

Depression can feel like an insurmountable darkness, a heavy burden that saps our strength and hope. For many men, it's a silent struggle, often hidden beneath a facade of strength and stoicism. Yet, in our lowest moments, we are not alone. God's presence is a beacon of hope and a source of strength, even when we feel utterly lost.

Victory over depression is not always instantaneous; it's a journey that requires courage, faith, and the willingness to seek help. God understands our pain and is with us in every step, offering His unfailing love and comfort. By leaning on Him and allowing His light to penetrate our darkness, we can find the strength to overcome and the hope to keep moving forward.

Action Plan:

Today, acknowledge your feelings and bring them before God in prayer. Don't be afraid to be vulnerable with Him—He knows your heart and is ready to comfort you. Consider reaching out to a trusted friend, family member, or counselor who can support you in this journey.

Heavenly Father, in our darkest moments, we thank You for being our light and our strength. Fill us with Your peace and hope, and help us to see the light of Your presence in our journey towards victory over depression. In Jesus' name, Amen.

DAY 320

Overcoming Worries

"Do not be anxious about anything, but in every situation, by prayer and petition, with thanksgiving, present your requests to God. And the peace of God, which transcends all understanding, will guard your hearts and your minds in Christ Jesus." - Philippians 4:6-7 (NIV)

Life often brings challenges that stir up worry and anxiety within us. Whether it's concerns about our jobs, families, health, or future, these worries can weigh heavily on our hearts and minds.

Overcoming worries is about shifting our focus from our problems to God's promises. It's an act of faith, where we choose to trust in God's sovereignty and His perfect plan for our lives. When we present our worries to God, we are acknowledging our dependence on Him and inviting His peace to reign in our hearts.

Action Plan:

Today, identify specific worries that are troubling you. Write them down and then bring each one to God in prayer. Express your concerns honestly, but also take time to thank Him for His past faithfulness and for the peace He promises.

: Heavenly Father, we come before You with our worries and anxieties, knowing that You care deeply for us. Teach us to rely on Your strength and to rest in Your love. May Your peace reign in our lives today and always. In Jesus' name, Amen.

DAY 321

The Importance of Prayer

"Do not be anxious about anything, but in every situation, by prayer and petition, with thanksgiving, present your requests to God." - Philippians 4:6 (NIV)

Prayer is the heartbeat of our relationship with God. It is through prayer that we communicate with our Creator, expressing our deepest needs, fears, hopes, and gratitude. Prayer is not just a ritual; it is a powerful and intimate connection with the divine.

Through prayer, we align our hearts with His, finding peace amid chaos and clarity in confusion. Prayer transforms us from the inside out, shaping our character and renewing our minds. It is a constant reminder that we are not alone, that the God of the universe hears us and cares deeply about every aspect of our lives.

Action Plan:

Today, commit to deepening your prayer life. Set aside a specific time each day to pray, making it a non-negotiable part of your routine. Find a quiet place where you can be alone with God, free from distractions. Begin with gratitude, thanking God for His blessings and faithfulness.

Heavenly Father, thank You for the gift of prayer, for the privilege of coming before You with our hearts wide open. Help us to understand the importance of this sacred communication and to prioritize it in our daily lives. In Jesus' name, Amen.

DAY 322

Lessons from Paul Ministry

"But the Lord said to him, 'Go, for he is a chosen instrument of mine to carry my name before the Gentiles and kings and the children of Israel.'" - Acts 9:15 (ESV)

The life and ministry of Paul, once known as Saul, is a powerful testament to the transformative power of God's grace and the unyielding commitment to spreading the Gospel. Paul's journey from a fierce persecutor of Christians to one of the most devoted apostles of Christ is filled with profound lessons of faith, resilience, and purpose.

His letters to the early churches are rich with wisdom, encouragement, and exhortations to live a life worthy of our calling. Paul's life exemplifies how God can use anyone, regardless of their past, to fulfill His divine purposes and how our weaknesses can be made perfect in His strength.

Action Plan:

Today, reflect on your own journey and the ways God has transformed your life. Read Acts 9:1-22 to gain a deeper understanding of Paul's conversion and calling. Identify areas where you feel called to serve but may be holding back due to fear or doubt.

Heavenly Father, thank You for the powerful example of Paul's life and ministry. Give us the courage to step out in faith, trusting in Your strength and guidance. May our lives be a testament to Your grace and love, bringing glory to Your name in all we do. In Jesus' name, Amen.

DAY 323

The Role of Forgiveness

"Be kind and compassionate to one another, forgiving each other, just as in Christ God forgave you." - Ephesians 4:32 (NIV)

Forgiveness is a cornerstone of the Christian faith, a powerful act that reflects the heart of God's love and grace. For men, forgiveness can often feel like a difficult and daunting task, especially when faced with deep wounds and betrayals.

Forgiveness is not about condoning the wrongs done to us or forgetting the pain we have endured. Instead, it is a deliberate decision to release our right to hold onto anger and seek retribution. It is an act of obedience to God, recognizing that we, too, have been forgiven through the sacrificial love of Jesus Christ.

Action Plan:

Today, take time to reflect on anyone you need to forgive, whether it's a friend, a family member, or even yourself. Write down the names and the specific hurts you are holding onto. Bring these to God in prayer, asking Him for the strength and grace to forgive. Remind yourself of Ephesians 4:32 and the forgiveness you have received through Christ.

Heavenly Father, thank You for the boundless forgiveness You have given us through Your Son, Jesus Christ. We acknowledge our struggles with forgiveness and ask for Your help in releasing our hurts and grudges. Heal our wounds and restore our relationships, making us instruments of Your peace. In Jesus' name, Amen.

DAY 324

The Power of Studying

"Your word is a lamp to my feet and a light to my path." - Psalm 119:105 (NIV)

God's Word provides clarity amidst confusion, strength in times of weakness, and direction when we feel lost. It is through diligent study that we deepen our relationship with God, understand His will for our lives, and equip ourselves to face life's challenges with faith and confidence.

The Bible is a living document, speaking to us in our unique circumstances, offering timeless truths and practical guidance. Through regular study, we cultivate a discipline that draws us closer to God, enabling us to live out our faith more authentically and powerfully.

Action Plan:

Today, commit to setting aside dedicated time for studying the Bible. Start with a specific book or passage that resonates with you. Use a study guide or commentary to deepen your understanding. Take notes, reflect on what you read, and pray for insight and application.

Heavenly Father, thank You for the gift of Your Word, a lamp to our feet and a light to our path. We ask for a renewed passion for studying Scripture, that we may grow in wisdom and understanding. May it transform us and draw us closer to You. In Jesus' name, Amen.

DAY 325

Embracing Evangelism

*"But you will receive power when the Holy Spirit comes on you;
and you will be my witnesses in Jerusalem, and in all Judea and
Samaria, and to the ends of the earth." - Acts 1:8 (NIV)*

This mission is not just for a select few but for all who believe in
Him. Evangelism is a powerful act of love and obedience, where
we share the hope, peace, and transformation we have found in
Christ with those who have yet to experience it.

The thought of evangelism can be daunting, as it often involves
stepping out of our comfort zones and facing potential rejection or
discomfort. However, Jesus assures us that we are not alone in this
task. The Holy Spirit empowers us, giving us the courage, wisdom,
and words to speak.

Action Plan:

Today, begin by praying for opportunities to share your faith. Ask
God to open your eyes to the needs around you and to give you
boldness and sensitivity in your interactions. Identify one person in
your life who does not yet know Christ and commit to praying for
them daily.

*Heavenly Father, thank You for the incredible privilege of being
Your witnesses. We ask for Your Holy Spirit to fill us with power,
courage, and love as we step out in faith to share the Good News.
May our lives be a testament to Your transforming power and may
many come to know You through our witness. In Jesus' name,
Amen.*

DAY 326

The Cost of a Soul

"What good will it be for someone to gain the whole world, yet forfeit their soul? Or what can anyone give in exchange for their soul?" - Matthew 16:26 (NIV)

The cost of a soul is immeasurable, a treasure beyond the reach of earthly wealth and power. Jesus' profound question in Matthew 16:26 challenges us to reflect on our priorities and the true value of our lives

Understanding the cost of a soul shifts our perspective, guiding us to focus on what truly matters—our relationship with God and our eternal destiny. It prompts us to consider the choices we make daily and how they impact our spiritual well-being.

Action Plan:

Today, take time to evaluate your life's priorities. Ask yourself if there are areas where you have been placing material pursuits or worldly success above your spiritual health. Write down these areas and bring them before God in prayer, asking for His guidance and wisdom to realign your focus.

Heavenly Father, thank You for the reminder of the eternal value of our souls. Help us to see beyond the temporary allure of worldly success and to prioritize our relationship with You above all else. Guide us in making choices that honor You and nurture our spiritual well-being. In Jesus' name, Amen.

DAY 327

Dealing with Lust

"Create in me a pure heart, O God, and renew a steadfast spirit within me." - Psalm 51:10 (NIV)

Lust, in its various forms, can lead us away from God's plan for our lives and damage our relationships with others. However, through prayer, self-reflection, and reliance on God's grace, we can cultivate purity of heart and live in alignment with His will.

Understanding the roots of lust involves recognizing its triggers and the underlying desires it represents. It's about acknowledging our vulnerability and seeking God's help in resisting temptation.

Action Plan:

Today, take time to reflect on any areas in your life where lust has a foothold. Be honest with yourself and with God about the struggles you face. Journal about your thoughts and feelings, and bring them to God in prayer. Ask Him to purify your heart and renew your spirit, empowering you to resist temptation and pursue purity in your thoughts and actions.

Gracious Father, we come before You with humble hearts, acknowledging our struggles with lust. Create in us pure hearts, O God, and renew steadfast spirits within us. Give us the strength to resist temptation and the wisdom to discern Your will in every situation. May Your grace empower us to walk in purity and integrity each day. In Jesus' name, Amen.

DAY 328

Hunger for God's Word

"Like newborn babies, crave pure spiritual milk, so that by it you may grow up in your salvation." - 1 Peter 2:2 (NIV)

The hunger for God's Word is a deep longing within our souls, a desire to nourish ourselves with the timeless truths and wisdom found in Scripture. Just as a newborn baby instinctively craves milk for sustenance and growth, so too should we crave God's Word to feed our spirits and strengthen our faith.

When we hunger for God's Word, we prioritize time in His presence, eagerly seeking to hear His voice and understand His will for our lives. We recognize that His Word is living and active, capable of speaking directly to our hearts and guiding us in every aspect of our journey.

Action Plan:

Today, commit to cultivating a hunger for God's Word in your life. Set aside dedicated time each day to read and study Scripture, even if it's just a few verses. Consider joining a Bible study group or finding a devotional plan that will help you dive deeper into God's Word and stay consistent in your reading.

Gracious God, thank You for the precious gift of Your Word, which nourishes our souls and guides us in the way of truth. Stir within us a hunger for Your Word, a longing to know You more deeply and to walk in Your ways. May Your Word be a lamp to our feet and a light to our path, leading us ever closer to You. In Jesus' name, Amen.

DAY 329

Meekness

"Blessed are the meek, for they will inherit the earth." - Matthew 5:5 (NIV)

Meekness is often misunderstood as weakness, but in the eyes of God, it is a powerful virtue that embodies strength under control. It is the humble recognition of our dependence on God and the gentle surrender of our will to His.

When we embrace meekness, we mirror the character of Christ, who humbly submitted Himself to the will of the Father, even to the point of death on the cross. Meekness allows us to navigate life with grace and dignity, even in the face of adversity or injustice.

Action Plan:

Today, reflect on areas of your life where you struggle with pride, self-will, or the desire to control outcomes. Surrender those areas to God in prayer, asking Him to cultivate a spirit of meekness within you. Practice patience and gentleness in your interactions with others, seeking to understand before being understood.

Heavenly Father, thank You for the example of meekness displayed by Your Son, Jesus Christ. Teach us to follow in His footsteps, humbly submitting our lives to Your will. May Your Spirit work within us, transforming our hearts and molding us into vessels of Your grace and love. In Jesus' name, Amen.

DAY 330

Obeying God's Command

"As the heavens are higher than the earth, so are my ways higher than your ways and my thoughts than your thoughts." - Isaiah 55:9 (NIV)

Obeying God's command is not merely about adhering to a set of rules or regulations; it's about aligning our will with His divine purpose and trusting in His wisdom and guidance. God's commands are rooted in His perfect love for us and His desire for our ultimate good.

When we choose to obey God's commands, we demonstrate our love and reverence for Him. It's an act of surrender, acknowledging His authority in our lives and placing our trust in His sovereignty. Obedience requires humility, as we set aside our own desires and submit ourselves wholeheartedly to God's will.

Action Plan:

Today, take time to reflect on areas of your life where you may be struggling to obey God's commands. Identify any areas where you have been resisting His guidance or compromising His principles.

Heavenly Father, Your ways are higher than our ways, and Your thoughts are beyond our understanding. Give us the wisdom and discernment to recognize Your commands and the courage to obey them wholeheartedly. May our obedience bring glory to Your name and draw others closer to You. In Jesus' name, Amen.

DAY 331

Discipleship

"Then Jesus said to his disciples, 'Whoever wants to be my disciple must deny themselves and take up their cross and follow me.'" - Matthew 16:24 (NIV)

Discipleship is a transformative journey of surrender and commitment, where we walk closely with Jesus, learning from Him, and becoming more like Him in every aspect of our lives. It's not merely about acquiring knowledge or following a set of rules; it's about a deep, intimate relationship.

To be a disciple of Jesus means to embrace His teachings, His values, and His mission. It's about living in obedience to His word and allowing His love to overflow from our hearts into the world around us. It's a lifelong journey of growth and transformation, as we continually surrender our will to His and allow His Spirit to work in and through us.

Action Plan:

Today, take some time to reflect on what it means to be a disciple of Jesus. Consider areas in your life where you may be holding back or resisting His call to follow wholeheartedly. Surrender those areas to Him in prayer, asking for His strength and guidance to walk in obedience.

Gracious Lord, thank You for calling us to be Your disciples and for the privilege of walking closely with You. May our lives be a reflection of Your love and grace, drawing others into relationship with You. In Jesus' name, Amen.

DAY 332

Beacon of Hope

"The Lord is my light and my salvation—whom shall I fear? The Lord is the stronghold of my life—of whom shall I be afraid?" - Psalm 27:1 (NIV)

He is the unwavering source of strength and comfort, illuminating our path and dispelling the shadows of fear and doubt. As men navigating the challenges of this world, we can take solace in the assurance that God is our constant companion, our guiding light in the storm.

Understanding God as our beacon of hope transforms our perspective on life's difficulties. It reminds us that no matter how bleak our circumstances may seem, there is always hope to be found in Him. His light shines brightest in our darkest moments, providing us with the courage and resilience to press on.

Action Plan:

Today, take some time to meditate on Psalm 27:1. Reflect on the areas of your life where you are currently facing challenges or feeling overwhelmed. Surrender those burdens to God in prayer, asking Him to be your guiding light and source of hope.

Heavenly Father, thank You for being our beacon of hope in the midst of life's storms. Use us as vessels of Your hope, Lord, shining Your light into the lives of those who need it most. May Your hope reign in our hearts and radiate through us to a world in need. In Jesus' name, Amen.

DAY 333

The Importance of Giving

"Each of you should give what you have decided in your heart to give, not reluctantly or under compulsion, for God loves a cheerful giver." - 2 Corinthians 9:7 (NIV)

The importance of giving is woven into the fabric of our faith journey. Giving is not just about material offerings; it encompasses our time, talents, and resources, offered with a willing and cheerful heart.

When we give, we participate in God's work of love and redemption in the world. Our generosity becomes a tangible expression of our faith, spreading hope and joy to those in need. Moreover, giving transforms us from being self-centered to others-centered, breaking the chains of greed and materialism that can hinder our spiritual growth.

Action Plan:

Today, take some time to reflect on 2 Corinthians 9:7. Consider the ways in which you can give back to God and others with a joyful heart. Whether it's donating to a charity, volunteering your time to serve others, or sharing your talents with those in need, make a commitment to give sacrificially and cheerfully.

Gracious God, thank You for the countless blessings You have poured out upon us. Help us to be cheerful givers, freely offering our time, talents, and resources for Your kingdom purposes. Guide us in finding ways to give sacrificially and joyfully, that Your name may be glorified. In Jesus' name, Amen.

DAY 334

The Power of God's Presence

"The Lord is near to all who call on him, to all who call on him in truth." - Psalm 145:18 (ESV)

The power of God's presence is a source of strength, comfort, and guidance in our lives. His presence is not bound by time or space but is accessible to us at all times, ready to envelop us in His love and peace.

God's presence brings a sense of security and assurance, knowing that we are never alone and that He is always with us, walking alongside us through every trial and triumph. In His presence, we find refuge from the storms of life, a sanctuary where we can pour out our hearts and find solace in His embrace.

Action Plan:

Today, set aside time to intentionally seek God's presence. Find a quiet place where you can be alone with Him, free from distractions. Begin by meditating on Psalm 145:18 and inviting God to draw near to you. Spend time in prayer, pouring out your heart to Him and listening for His voice.

Gracious God, thank You for the gift of Your presence in our lives. We are grateful for the assurance that You are always near, ready to comfort us in times of need and guide us along the path of righteousness. May Your presence be our strength and our refuge, now and forevermore. In Jesus' name, Amen.

DAY 335

Embracing God's Plan

"For I know the plans I have for you," declares the Lord, "plans to prosper you and not to harm you, plans to give you hope and a future." - Jeremiah 29:11 (NIV)

Embracing God's plan is an act of faith and surrender, trusting in His wisdom and sovereignty over our lives. It's recognizing that God has a purpose for each of us, a unique path tailor-made to fulfill His greater plan for His kingdom.

God's plan often differs from our own expectations or desires, but it is always for our ultimate good. It may lead us through valleys of struggle or uncertainty, but it also guides us to mountaintops of joy and fulfillment.

Action Plan:

Today, spend time in prayer and reflection, seeking God's guidance and wisdom for your life. Surrender your plans, dreams, and desires to Him, asking for clarity and discernment to understand His will. As you go about your day, remain open to God's leading and promptings, being willing to follow wherever He may lead.

Heavenly Father, thank You for the assurance that Your plans for us are good and filled with hope. Help us to trust in Your wisdom and sovereignty, even when we don't understand Your ways. Guide us each step of the way, Lord, and may Your plan unfold in our lives according to Your perfect timing. In Jesus' name, Amen.

DAY 336

The Importance of Commitment

"Commit your way to the Lord; trust in him, and he will act." -
Psalm 37:5 (ESV)

Commitment requires trust—trust in ourselves, trust in others, and ultimately, trust in God. It is a decision to persevere even when the journey becomes difficult, knowing that our efforts are not in vain. Just as God is faithful to His promises, we are called to be faithful in our commitments, honoring our word and demonstrating integrity in all that we do.

Through commitment, we experience growth, resilience, and fulfillment. It shapes our character, strengthens our resolve, and empowers us to overcome obstacles that stand in the way of our goals and aspirations. It is through our commitment that we leave a lasting impact on the world around us, inspiring others to follow in our footsteps and pursue their own commitments with courage and determination.

Action Plan:

Today, reflect on the commitments you have made in your life—both to God and to others. Are there areas where you have been hesitant or inconsistent in your commitment? Take time to prayerfully consider how you can renew your dedication and trust in these commitments.

Heavenly Father, thank You for the gift of commitment and the opportunities it presents for growth and transformation. May our lives be a testimony to Your faithfulness and grace, inspiring others to trust in You and follow Your path. In Jesus' name, Amen.

DAY 337

Trusting in God's Supremacy

"The Lord is my rock, my fortress and my deliverer; my God is my rock, in whom I take refuge, my shield and the horn of my salvation, my stronghold." - Psalm 18:2 (NIV)

Trusting in God's supremacy is an acknowledgment of His sovereignty and authority over all things. He is the Alpha and the Omega, the beginning and the end, the Creator and Sustainer of the universe. When we trust in God's supremacy, we recognize that He is in control of every aspect of our lives, and we surrender our will to His divine plan.

Trusting in God's supremacy also empowers us to live with confidence and boldness. When we know that God is for us, who can be against us? We can face any challenge, overcome any obstacle, and walk through any trial with the assurance that God is with us, guiding us every step of the way.

Action Plan:

Today, reflect on Psalm 18:2 and meditate on the attributes of God as your rock, fortress, and deliverer. Write down any areas of your life where you struggle to trust in God's supremacy and surrender them to Him in prayer.

Heavenly Father, thank You for Your supreme power and authority over all things. Help us to trust in Your sovereignty, knowing that You are our rock and our refuge in every circumstance. Strengthen our faith, Lord, and enable us to surrender our lives fully to Your divine plan. In Jesus' name, Amen.

DAY 338

The Power of God's Spirit

"The Spirit of God has made me, and the breath of the Almighty gives me life." - Job 33:4 (NIV)

The power of God's Spirit is a force that breathes life into every aspect of our existence. It is the divine presence within us, guiding, empowering, and transforming us from the inside out. Just as the breath of the Almighty gave life to humanity in the beginning, His Spirit continues to infuse us with vitality, purpose, and divine wisdom.

Understanding the power of God's Spirit is essential for men seeking to live a life of significance and impact. It is through His Spirit that we are equipped to face the challenges of life with courage, wisdom, and resilience. His Spirit empowers us to overcome obstacles, to persevere in the face of adversity, and to live with integrity and honor in all that we do.

Action Plan:

Today, take time to meditate on Job 33:4 and reflect on the presence of God's Spirit within you. Journal about moments in your life where you have felt His guidance and empowerment. Then, identify areas where you need His Spirit's help and guidance—whether it's in your relationships, your work, or your personal struggles.

Heavenly Father, we thank You for the gift of Your Spirit, which gives us life and empowers us to live for Your glory. May Your Spirit guide us, strengthen us, and inspire us to live lives that honor You. In Jesus' name, Amen.

DAY 339

Living with Faith

"Trust in the Lord with all your heart and lean not on your own understanding; in all your ways submit to him, and he will make your paths straight." - Proverbs 3:5-6 (NIV)

Living with faith is a profound journey of trusting in God's wisdom and guidance, even when the path ahead seems uncertain or challenging. Faith is not merely a passive belief; it's an active choice to rely on God's promises and to walk confidently in His will.

When we live with faith, we experience a profound sense of peace and assurance, knowing that we are not alone in our struggles. It transforms our perspective, allowing us to see beyond our current circumstances and to trust in God's provision and timing.

Action Plan:

Today, take a moment to reflect on areas of your life where you struggle to trust God completely. Write down any doubts or fears you have been holding onto and surrender them to Him in prayer. Ask God to increase your faith and to help you trust in His perfect plan for your life.

Heavenly Father, we thank You for the gift of faith and for Your promise to guide us on the path of righteousness. Help us to trust in You with all our hearts, leaning not on our own understanding but acknowledging You in all our ways. May our lives be a testimony to Your goodness and grace. In Jesus' name, Amen.

DAY 340

Being Courageous

"Be strong and courageous. Do not be afraid or terrified because of them, for the Lord your God goes with you; he will never leave you nor forsake you." - Deuteronomy 31:6 (NIV)

Being courageous is not merely about facing physical dangers or challenges; it's about having the inner strength and conviction to stand firm in our faith and convictions, even in the face of adversity. As men of God, we are called to be courageous in our daily lives, trusting in the promises of God and stepping out in faith to fulfill His purposes for us.

Courage often requires us to confront our fears and insecurities, to push past the limitations we place on ourselves, and to boldly pursue the paths that God has laid before us.. When we embrace courage, we align ourselves with God's will and invite His power and presence to work through us.

Action Plan:

Today, reflect on areas in your life where fear may be holding you back from fully living out God's calling. Write down those fears and take them to God in prayer, asking for His strength and courage to overcome them.

Heavenly Father, thank You for the assurance that You go with us wherever we go and that You will never leave us nor forsake us. Help us to trust in Your power and to step out in faith, knowing that You are always by our side. May our lives be a testimony to Your goodness and faithfulness. In Jesus' name, Amen.

DAY 341

The Importance of Joy

"May the God of hope fill you with all joy and peace as you trust in him, so that you may overflow with hope by the power of the Holy Spirit." - Romans 15:13 (NIV)

Joy is not just a fleeting emotion; it is a deep-seated sense of contentment and fulfillment that comes from knowing and trusting in God. In a world filled with uncertainty and chaos, joy becomes an anchor for our souls, grounding us in the assurance of God's love and faithfulness.

The importance of joy for men cannot be overstated. It is not merely about putting on a happy face or pretending that everything is fine, but rather it is about cultivating a joy that runs deep within our hearts, regardless of our circumstances. This joy is found in our relationship with God, in the knowledge that we are loved unconditionally and that His plans for us are good.

Action Plan:

Today, take a moment to reflect on the source of your joy. Is it found in external circumstances or in your relationship with God? Spend time in prayer, asking God to fill you with His joy and peace as you trust in Him.

Gracious God, thank You for the gift of joy that comes from knowing You. Fill us with Your joy and peace as we trust in You, Lord. May our joy be contagious, spreading hope and encouragement wherever we go. In Jesus' name, Amen.

DAY 342

Trusting God's Mercies

"For the Lord is good; his steadfast love endures forever, and his faithfulness to all generations." - Psalm 100:5 (ESV)

Trusting in God's mercies is an act of faith that anchors us in the unchanging goodness of our Creator. His mercies are not temporary or conditional; they endure forever, flowing from His boundless love and faithfulness.

In times of uncertainty and adversity, trusting in God's mercies brings comfort and hope. It reassures us that even in the darkest moments, God's love shines brightly, guiding us through the storms of life. When we face challenges that seem insurmountable, His mercies sustain us, reminding us that we are never alone.

Action Plan:

Today, take a moment to reflect on Psalm 100:5 and meditate on the steadfast love and faithfulness of God. Journal about a time when you experienced God's mercies in your life and how it strengthened your faith.

Gracious God, we thank You for Your enduring love and faithfulness that sustain us through every season of life. Help us to trust in Your mercies wholeheartedly, knowing that You are always working for our good. Strengthen our faith, Lord, and fill us with confidence in Your promises. May we live each day with gratitude for Your mercies, sharing Your love and grace with those around us. In Jesus' name, Amen.

DAY 343

The Role of Spiritual Strength

"The Lord is my strength and my shield; my heart trusts in him, and he helps me. My heart leaps for joy, and with my song I praise him." - Psalm 28:7 (NIV)

Spiritual strength is not about relying solely on our own abilities, but rather, it's about placing our trust in God and drawing from His infinite power. It's about cultivating a deep, intimate relationship with our Heavenly Father through prayer, meditation, and studying His Word. As we lean on God for strength, He equips us with the courage, wisdom, and perseverance needed to fulfill His purpose for our lives.

In a world that often values external success and achievement, spiritual strength reminds us of what truly matters—the condition of our hearts and our relationship with God. It's what enables us to remain steadfast in our faith, even in the midst of adversity, and to be a source of encouragement and support to those around us.

Action Plan:

Today, take time to assess your spiritual strength. Reflect on areas where you feel weak or weary, and bring them to God in prayer, asking Him to strengthen you.

Gracious Father, thank You for being our strength and our shield. Help us to trust in You wholeheartedly, knowing that You are always there to help us. May Your Spirit empower us to face each day with courage and faith, and may we be a shining light of Your love and grace to the world. In Jesus' name, Amen.

DAY 344

The Power of God's Love

"For God so loved the world that he gave his one and only Son, that whoever believes in him shall not perish but have eternal life."
- John 3:16 (NIV)

God's love is transformative. It has the power to heal the brokenhearted, restore the lost, and bring hope to the hopeless. When we truly grasp the depth of God's love for us, it changes how we see ourselves and others. We are no longer defined by our mistakes or shortcomings but by the immense love God has lavished upon us through Christ.

Understanding the power of God's love calls us to action. It compels us to love others as He has loved us—selflessly, sacrificially, and unconditionally. It challenges us to extend grace, forgiveness, and compassion to those around us, regardless of their circumstances or background.

Action Plan:

Today, take time to reflect on the magnitude of God's love for you. Meditate on John 3:16 and allow it to sink deep into your heart. Consider how God's love has impacted your life and thank Him for His unending grace.

Heavenly Father, thank You for Your incomprehensible love that knows no bounds. Help us to grasp the depth and breadth of Your love for us, that we may be transformed by it. May Your love shine through us, bringing hope and healing to a broken world. In Jesus' name, Amen.

DAY 345

Praying Always

"Rejoice always, pray continually, give thanks in all circumstances; for this is God's will for you in Christ Jesus." - 1 Thessalonians 5:16-18 (NIV)

The command to pray always is not just a suggestion, but a powerful invitation to cultivate a deep and intimate relationship with God. Prayer is the lifeline of our faith, the avenue through which we communicate with our Creator, pouring out our hearts, sharing our joys and sorrows, and seeking His guidance and presence in every aspect of our lives.

When we pray always, we acknowledge our dependence on God and recognize His sovereignty over every situation. It's in those moments of prayer, whether in times of joy or trials, that we experience His peace that surpasses all understanding and find strength to persevere.

Action Plan:

Today, commit to making prayer a priority in your life. Start by setting aside specific times each day to pray, whether it's in the morning before you begin your day, during your lunch break, or before you go to bed. Find a quiet place where you can be alone with God and pour out your heart to Him.

Gracious Father, thank You for the privilege of prayer and the opportunity to commune with You at all times. Guide us by Your Spirit as we seek Your face and surrender our lives to Your will. In Jesus' name, Amen.

DAY 346

Lesson from The Ten Virgins

"Watch therefore, for you know neither the day nor the hour." -
Matthew 25:13 (ESV)

The parable of the Ten Virgins serves as a poignant reminder of the importance of spiritual preparedness and vigilance in our lives. In this parable, Jesus compares the kingdom of heaven to ten virgins who were awaiting the arrival of the bridegroom. Five of them were wise, prepared with enough oil for their lamps, while the other five were foolish, lacking oil and unprepared for the bridegroom's arrival. When the bridegroom finally came, the wise virgins entered the wedding feast with him, while the foolish virgins were left outside in the darkness.

This parable teaches us that we must be ready for the return of Christ at all times, as we do not know the exact hour of His coming. It underscores the importance of spiritual readiness and living in constant anticipation of His arrival. Just as the wise virgins kept their lamps burning with an ample supply of oil, we must keep our hearts and lives filled with the oil of faith, prayer, and obedience to God's Word. We must be vigilant in our faith, constantly seeking to grow closer to God and live according to His will.

Action Plan:

Today, take inventory of your spiritual life. Reflect on whether you are living in a state of readiness for the return of Christ. Are there areas of your life where you need to refocus your attention and commitment to God? Spend time in prayer, asking God to reveal any areas of spiritual complacency or neglect. Then, make a commitment to deepen your relationship with God through daily prayer, reading Scripture, and seeking opportunities to serve others. Live each day with a sense of expectancy and readiness for Christ's return, knowing that He could come at any moment.

Heavenly Father, thank You for the reminder to watch and be prepared for the return of Your Son, Jesus Christ. Forgive us for the times when we have become spiritually complacent or distracted by the cares of this world. Help us to keep our lamps burning bright with the oil of faith and obedience, that we may be ready to meet You when You come. Give us a sense of urgency in our faith and a deep longing for Your kingdom. In Jesus' name, Amen.

DAY 347

Becoming Fruitful

"Remain in me, as I also remain in you. No branch can bear fruit by itself; it must remain in the vine. Neither can you bear fruit unless you remain in me." - John 15:4 (NIV)

Becoming fruitful is not just about achieving success or accomplishing goals; it's about living a life that bears lasting, meaningful impact. In John 15, Jesus uses the metaphor of a vine and branches to illustrate the importance of remaining connected to Him in order to bear fruit.

To become fruitful means to align our lives with God's purposes and to allow His Spirit to work in and through us. It requires a commitment to remain connected to Jesus through prayer, study of His Word, and obedience to His commands.

Action Plan:

Today, take time to evaluate your connection to Christ. Reflect on areas of your life where you may have become disconnected or distracted. Commit to spending intentional time in prayer and meditation, allowing God to speak to your heart and guide your steps.

Heavenly Father, help us to abide in You and to remain connected to the true vine, Jesus Christ. May Your Spirit work in us, producing fruit that glorifies Your name and blesses those around us. May our actions reflect Your love and grace, drawing others into relationship with You. In Jesus' name, Amen.

DAY 348

The Power of Tithe

"Bring the whole tithe into the storehouse, that there may be food in my house. Test me in this," says the Lord Almighty, "and see if I will not throw open the floodgates of heaven and pour out so much blessing that there will not be room enough to store it." - Malachi 3:10 (NIV)

The power of tithe is not just about giving a portion of our income to God; it's about acknowledging His ownership of everything we have and trusting in His provision. Tithing is an act of faith that demonstrates our obedience and gratitude to God for His blessings in our lives.

When we tithe faithfully, we open ourselves up to the abundant blessings that God promises to pour out upon us. It's not just about material blessings, but also spiritual growth, peace of mind, and a deeper intimacy with God.

Action Plan:

Today, take a moment to prayerfully consider your attitude towards tithing. Reflect on Malachi 3:10 and the promises God makes to those who trust Him with their finances. If you haven't been tithing regularly, commit to starting today, trusting in God's faithfulness to provide for your needs.

Gracious God, thank You for the privilege of stewardship and the opportunity to participate in Your kingdom work through tithing. May our tithes and offerings be a pleasing sacrifice to You and a testament to Your faithfulness. In Jesus' name, Amen.

DAY 349

Living with Discernment

"Trust in the Lord with all your heart and lean not on your own understanding; in all your ways submit to him, and he will make your paths straight." - Proverbs 3:5-6 (NIV)

Living with discernment is about cultivating a deep awareness of God's will and guidance in our lives. It involves seeking His wisdom and understanding in all aspects of our existence, from the big decisions to the seemingly mundane moments.

When we live with discernment, we allow God to direct our steps and guide our choices. It's about aligning our desires and ambitions with His perfect plan for us, rather than relying solely on our own limited understanding.

Action Plan:

Today, commit to seeking God's guidance in every area of your life. Start by setting aside time for prayer and meditation, asking God to grant you wisdom and discernment. Reflect on Proverbs 3:5-6 and consider any areas where you may be leaning on your own understanding instead of trusting in God completely.

Heavenly Father, we thank You for the gift of discernment and Your promise to guide us along straight paths. Help us to trust in You with all our hearts and to submit to Your will in every area of our lives. May we live with clarity and purpose, knowing that You are leading us every step of the way. In Jesus' name, Amen.

DAY 350

Power of Building an Altar

"And he built an altar there and called on the name of the Lord and pitched his tent there. And there Isaac's servants dug a well." - Genesis 26:25 (ESV)

The power of building an altar lies in its significance as a symbol of devotion, worship, and communion with God. Throughout the Bible, we see men of faith erecting altars as places of encounter with the divine, where they offer sacrifices, seek guidance, and express gratitude to God. These altars serve as tangible reminders of God's faithfulness and presence in their lives.

Building an altar is not merely about constructing a physical structure; it's about creating a sacred space in our hearts where we can meet with God. It's about prioritizing our relationship with Him above all else and intentionally setting aside time and space for worship and prayer.

Action Plan:

Today, find a quiet space where you can create your own altar of devotion. It could be a corner of your home, a spot in nature, or simply a designated chair where you can spend time with God each day.

Gracious God, we thank You for the privilege of coming into Your presence and building altars of devotion where we can commune with You. May our lives be living altars, continually devoted to Your glory. In Jesus' name, Amen.

DAY 351

Staying Vigilant

"Be alert and of sober mind. Your enemy the devil prowls around like a roaring lion looking for someone to devour." - 1 Peter 5:8 (NIV)

Staying vigilant is not merely a suggestion; it's a command woven into the fabric of our spiritual journey. The scripture reminds us of the reality of spiritual warfare and the constant battle between good and evil. As men of faith, we are called to be vigilant, to be watchful, and to stand firm against the schemes of the enemy.

Being vigilant means being aware of the spiritual forces at work around us and being intentional in guarding our hearts, minds, and actions. It requires us to stay grounded in God's truth, to resist temptation, and to remain steadfast in prayer.

Action Plan:

Today, commit to staying vigilant in your spiritual walk. Start by examining your heart and identifying any areas where you may be vulnerable to temptation or spiritual attack. Arm yourself with the Word of God by spending time in Scripture daily and meditating on its truths.

Heavenly Father, we thank You for the gift of Your Word, which guides us and strengthens us in our spiritual battles. Grant us the wisdom and discernment to stay vigilant against the schemes of the enemy. May we walk in victory, knowing that You are with us every step of the way. In Jesus' name, Amen.

DAY 352

Saved by Grace

"For it is by grace you have been saved, through faith—and this is not from yourselves, it is the gift of God." - Ephesians 2:8 (NIV)

Saved by grace—three simple words that hold the weight of eternity. This scripture encapsulates the heart of the gospel message: that our salvation is not earned through our own efforts or merits but is a gift freely given by God through His grace.

Understanding that we are saved by grace transforms our perspective on ourselves, others, and our relationship with God. It shatters the illusion of self-sufficiency and self-righteousness, leading us to a place of humility and gratitude.

Action Plan:

Today, take a moment to reflect on the meaning of God's grace in your life. Journal about specific moments where you have experienced His grace and mercy. Spend time in prayer, thanking God for His indescribable gift of salvation through Jesus Christ.

Gracious Father, we thank You for Your incomprehensible grace that has saved us from our sins and brought us into relationship with You. Help us to fully grasp the depth of Your love and the magnitude of Your grace. Let Your grace flow through us, touching the lives of those around us and bringing glory to Your name. In Jesus' name, Amen.

DAY 353

The Role of Spiritual Wisdom

"The fear of the Lord is the beginning of wisdom, and knowledge of the Holy One is understanding." - Proverbs 9:10 (NIV)

Spiritual wisdom is not just about acquiring knowledge; it's about understanding and applying God's truth to every aspect of our lives. It is rooted in reverence for God and a deep desire to align our thoughts, words, and actions with His will.

Understanding the role of spiritual wisdom is essential for men seeking to live a life of purpose and honor. It empowers us to make wise decisions, to lead with humility and compassion, and to build meaningful relationships founded on love and grace.

Action Plan:

Today, commit to seeking spiritual wisdom through prayer, study, and reflection. Set aside time each day to read Scripture and meditate on its teachings, asking God to grant you wisdom and understanding.

Heavenly Father, we thank You for the gift of spiritual wisdom, which illuminates our minds and directs our paths. Grant us a deep reverence for You, Lord, and a hunger for Your truth. May we seek Your wisdom above all else, trusting in Your guidance and understanding. Fill us with Your Spirit, that we may live lives worthy of Your calling and bring glory to Your name. In Jesus' name, Amen.

DAY 354

The Power of Consistency

"Let us not become weary in doing good, for at the proper time we will reap a harvest if we do not give up." - Galatians 6:9 (NIV)

The power of consistency lies in its ability to cultivate discipline, perseverance, and growth in our lives. Consistency is not about perfection but about faithfully showing up day after day, even when it's hard or we don't see immediate results.

Consistency is a spiritual discipline that strengthens our character and deepens our relationship with God. When we are consistent in prayer, in reading God's Word, and in living out our faith, we create space for God to work in and through us.

Action Plan:

Today, commit to being consistent in your faith walk. Start by setting aside dedicated time each day for prayer and reading Scripture, even if it's just a few minutes. Choose a specific area of your life where you want to see growth or change, whether it's in your relationships, your work, or your spiritual life, and commit to taking small, consistent steps towards that goal.

Gracious God, we thank You for Your faithfulness and Your steadfast love that never fails. Help us to be consistent in our pursuit of You and Your purposes for our lives. May our lives be a testimony to Your faithfulness and grace. In Jesus' name, Amen.

DAY 355

Embracing God's Love

"For I am convinced that neither death nor life, neither angels nor demons, neither the present nor the future, nor any powers, neither height nor depth, nor anything else in all creation, will be able to separate us from the love of God that is in Christ Jesus our Lord."
- Romans 8:38-39 (NIV)

Embracing God's love is a transformative journey that reshapes our understanding of ourselves, others, and the world around us. This scripture from Romans reminds us of the incomparable depth and breadth of God's love—a love that transcends all boundaries, defies all odds, and endures through every trial and tribulation.

God's love is not dependent on our performance or worthiness; it is freely given to us as His cherished children. It is a love that knows no limits, no conditions, and no end. Embracing God's love means accepting ourselves as beloved sons of the Most High, worthy of His affection and grace.

<u>*Action Plan:*</u>

Today, take time to meditate on Romans 8:38-39 and allow its truth to sink deep into your heart. Reflect on moments in your life where you have experienced God's love in tangible ways and thank Him for His faithfulness.

Heavenly Father, thank You for the overwhelming gift of Your love that knows no bounds. May Your love transform our hearts, our relationships, and our world, shining brightly as a beacon of hope and grace. In Jesus' name, Amen.

DAY 356

The Importance of Reflection

"For if anyone is a hearer of the word and not a doer, he is like a man who looks intently at his natural face in a mirror. For he looks at himself and goes away and at once forgets what he was like. But the one who looks into the perfect law, the law of liberty, and perseveres, being no hearer who forgets but a doer who acts, he will be blessed in his doing." - James 1:23-25 (ESV)

Reflection is a vital aspect of our spiritual journey as men of faith. Just as a mirror reflects our physical appearance, reflection allows us to examine our hearts, minds, and actions in light of God's truth. It is through reflection that we gain insight into our strengths and weaknesses, discern God's guidance in our lives, and grow closer to Him.

Taking time for reflection enables us to pause amidst the busyness of life, to silence the distractions around us, and to listen attentively to the voice of God. It is in these moments of introspection that we can evaluate our thoughts, attitudes, and behaviors, aligning them with the values and principles found in Scripture.

Action Plan:

Today, carve out intentional time for reflection in your daily routine. Find a quiet space where you can be alone with God, free from distractions. Begin by prayerfully reading a passage of Scripture or a devotional thought, allowing God's Word to penetrate your heart.

Gracious God, thank You for the gift of reflection, which allows us to draw closer to You and grow in our faith. May our reflections lead to transformation and a deeper relationship with You. In Jesus' name, Amen.

DAY 357

Trusting in God's Promises

"For no matter how many promises God has made, they are 'Yes'
in Christ. And so through him the 'Amen' is spoken by us to the
glory of God." - 2 Corinthians 1:20 (NIV)

Trusting in God's promises is an anchor for the soul, a firm foundation upon which we build our faith and hope. Throughout the pages of Scripture, God has given us countless promises—promises of love, provision, protection, and eternal life. These promises are not merely wishful thinking; they are declarations of God's faithfulness and His unchanging nature.

When we trust in God's promises, we are placing our confidence in His character and His ability to fulfill what He has spoken. It requires us to let go of our doubts and fears, to surrender our need for control, and to rest in the assurance that God is faithful to His word.

Action Plan:

Today, take time to meditate on some of God's promises found in Scripture. Write down a few that resonate with you personally, and reflect on how they have been fulfilled in your life or how you are trusting God to fulfill them in the future.

Gracious Father, we thank You for Your faithfulness and the
countless promises You have given us in Your word. May Your
promises be a source of hope and encouragement for us each day,
as we live to glorify Your name. In Jesus' name, Amen.

DAY 358

The Power of God's Grace

"For it is by grace you have been saved, through faith—and this is not from yourselves, it is the gift of God— not by works, so that no one can boast." - Ephesians 2:8-9 (NIV)

The power of God's grace is a profound and transformative force in our lives. Grace is the unmerited favor and love that God freely gives us, despite our unworthiness. It is through His grace that we are saved, redeemed, and made new.

Understanding the power of God's grace changes how we view ourselves and our relationship with God. It humbles us, reminding us that we are completely dependent on His grace for salvation and forgiveness. It fills us with gratitude, knowing that we don't deserve His love, yet He chooses to lavish it upon us anyway.

Action Plan:

Today, take a moment to reflect on Ephesians 2:8-9. Meditate on the depth of God's grace and how it has impacted your life. Spend time in prayer, thanking God for His grace and asking Him to help you fully embrace it.

Heavenly Father, we thank You for the immeasurable gift of Your grace. Help us to fully grasp the depth of Your love and forgiveness, and to live each day in gratitude for Your unmerited favor. May Your grace continue to transform our hearts and draw us closer to You. In Jesus' name, Amen.

DAY 359

Living with Joy

"May the God of hope fill you with all joy and peace as you trust in him, so that you may overflow with hope by the power of the Holy Spirit." - Romans 15:13 (NIV)

Living with joy is not just about experiencing fleeting moments of happiness; it's about cultivating a deep-seated sense of contentment and gratitude that transcends circumstances. As men of faith, we are called to live joyfully, not because life is always easy or perfect, but because we trust in the God who is our source of true and everlasting joy.

Joy is a fruit of the Spirit, a gift that God graciously bestows upon those who abide in Him. It is found not in the pursuit of worldly pleasures or achievements, but in the abiding presence of God and the assurance of His promises. Jo

Action Plan:

Today, choose to intentionally cultivate joy in your life. Begin by counting your blessings and focusing on the things you are grateful for, no matter how small. And finally, choose to let go of negativity and worry, trusting in God's sovereignty and His promise to fill you with joy through the power of the Holy Spirit.

Gracious Father, thank You for the gift of joy that You freely give to those who trust in You. Help us to live with gratitude and contentment, knowing that our ultimate joy is found in You alone. In Jesus' name, Amen.

DAY 360

Overcoming Fear and Anxiety

"Have I not commanded you? Be strong and courageous. Do not be afraid; do not be discouraged, for the Lord your God will be with you wherever you go." - Joshua 1:9 (NIV)

Fear and anxiety are common struggles that many men face, but we are not called to be slaves to these emotions. The scripture from Joshua reminds us of God's command to be strong and courageous, knowing that He is always by our side.

To overcome fear and anxiety, we must first acknowledge them and bring them before God in prayer. We can pour out our hearts to Him, expressing our fears and asking for His peace to fill us. Then, we can meditate on His Word and remind ourselves of His faithfulness throughout history.

Action Plan:

Today, take a moment to identify any fears or anxieties that have been weighing on your heart. Write them down and bring them to God in prayer, asking Him to replace them with His peace and courage. Spend time reading and meditating on scriptures that speak to overcoming fear, such as Joshua 1:9, Psalm 23:4, and Isaiah 41:10.

Heavenly Father, we thank You for Your promise to be with us always, even in the midst of our fears and anxieties. Fill us with Your peace that surpasses all understanding, and empower us to live boldly for Your glory. In Jesus' name, Amen.

DAY 361

Saved by Grace

"For it is by grace you have been saved, through faith—and this is not from yourselves, it is the gift of God—not by works, so that no one can boast." - Ephesians 2:8-9 (NIV)

Saved by grace—it's a concept that defines the very core of our faith journey. In these verses, we are reminded that our salvation is not earned through our own efforts or good deeds, but it is a gift from God, freely given to us out of His boundless love and mercy.

Understanding the depth of God's grace transforms our perspective on life. It humbles us, reminding us that we are utterly dependent on God's mercy for our salvation. It fills us with gratitude, knowing that we don't deserve His love, yet He offers it to us unconditionally.

Action Plan:

Today, take a moment to reflect on the grace of God in your life. Consider the ways He has forgiven you, sustained you, and blessed you beyond measure. Write down a prayer of thanksgiving, expressing your gratitude for His grace and mercy.

Heavenly Father, we thank You for the gift of Your grace, which saves us and sustains us each day. Help us to fully grasp the depth of Your love and mercy, and to live lives that reflect Your grace to the world around us. May Your grace continue to transform us from the inside out, drawing us closer to You and shaping us into the men You have called us to be. In Jesus' name, Amen.

DAY 362

Modesty

"Do not let your adorning be external—the braiding of hair and the putting on of gold jewelry, or the clothing you wear— but let your adorning be the hidden person of the heart with the imperishable beauty of a gentle and quiet spirit, which in God's sight is very precious." - 1 Peter 3:3-4 (ESV)

Modesty is a virtue that speaks to the character of a man's heart rather than the outward appearance. In a world that often prioritizes physical attractiveness and material possessions, God calls us to a deeper standard of modesty—one that reflects the beauty of a humble and gentle spirit.

True modesty goes beyond clothing choices; it encompasses our attitudes, behaviors, and the way we carry ourselves. It is about honoring God in all aspects of our lives and recognizing that our worth is not defined by external adornments but by the condition of our hearts.

Action Plan:

Today, reflect on the concept of modesty and consider how it is manifested in your life. Examine your motivations and intentions behind your choices in clothing, speech, and actions.

Heavenly Father, thank You for reminding us of the true beauty that comes from a gentle and humble spirit. Give us the wisdom to prioritize modesty in our lives, turning away from the fleeting standards of the world and seeking instead to please You in all things. In Jesus' name, Amen.

DAY 363

Trusting God's Plan

"Trust in the Lord with all your heart and lean not on your own understanding; in all your ways submit to him, and he will make your paths straight." - Proverbs 3:5-6 (NIV)

Trusting God's plan is an act of surrender and faith, acknowledging that His wisdom far surpasses our own and His ways are higher than ours. It requires us to let go of our need for control and to embrace His sovereignty over our lives.

Trusting God's plan doesn't mean that life will be without challenges or difficulties. In fact, it often means walking through valleys and facing obstacles that seem insurmountable. But even in the darkest moments, we can trust that God is working all things together for our good and His glory. His plan for us is perfect, even when we can't see the bigger picture.

Action Plan:

Today, make a conscious decision to surrender your plans and desires to God. Spend time in prayer, asking Him to reveal His will for your life and to give you the faith to trust in His plan. Reflect on times in the past when God has been faithful, even when His ways didn't make sense at the time.

Gracious God, we thank You for Your perfect plan for our lives, even when we can't see it clearly. Help us to trust in Your wisdom and Your goodness, knowing that You always have our best interests at heart. May Your will be done in our lives, Lord, as we trust in Your unfailing love. In Jesus' name, Amen.

DAY 364

Committing your Ways into God's Hands

"Commit your way to the Lord; trust in him and he will do this: He will make your righteous reward shine like the dawn, your vindication like the noonday sun." - Psalm 37:5-6 (NIV)

Committing our ways into God's hands is an act of surrender and trust. It's about relinquishing our control and placing our lives, dreams, and plans into the loving and capable hands of our Heavenly Father. This scripture assures us that when we entrust our paths to God, He will guide us, protect us, and ultimately bring about His perfect plan for our lives.

When we commit our ways into God's hands, we are acknowledging His sovereignty and wisdom. We recognize that His ways are higher than our ways, and His thoughts are higher than our thoughts (Isaiah 55:8-9).

Action Plan:

Today, take a moment to reflect on areas of your life where you may be holding onto control instead of trusting God. Write down specific goals or plans you have for the future and commit them into God's hands, trusting that He will work all things together for your good (Romans 8:28).

Gracious Father, we thank You for Your faithfulness and goodness in our lives. Help us to trust You more deeply and to surrender our ways into Your hands. May Your perfect will be done in our lives, and may Your name be glorified in all that we do. In Jesus' name, Amen.

DAY 365

Embracing God's Direction

"Trust in the Lord with all your heart and lean not on your own understanding; in all your ways submit to him, and he will make your paths straight." - Proverbs 3:5-6 (NIV)

Embracing God's direction is an act of surrender and trust, allowing Him to guide our steps and lead us on the path He has prepared for us. It's about relinquishing our own plans and desires, and instead, aligning our hearts with His will.

God's direction may not always be clear or easy to follow, but it is always purposeful and for our ultimate good. It requires humility to set aside our own agendas and seek His guidance earnestly through prayer, meditation on His Word, and listening to the prompting of His Spirit.

Action Plan:

Today, begin by surrendering your plans and desires to God in prayer. Ask Him to reveal His direction for your life and to give you the wisdom and courage to follow it faithfully. Spend time in Scripture, seeking guidance and insight into His will for you.

Heavenly Father, we humbly come before You, acknowledging Your wisdom and sovereignty over our lives. Give us the faith and courage to follow where You lead, knowing that Your ways are always good and true. In Jesus' name, Amen.

FINAL WORDS

In the pages of this daily devotional for 2025, we've embarked on a profound journey—a journey of faith, reflection, and transformation. Each day, we've explored themes that resonate with the essence of what it means to be a child of God in the year 2025. We've delved into the depths of our hearts, seeking wisdom, courage, and purpose in a world filled with challenges and opportunities.

As we conclude this devotional, let's take a moment to reflect on the lessons we've learned, the moments of inspiration, and the growth we've experienced along the way. We've explored topics like facing fear, pursuing God's calling, enduring through trials, and giving with an open heart. Through these daily reflections, we've sought to strengthen our faith, deepen our relationship with God, and become better stewards of the gifts He's entrusted to us.

Heavenly Father,

As we conclude this devotional journey, we come before you with hearts filled with gratitude and renewed purpose. You have been our constant companion, guiding us through the trials and triumphs of life. We thank you for the inspiration and insights we've gained along the way.

Lord, continue to mold us into men of courage, purpose, and unwavering faith. May the lessons we've learned and the truths we've embraced continue to resonate in our hearts and shape our daily lives.

Help us carry the light of your love, grace, and truth into the world, touching the lives of those around us. May our journey of faith be a testament to your goodness and faithfulness.

As we move forward, Lord, we ask for your continued guidance and strength. Lead us in the paths of righteousness, and may your presence be our constant source of inspiration and hope.

In Jesus' name, we pray.

Amen.

LEAVE US A REVIEW

At Mount Hermon Publications, your feedback matters. We believe that the best way to improve our devotionals and resources is by hearing from you, our valued readers. We invite you to share your thoughts, insights, and experiences by leaving a review.

Your reviews are more than just words on a screen; they are the compass that guides us toward creating better, more impactful devotionals for men like you.

So, if you've found inspiration, wisdom, or transformation within the pages of our devotionals, we encourage you to take a moment to drop a review. Let us know what you loved, what spoke to your heart, and even areas where you think we can improve.

Your voice matters, and we look forward to hearing from you.

Don't forget to follow our Author page on Amazon [Mount Hermon Publication], to get updated information concerning our devotionals, Prayer books, and also when we launch a discount. We would appreciate that.

ABOUT MOUNT HERMON PUBLICATION

Mount Hermon Publications is dedicated to the creation and dissemination of inspirational devotionals and spiritual resources designed to empower and uplift every Christian in their faith journeys. Our mission is to provide Christians with practical, faith-based guidance for navigating the complexities of life while nurturing their spiritual growth.

We understand that being a believer of Christ in today's world comes with unique challenges and opportunities. That's why we are committed to producing thoughtfully crafted devotionals, books, and resources that resonate with the hearts of Christians, offering guidance, inspiration, and practical wisdom to help them live out their faith in meaningful ways.

Our devotionals are designed to be more than just daily readings; they are companions for the journey—faithful allies that walk alongside Men, Women, Boys, Girls, Families, Couples as they seek deeper connections with God and endeavor to live purposeful and impactful lives. We believe in the power of reflection, action, and community to foster spiritual growth, and our devotionals reflect these principles.

Mount Hermon Publications is dedicated to nurturing a community of Christians who strive to be courageous, purpose-driven, and deeply connected to their Creator. We are committed to supporting every Believer as they face life's challenges with faith, embrace their unique callings, and leave a positive impact on the world around them.

With each publication, we aim to inspire Christians to live out their faith with intention, to become better husbands, fathers, mothers, wife, kids, teens, friends, and leaders, and to leave a legacy of love, grace, and truth. We invite you to explore our devotionals and resources, and we look forward to being a part of your spiritual journey.

Together, let us seek to grow in faith, reflection, and action, living as Christians who are anchored in the love of God and empowered to make a difference in the world.

Thank you for joining us in this journey of spiritual building.
May God continue to build and uphold you.
God bless you.

Made in the USA
Columbia, SC
09 December 2024

48882234R00243